M. Shah
"the daylight of consciousness

understanding of the cultural and economic history of Islamic and European societies, and of influential contemporary scholarship and debate. The analysis is careful and serious, and will be of considerable value to anyone concerned with the crucial and timely issues that Alam addresses, whether they come to agree with his conclusions or not.

—Noam Chomsky
Professor of Linguistics, MIT

"In the face of race-baiting, bigotry and official hysteria, M. Shahid Alam offers reason, analysis and genuine compassion for those who have been steamrolled by the imperial machine as it rampages across the globe. This urgent collection of essays proves that clear and courageous writing can still be a powerful force for change."

—Jeffrey St. Clair
Coeditor CounterPunch, and coauthor, Imperial Crusades (2004)

M. Shahid Alam is a truth-teller and powerful writer. Without fear, and in defiance of all attempts to censor him, he explains to us the origins of our present dangerously deteriorating situation. Read these essays and you will come away with a level of awareness that you cannot get from the world's corporate media. The essays may disturb you and they may anger you, but hopefully they will also lead you to ask what you can do to act against the stereotypes, prejudices, and lies that now dominate the policies of the world's sole superpower.

—Lawrence Davidson
West Chester University, Pennsylvania

THE AUTHOR

M. Shahid Alam is Professor of Economics at Northeastern University, Boston. His writings have appeared in leading journals in the social sciences, including American Economic Review, Cambridge Journal of Economics, Kyklos, Science and Society and Journal of World Systems Research; in newspapers and webzines, including Dawn, Jang, Holiday, The Star, Al-Ahram, Asia Times, CounterPunch, Commondreams, Tehelka and OutlookIndia; and in literary magazines, including Chicago Review, Marlboro Review and Beloit Poetry Journal. His previous books include *Poverty from the Wealth of Nations* (Macmillan, 2000) and *Governments and Markets in Economic Development Strategies* (Praeger, 1989).

Challenging the

New Orientalism:

Dissenting Essays
on the
"War Against Islam"

M. Shahid Alam

Islamic Publications International
North Haledon, New Jersey
iPi

Islamic Publications International
5 Sicomac Road, Suite 302
North Haledon, NJ 07508, USA
Telephone: 800-568-9814
Fax: 800-466-8111
Email: ipi@onebox.com
Website: www.islampub.com

Director of Publications
Moin Shaikh

Book Design
Nancy Windesheim

Book Layout
David Van Ness

Index
Katherine Jensen

Copyright © 2006   M. Shahid Alam

Printed in the United Sates of America

Library of Congress Cataloging-in-Publication Data

Alam, M. Shahid (Mohammad Shahid), 1950-
    The new orientalism: dissenting essays on the "War against Islam" / M. Shahid Alam.—1st ed.
    p. cm.
Includes index.
Previously published as *Is there an Islamic problem?* (Kuala Lumpur: The Other Press, 2004).
ISBN 1-889999-45-8 (pbk.) — ISBN 1-889999-46-6 (hardback)
    1. Islamic countries–Foreign relations–United States. 2. United States–Foreign relations–
Islamic countries. 3. September 11 Terrorist Attacks, 2001–Causes. 4. Terrorism–United States.
5. Terrorism–Israel. I. Title.
    DS35.74.U6A433 2006
    909.83'1–dc22
                                    2006021319

*"O ye, who believe! Be ye staunch
in justice, witnesses for Allah,
even though it be against yourselves
or (your) parents or (your) kindred,
or whether (the case be of) a rich man
or a poor man, for Allah is nearer
unto both (than ye are)."*

—Qur'an: 4: 135

CONTENTS

PREFACE
TO SECOND EDITION

"And if Allah had not repelled some men by others the earth would have been corrupted. But Allah is the Lord of kindness to (His) creatures."
—Qur'an: 2: 251[1]

July 2006

A new edition of these essays requires a word of explanation. Several essays have been added to this volume but they do not introduce entirely new themes; and the revisions are minor and stylistic. However, the new title under which these essays are now collected, *Challenging the New Orientalism*, claims a thematic unity for the essays which was missing in the old title, *Is There An Islamic Problem*? Perhaps, it might be useful to explain what I mean by this new Orientalism.

The West has never had an easy time coming to terms with Islam or Islamicate societies.[2] There was a long period, lasting more than a millennium, when the two were seen as existential threats. In order to mobilize the energy to contain and then roll back these threats – first from the 'Holy Lands' and Southwestern Europe and later from Southeastern Europe – European writers presented Islam as a Christian heresy, a devil-worshipping religion, Mahomet's trickery, a militant and militarist cult crafted for Bedouin conquests. To this list of dark qualities the thinkers of the Renaissance and the Enlightenment added a few more. Now Islamicate societies were also seen as despotic, fatalistic, fanatical, irrational, uncurious, opposed to science, and inimical to progress. When Europe gained the upper hand militarily in the nineteenth century, this complex of Orientalist ideas would be used to justify the conquest and colonization of Islamicate lands.

Starting in the nineteenth century, a small minority of European thinkers began to reject the standard Orientalist constructs of Islam and

---

1 *The Glorious Qur'an: Arabic Text and English Rendering, Text and Explanatory Translation by* Mohammad M. Pickthall (Des Plaines, IL.: Library of Islam, 1994). All Qur'anic references are to this translation.

2 Where appropriate, following Marshall Hodgson (1974), I replace the terms 'Islam' and 'Islamic' with 'Islamdom' and 'Islamicate.' This is an attempt to introduce a distinction between the faith (or activities derived from its norms) and a society (consisting mostly of Muslims) or some aspect of such a society, which may or may not derive from Islam as a faith. Marshall Hodgson, *The Venture of Islam*, volume 1 (Chicago: University of Chicago, 1974).

Islamicate societies. They began to look at Islam and Islamicate societies as they were described in Muslim sources; they wrote of Islamic achievements in philosophy, the sciences, arts and architecture; they emphasized Islam's egalitarian spirit, its emphasis on racial equality, and greater tolerance of other religious communities. Many of these Europeans who had chosen to give Islam its due were Jews who had only recently escaped from the ghettoes to enter into Europe's academies. In part, these Jews were appropriating for themselves the achievements of another Semitic people. In calling attention to the tolerance of Islamic societies, they were also gently reminding the Europeans that they had far to go towards creating a bourgeois civilization based on humane values. Less charitably, one might say that the Jewish dissenters were undermining the Christian West by elevating its opposite, the Islamic East.

A second shift in the temper of Orientalism that began in the 1950s would become more pervasive. From now on, a growing number of mainstream scholars of Islam and Islamicate societies would try to escape the essentializing mental habits of earlier Orientalists. This shift was the work of at least three forces. The most powerful of these forces was the struggle of the colonized peoples in the post-War period to free themselves from the yoke of colonialism. In the context of the Cold War, the political and economic interests of Western powers now demanded greater sensitivity to the culture, religion and history of the peoples they had denigrated over the previous four centuries. A show of respect for their subjects had now become a virtue in the writings of Orientalists.

The Orientalists were also being put on notice by the entry into Western academia of scholars of Middle Eastern and South Asian origins – including Phillip K. Hitti, Albert Hourani, George Makdisi, Muhsin Mahdi, Syed Hussein Nasr and Fazlur Rahman – who brought greater empathy and understanding to their studies on Islamicate societies. Edward Said too was a member of this group; his distinctive contribution consisted of his erudite and sustained critique of the methods of Orientalism. Said's critique belongs also to a broader intellectual movement – fueled in part by scholars from the non-Western world – that not only debunked the distortions of Orientalists but also sought to remedy their errors by writing a more sympathetic history of Asian and African societies. In other words, during this period some sections of the West began to acknowledge with some consternation the racism and bigotry that permeated much of the social sciences and humanities.

Starting in the 1950s, Islam also attracted the attention of several spiritual explorers from the West who were led hither by their disappointment with the poverty of living spiritual traditions in their own societies. The deep understanding of Islam they acquired through association with authentic Sufis – Muslims who cultivated, in addition to their meticulous observance of the Shariah, the inner dimensions of Islam – allowed them to write several outstanding books on the metaphysical and spiritual perspectives of Islam, both as they are practiced by its living exponents and as they are reflected in the calligraphy, architecture and the still surviving traditional crafts of the Islamic world. The writings of Rene Guenon, Titus Burckhardt, Frithjof Schuon, Martin Lings, Charles Le Gai Eaton, among others, demonstrate conclusively that Islam offers an original spiritual perspective that is fully capable of supporting a deeply religious life.

Yet, running counter to these developments, a new Orientalism was also taking shape in the post-War era. It was not based on any strikingly new the-sis about Islam. Instead, it was mostly a repackaging of the old Orientalism designed to renew a more intrusive dual US-Israeli control over the Middle East. Led by Bernard Lewis, the new Orientalists claim that the Islamicate world is a failed civilization. Among other things, they argue that Islamicate societies have failed to modernize because Islam's mixing of religion and politics makes it incompatible with democracy; Islam does not support equal rights for women and minorities; and Islam commands Muslims to wage war until the whole world is brought under the sway of Islamic law. In short, because of its intransigence and failure to adapt to the challenges of modernity, Islam has become the greatest present threat to civilization, that is, to Western interests.

What makes this repackaged Orientalism new are its intentions, its propo-nents, and the enemy it has targeted for destruction. Its intention is to mobi-lize the United States behind a scheme to balkanize the Middle East into ethnic, sectarian and religious micro states, a new system of client states that would facilitate Israel's long-term hegemony over the region. Ironically, the scholars who have dominated this repackaging of the old Orientalism are mostly Jewish, a reversal of roles that flows directly from the creation of a Jewish colonial-settler state in the heart of the Middle East. Once they had succeeded in creating Israel, the Zionists knew that its long-term survival depended on fomenting wars between the West and Islam. Zionism has pursued this goal by its own wars against Arabs and, since 1967, a brutal occupation of the West Bank and Gaza; but equally, it has pulled out all the stops to convince the United States to support unconditionally Israel's depredations against Arabs.

The target of the war that the new Orientalists want to wage are what they variously call Islamists, Islamic fundamentalists, Islamic militants, Islamofascists, or Islamic terrorists. Whatever the term, it embraces all Islamicate movements – no matter what their positions on the political uses of violence – that appeal to Islamic symbols to mobilize local, national, and pan-Islamicate resistance against the wars that the United States and Israel have jointly waged against the Middle East since 1945. These Islamicate resistance movements, which are both national and transcend national boundaries, have replaced the secular nationalists who, after failing to achieve their objectives, were co-opted by the United States and Israel to destroy the Islamicate resistance.

The events that have unfolded over the past few decades – the rise of the Islamicate resistance, the strategic cooperation between the United States and Israel, the new Orientalism, and the war that is now being waged against the Islamicate world – could have been foreseen, and indeed were foreseen, when the British first made a commitment to create a Jewish state in Palestine. An American writer on international affairs, Herbert Adams Gibbons, showed more acuity on the long-term fallout of Britain's Zionist plans than the leading Western statesmen of the times. In January 1919, he wrote: "If the peace conference decides to restore the Jews to Palestine, immigration into and development of the country can be assured only by the presence of a considerable army for an *indefinite* period. Not only the half million Moslems living in Palestine, but the millions in surrounding countries, will have to be cowed into submission by the constant show and occasional use of force (italics added)."[3] Even more prophetically, Anstruther MacKay,

---

3   Herbert Adams Gibbons, "Zionism and the World Peace," in: Richard P. Stevens, ed., *Zionism and Palestine Before the Mandate: A Phase of Westernlimperialism* (Beirut: The Institute of Palestine Studies, 1972): 63, reprinted from: *Century* 97, 3 (January 1919).

military governor of part of Palestine during World War I, wrote that the Zionist project would "arouse fierce Moslem hostility and fanaticism against the Western powers that permitted it. The effect of this hostility would be felt through the Middle East, and would cause trouble in Syria, Mesopotamia, Egypt, and India. To this might be ascribed by future historians the outbreak of a great war between the white and the brown races, *a war into which America would without doubt be drawn* (italics added)."[4] We are now living in the future predicted by Gibbons and MacKay. The Islamicate resistance has been slow in developing but it has now spread in one form or another beyond Syria, Mesopotamia, Egypt and India to the farthest corners of the Islamicate world – and even into the Islamicate diaspora in the West.

Only when I was preparing the new edition of these essays did I realize that the unifying theme, which I had missed before, consisted of my attempts to define, locate, contextualize, debunk and challenge the New Orientalism that I have briefly described here. In doing so my aim constantly has been to provide historical perspective to the wars that Western nations including the Zionists have waged, directly and indirectly, against the Middle East since 1917. History is always the ally of oppressed peoples; they can tell it as it was. It is the oppressors who deny their history; they have to make it up to deny the torments they have inflicted on their victims. They must speak constantly, unremittingly of the need to put down insurgencies, terrorists, threats to world peace, and violence against the civilized order. The essays in this volume espouse the aim of uncovering the sources, the methods and the aims of the new Orientalism. The aim is immodest, but I am aware that my reach is at best modest. And this too is a debt I owe to my *Rabb* and *Khaaliq*.[5]

---

4   Richard P. Stevens, ed., *Zionism and Palestine Before the Mandate*: 47-48, reprinted from: Anstruther MacKay, "Zionist Aspirations in Palestine," *Atlantic* 216 (July 1920): 123-25.
5   Lord and Creator.

*"O David! Lo! We have set thee as a viceroy in the earth; therefore judge
aright between mankind, and follow not desire that it beguile thee from the
way of Allah. Lo! those who wander from the way of Allah have an awful doom,
forasmuch as they forgot the Day of Reckoning."*
—Qur'an: 38: 26

May 2004

I have brought together in this book some of the essays I wrote after
September 11, 2001, essays in which I have tried to make sense – historical sense – of the events which transpired on the morning of that
fateful day, between 8:45 AM and 9:43 AM, when three hijacked air-
liners, converted into missiles, crashed into the Twin Towers and the
Pentagon, killing 2752 people.[1]

Articulating their fear and dread, many Americans felt that the attacks
of 9-11 had "changed the world forever." In large measure, this was true.
Most Americans had never known what it felt to be victims; they had
never lived in fear of attacks from bombs, missiles and artillery shells.
Only Americans had the right to deliver destruction to others; in any
case, only they had the power to do this to anyone, at any time. Now,
for the first time, death and destruction had been delivered to two
iconic addresses in America. This was not expected. It was unfair. It
was unnerving.

There are few moments in history, few horrors, that crystallize the contradictions of the reigning capitalist paradigm – contradictions that are
concealed, papered over by the ideologues of that paradigm – the way
that the attacks of 9-11 have done. I am referring here to the symbol-
ism of these attacks. They would retain their symbolic value even if
the attacks had occurred at night – when the Twin Towers were empty
– and they inflicted no human casualties.

Only a few years back, Francis Fukuyama had announced to the world
that man had finally reached the 'end of history,' that Hegel's Zeitgeist,

---

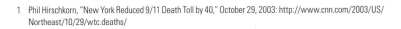

1   Phil Hirschkorn, "New York Reduced 9/11 Death Toll by 40," October 29, 2003: http://www.cnn.com/2003/US/
    Northeast/10/29/wtc.deaths/

after successively wrestling and defeating the fascist and communist challenges to freedom, had delivered history into the long-awaited Valhalla
of liberal capitalism. The American model, combining free markets and
democracy, had triumphed.[2] There might be a few road bumps ahead, but
henceforth, humanity would travel a straight and narrow path, paved with
peace, prosperity, and, not to forget, unchallenged American supremacy.

Perhaps, the attacks of September 11 have ended this end-of-history fan-
tasy. At least, some oracles are now proclaiming that history could not be
sent into retirement; not just yet. Sorry, there is one more dragon to slay.
A new fascism has reared its ugly head. It is fascism in its Islamic vari-
ant. Saint George must again sharpen his lance to slay the Islamic dragon.
Why this unseemly retreat from a triumph that seemed complete just a few
years back?

The attacks of September 11 are like an eruption, a volcanic eruption that
has thrust lava and ashes from our netherworld, the dark netherworld of
the Periphery, into the rich and tranquil landscape of America. In the past,
we had succeeded in containing these eruptions *inside* the Periphery. The
attacks of September 11 speak of a massive failure in a paradigm that has
worked for two hundred years to keep the Periphery in its place, to contain
the resistance against the Core within the bounds of the Periphery.

At first, and for the longest period, the Core kept the Periphery in check
through colonization: through massacres, ethnic cleansings, concentration
camps, apartheid and racism. We sent our men into the Periphery to do the
job, telling them that they were on a civilizing mission; they were bringing
good governance to the savages. We could always find natives to collaborate
with us against their own kin and class. In time, the natives understood the
game; they understood that they only labored for our profit. Taking advantage of our squabbles, the Periphery broke lose, starting in the 1940s.

This setback was temporary. In large part, the system managed to restore
the *status quo ex ante*. Steadily, inevitably, Core capital took over the capital in
the Periphery or bound it in a hundred ties of clientage, in unalterable relations of dependence. The Periphery was now run by native thugs who were
our men. We armed them, trained them, provided them with intelligence,

---

2   Francis Fukuyama, "The End of History?" *The National Interest*, (Summer 1989): 3-18. This was later written up into a book,
    The End of History and the Last Man (London: Hamish Hamilton, 1992).

and, when they misbehaved, we knew how to get rid of them. The CIA took care of that.

When the Soviet Union collapsed in 1991, the Core was free, as it had never been before, to impose global rules that best served its corporate interests. Henceforth, all capital would be privatized; capital, goods and services would be free to move across all borders; indigenous capital in the Periphery would receive no preferences; and property rights in intellectual capital would be strengthened. In 1994, the World Trade Organization (WTO) was created to join the IMF and World Bank in imposing these rules on the Periphery.

Once this new framework was in place, the Core encouraged elections everywhere, barring the Arab world. Democracy in the Periphery was now functional. It gave a measure of legitimacy to the branch-plant governments in the Periphery while ensuring that they would have no real power to challenge Core capital. Core capital never had a better deal. This was Valhalla.

Why did September 11 disturb the bliss of this Valhalla?

Directly and indirectly, the essays in this book provide answers to this question. September 11 brings into the open, forcing into the daylight of consciousness, the legacies of history – of racial hubris, of disequilibria imposed by wars, of messianism, of reincarnated fossils, of tribalism sanctified by religion, of social science in the service of power, of naked greed disguised in the rhetoric of the civilizing mission, of citizens fed on lies and sedated by amusements, of cruelty cultivated as a racial virtue, of injustices that cannot be allowed to stand. September 11 establishes beyond reasonable doubt that the United States is deeply, irrevocably connected to the Arab world, the Islamicate world, in ways it cannot ignore or deny. These essays map out the connections.

Notwithstanding its horror, September 11 was a symbol that spoke unmistakably of the manifold connections that bind the United States – through Zionism, through its messianic fervor, through its links to an older past, through wars, through sanctions, through tens of billions of dollars in military aid, through coups, through partnerships with corrupt monarchies, through vetoes at the Security Council, through demonization of Islam, through the brothels of corporate media – to Palestinians, to Iraqis, to the

Arab world, to the Islamicate world, to Africa, Asia and Latin America: in a word, to the Periphery. September 11 was a souvenir from the dark dungeons of our secret history, a digitized, televised image from the lost and forgotten Abu Ghraibs of decades past.

The symbolic power of 9-11 had to be suppressed. Instantly, the President, followed by the brothels of corporate media and the ideologues who pimp for authority, was spinning a thick web of lies and obfuscations around 9-11. The hijackers were emissaries from an evil country, a demon world, whose inhabitants worship false idols, and in daily rituals of blood sacrifices imprecate our democracy, our freedoms, our rights, our traditions of infinite justice. These devils hate us because we are so good, so virtuous, and so Christian.

September 11 was also welcomed by some in Israel and America. Yes, it was welcomed. The words are unmistakable. In an interview he gave to the *New York Times*, Benjamin Netanyahu, former Prime Minister of Israel, said the attacks are "very good" for relations between the United States and Israel.[3] The attacks were also very good for the neoconservatives, many of them friends of Israel, who were waiting for a "galvanizing event" to launch their *Project for a New American Century*, which would make American power unchallengeable.[4] September 11 was their dream come true. In April 2003, they succeeded in leveraging 9-11 into an invasion of Iraq. That is now history. A few of the essays in this book are about this war too, its lies, its language, its links to the past, and its bitter legacy rapidly, unexpectedly unfolding before our eyes.

In gathering these essays, I am led to recall the support and friendship I received along the way, as I looked for publishing outlets, and as I faced the wrath of cliques who have long sought to censor – too often successfully – any references to the crimes of their favorite tribe. I owe my deepest thanks to the two bold and doughty editors of *Counterpunch*, Jeffrey St. Claire and Alexander Cockburn, who first launched these essays, giving me the audience that the censors in mainstream media were determined to deny me. *Counterpunch* is one of the few points of light in a media space that is dominated by black holes.

---

3 James Bennet, "Spilled Blood Is Seen as Bond That Draws 2 Nations Closer," *New York Times* (September 12, 2001), section A, p. 22. col. 5.

4 David Fitts, "Those Who Don't Remember History," *Ace Weekly* (April 10, 2003): www.aceweekly.com/Backissues_ACE-Weekly/2003/030410/cover_story 030410. html

I had few friends at Northeastern University before 9-11. I have fewer now. Only one colleague, Frank Naarendorp, Professor of Psychology, stood by my side during my travails with people who wanted me fired from my job. I lost one friend when he discovered, on the eve of America's invasion of Iraq, that I was deficient in the measure of patriotism that translates into automatic support for *all* American wars, once they have been launched. I lost a second friend when I signed my name to a petition calling for the academic boycott of Israel. Israel can do nothing to deserve our moral censure, unless we also censure its victims. Still, I remain grateful to Northeastern University for tolerating my free speech – for leaving me alone – at a time when many outside and a few inside Northeastern sought my dismissal for exercising that right in ways that they found disagreeable.

Judging from their comments on my teaching, I like to think that my students are better disposed towards my critiques of global capitalism and the ideologies that support it. An occasional student will demand that I love it or leave it. Many more are more appreciative; a few even claim that they have been transformed. But I suspect that their appreciation probably has a short shelf-life.

Among my friends, Paul de Rooij receives my warmest gratitude. Paul is an economist based in London, who, at about the same time as I, decided to enter the public discourse, impelled I think by the same events that had moved me. Paul has long been an indefatigable advocate of the Palestinians in their struggle against Israeli Occupation. Though divided by an ocean, with a little help from the internet, over the past two years Paul has been a comrade in arms, an invaluable resource, occasionally a demanding editor, but always a delightful companion.

Many friends and fellow travelers offered hope, encouragement and friendship when others proffered insults, invectives and intimidations. In particular, I would like to acknowledge with gratitude the many kindnesses I have received from Ahrar Ahmad, Mumtaz Ahmed, Mohammed Aleem, Abdul Cader Asmal, Rauf Azhar, Mona Baker, Ken Barney, Belal Baquie, Shelagh Bocoum, Ashfak Bokhari, Zeljko Cipris, Hamid Dabashi, Lawrence Davidson, Sundeep Dougal, John Esposito, Ahmad Faruqui, Ted Honderich, Rashid Khalidi, Anwar Shahid Khan, Rich LaRock, Aftab Malik, Muneeb Malik, Mustansir Mir, Enver Masud, Parviz Mirbaghi, Sheila Musaji, Ahmed

Nassef, Marghoob Quraishi, Saleem Rashid, Syed Shakeel, Sunil Sharma, Lille Singh, George Saliba, Teepu Siddique, Denis Sullivan, Gale Toensing, Pankaj Topiwala and Asad Zaman. Some of them are old friends; some new; some I have not met but hope to meet soon.

My final acknowledgement is paternal. It goes to my son, Junaid, from whom I have learnt far more than he has from me, at least in the years during which he was negotiating his rites of passage. Instead of writing poetry, as I did to ease my passage, he was reading Karl Marx and Leon Trotsky. I think it all started when a teacher gave him a copy of Frantz Fanon's *The Wretched of the Earth*. I may have helped it along by giving him access to my copy of Aimé Césaire. I have since been wondering about whatever happened to all my talk about Rumi and the contemplative life. Was it only talk?

I hope that these essays will bear witness, faint witness though it be, that I have endeavored to be true to my *Rabb*, the single Lord of all Creation, to whom belong the most beautiful names, and, conversely, that I have labored to reject the false deities of tribe and cult, of racism and bigotry, because He, who is *Rahman* and *Raheem*, created us "from a single soul and from it created its mate, and from them twain hath spread abroad a multitude of men and women."[5] As a Muslim, to believe is to bear witness to our single humanity: our creation from, and connection to, a single soul.

"Our Lord! Cause not our hearts to stray after Thou hast guided us, and bestow upon us mercy from Thy Presence. Lo! Thou, only Thou art the Bestower."[6]

---

5 Qur'an: 4:1.
6 Qur'an: 3:8.

THE NEW

CHAPTER ONE

Bernard Lewis:
Scholarship or Sophistry?[1]

"Confound not truth with falsehood, nor knowingly conceal the truth."
Qur'an: 2:42

February 2002

It would appear from the fulsome praise heaped by mainstream review-ers on Bernard Lewis's most recent and well-timed book, *What Went Wrong? Western Impact and Middle Eastern Response*, that the demand for Orientalism has reached a new peak.[2] America's search for new ene-mies that began soon after the end of the Cold War very quickly resur-rected the ghost of an old, though now decrepit, enemy, Islamdom. Slowly but surely, this revived the sagging fortunes of Orientalism, so that it speaks again with the treble voice of authority.

The mainstream reviewers describe Bernard Lewis as "the doyen of Middle Eastern studies," the "father" of Islamic studies, "arguably the West's most distinguished scholar on the Middle East," and "a Sage for the Age."[3] Lewis is still the reigning monarch of Orientalism, as he was some twenty-five years ago, when Edward Said dissected and exposed the intentions, modalities, deceptions, and imperialist connections of this ideological enterprise.[4] This Orientalist tiger has not changed his stripes over the fifty-odd years that he has been honing his predatory

---

1   This paper first appeared in *Studies in Contemporary Islam* 4, 1 (Spring 2002): 53-80.

2   Bernard Lewis, *What Went Wrong? Western Impact and Middle Eastern Response* (Oxford: Oxford University Press, 2002).

3   The first three quotes are from the *New York Times*, the *National Review*, and *Newsweek*, respectively, and are showcased on the Oxford University Press website: www.oup-usa.org/isbn/0195144201.html. The last quote is the title of an article from *Jewsweek*, 4 September 2002; available at www.jewsweek.com/ israel/ 092.htm.

4   Edward Said, *Orientalism* (New York: Vintage Books, 1978).

3

skills. Now at the end of his long career – only coincidentally, also the peak – he presents the summation, the quintessence of his scholarship and wisdom on Islam and the Middle East, gathered, compressed in the pages of this slim book that sets out to explain what went wrong with Islamicate history, and that has so mesmerized reviewers on the right.

Who Is Bernard Lewis?

We will return to the book in a moment, but before that, we need to step back some twenty-five years and examine how Edward Said, in *Orientalism*, has described this Orientalist tiger's stripes and his cunning ploys at concealment. Edward Said gets to the nub of Lewis's Orientalist project when he writes that his "work purports to be liberal objective scholarship but is in reality very close to being propaganda *against* his subject material." Lewis's work is "aggressively ideological." He has dedicated his entire career, spanning more than five decades, to a "project to debunk, to whittle down, and to discredit the Arabs and Islam." Said writes: "The core of Lewis's ideology about Islam is that it never changes, and his whole mission is to inform conservative segments of the Jewish reading public, and anyone else who cares to listen, that any political, historical, and scholarly account of Muslims must begin and end with the fact that Muslims are Muslims."

Although Lewis's objectives are ominous, his methods are subtle; he prefers to work "by suggestion and insinuation." In order to disarm his readers, he delivers frequent "sermons on the objectivity, the fairness, the impartiality of a real historian." However, this is only a cover, a camouflage, for his political propaganda. Once he is seated on his high Orientalist perch, he goes about cleverly insinuating how Islam is deficient in and opposed to universal values, which, of course, always originate in the West. It is because of this defect in their values that Arabs have trouble accepting a democratic Israel; it is always "democratic" Israel. Lewis can write "objectively" about the Arab's "ingrained" opposition to Israel without ever telling his readers that Israel is an imperialist creation, a racist and expansionist colonial-settler state that was founded on terror, wars and ethnic cleansing. Lewis's work on Islam represents the "culmination of Orientalism as a dogma that not only degrades its subject matter but also blinds its practitioners."[5]

---

5   All the quotes in this and the preceding paragraph are from Said (1978): 314-320.

Lewis's scholarly mask slips off rather abruptly when he appears on television, a feat that he accomplishes with predictable regularity. Once he is on the air, his polemical self, the Orientalist crouching tiger, takes over, all his sermons about objectivity forgotten, and then he does not shrink from displaying his sneering contempt for the Arabs and Muslims more generally, his blind partisanship for Israel, or his bristling hostility toward Iran. One recent example will suffice here. In a PBS interview broadcast on 16 April 2002, hosted by Charlie Rose, he offered this gem: "Asking Arafat to give up terrorism would be like asking Tiger to give up golf."[6] That is a statement whose malicious intent and vindictive meanness might have been excusable if it came from an Israeli official deflecting attention from the brutal Israeli Occupation of Palestinian lands.

After this background check, do we really want to hear from this "sage" about "what went wrong" with Islamicate societies? Why, after nearly a thousand years of expansive power and world leadership in many branches of the arts and sciences, they began to lose their élan, their military advantage, and their creativity and, starting in the nineteenth century, capitulated to their historical adversary, the West? Although Islamicate societies have regained their political independence, why has their economic and cultural decline proved so difficult to reverse? Yet, although our stomachs turn at the prospect, we must sample the gruel Lewis offers, taste it, and analyze it, if only to identify the toxins that it contains and that have poisoned far too many Western minds for more than fifty years.

Where Is the Context?

What went wrong with the Islamic societies? When our "doyen" of Middle Eastern studies asks this question – and right after the attacks of 11 September too – it is hard not to notice that this manner of framing the problem of the eclipse of Islamicate societies by the West is loaded with biases, value judgments and preconceptions; it also contains its own answer. There are two sets of "wrongs" in *What Went Wrong*? The first consists of "wrongs," deviations from what is just and good, that we confront in *contemporary* Islamicate societies. Lewis undoubtedly has in mind a whole slew of problems, includ-

---

6   Jay Nordlinger, "Arafat and Tiger, Nimoy and Shatner, Reagan and Wayne, &c.," *National Review Online,* 2 May 2002; available at www.nationalreview.com/impromptus/ impromptus050202.asp.

ing the political, economic and cultural failings of the Islamicate world. In addition, this question seeks to discover deeper "wrongs," deviations from what is just and good that are prior to and lie at the root of the present "wrongs." Lewis is concerned primarily with this second set of "wrongs" that have derailed Islamicate history.

The first problem one encounters in Lewis's narrative of Middle Eastern decline is the absence of a context. He never locates the problem of Islamicate backwardness in its global setting, where backwardness has been endemic to all societies in the Periphery, including the Indian, Chinese, Islamicate, African and Latin American. Instead, he seeks to create the impression that only Islamicate societies have failed to catch up with the West, that this is a specifically Islamic failure. This Middle Eastern focus reveals to all but the blinkered the *mala fides* of *What Went Wrong?* Lewis cannot deceive us with pious claims that a historian's "loyalties may well influence his choice of subject of research; they should not influence his treatment of it."[7] His exclusive focus on the decline of the Middle East is not legitimate precisely because it is designed to – and it unavoidably must – "influence his treatment of it."

Once Western Europe began to make the transition from a feudal-agrarian to a capitalist-industrial base, starting in the sixteenth century, the millennial balance of power among the world's major civilizations began to shift inexorably in favor of Western Europe. A feudal-agrarian society could not match the social power of societies with a capitalist-industrial base. Increasingly, the latter were organized into nation states, whose mercantilist pursuit of power constantly pushed them to augment their military power through industrial strength. To this end, they stimulated the development of a national bourgeoisie; promoted innovations in statecraft, bureaucracy, and civil and military technology; and took advantage of the growing knowledge of markets to design more effective industrial policies. In addition, as the nation states forged a national consciousness, they became better at commanding national resources in the pursuit of nationalist goals. Altogether, these developments made it difficult for non-Western societies to rise up to the challenge offered by Western power. It was unlikely that non-Western societies could simultaneously alter the foundations of their

---

7   Bernard Lewis, *Islam in History: Ideas, Men and Events in the Middle East* (London: Alcove Press, 1973): 65.

societies while fending off military attacks from Western states. Even as these feudal-agrarian societies sought to reorganize their economies and institutions, Western onslaughts against them escalated, and this made their reorganization increasingly difficult. It is scarcely surprising that the growing asymmetry between the two sides eventually led to the eclipse, decline or subjugation of nearly *all* non-Western societies.

Unlike Lewis, who studiously avoids any reference to this new disequalizing dynamic, another Western scholar of Islam – not driven by a compulsion "to debunk, to whittle down, and to discredit the Arabs and Islam" – understood this tendency quite well. I am referring here to Marshall Hodgson, whose *The Venture of Islam* shows a deep and, for its time, rare understanding of the interconnectedness, across space and time, amongst all societies in the Eastern hemisphere. He understood very clearly that the epochal changes underway in parts of Western Europe between 1600 and 1800 were creating an altogether new order based on markets, capital accumulation and technological change, which acted upon each other to produce cumulative growth. Moreover, this dynamic endowed the most powerful Western states with a degree of social power that no one could resist. Once this "Western Transmutation" got well under way, writes Hodgson, it "could neither be paralleled independently nor be borrowed wholesale. Yet it could not, in most cases, be escaped. The millennial parity of social power broke down, with results that were disastrous everywhere."[8]

Clearly, the absence of any comparative perspective in Lewis's narrative of Middle Eastern decline is a ploy. His objective is to whittle down world history, to reduce it to a primordial contest between two historical adversaries, the West and Islamicate societies. This is historiography in the Crusading mode; it purports to resume the Crusades and carry them to their unfinished conclusion, i.e., the extirpation of Islam in the one-time Christian lands of the Middle East. Once Lewis has established his framework, with its exclusive focus on a failing Islamicate civilization, it becomes necessary to cast the narrative of this decay as a uniquely Islamic phenomenon: a failure contained in the essence of Islam. The attacks of 9-11 created a large

---

8 Marshall Hodgson, *The Venture of Islam: Conscience and History in a World Civilization*, volume 3 (Chicago: University of Chicago Press, 1974): 200.

audience for such narratives in the United States. Lewis was ready to meet this demand. It is as if, all his life he had prepared for this occasion.

If Lewis had an interest in exploring the decline of the Middle East, he would be asking why the new, more dynamic capitalist society had emerged in the West and not in the Middle East, India, China, Italy or Africa. This question would have led him to explore the factors that might explain the rise of Western hegemony. However, Lewis ducks this question altogether. Instead, he makes the growing power of the West the starting point of his narrative and concentrates on demonstrating why the efforts of Islamicate societies to catch up with the West were both too little and too late. In other words, he seeks to explain a *generic* phenomenon – the overthrow of agrarian societies before the rise of a new historical system, based on capital, markets and technological change – as one that is *specific* to Islam and is due to specifically Islamic "wrongs."[9]

Clearly, the Middle Eastern response to the Western challenge was inadequate. The Ottoman Empire, once the most powerful in the Islamicate world, had lost nearly all its European territories by the end of the nineteenth century, and the remnants of its Arab territories were lost during the First World War. Worse still, at the end of the War, the European powers threatened the Turks in their Anatolian heartland, with the British and French occupying Istanbul, the Greeks marching towards Ankara, the Armenians pushing westward in eastern Anatolia, and the French pushing north into Cilicia. Faced with extinction, the Turks mobilized before it was too late; they rallied in central Anatolia after the War and fought tooth and nail to push back the Bulgarians, Greeks, French and Armenians. In 1922, they succeeded in establishing a new and modern Turkish nation-state over Istanbul, Thrace and all of Anatolia. The Iranians had more luck in preserving their territories, though, like the Ottomans, they too had lost control over their economic policies in the first decades of the nineteenth century.

Nevertheless, in a comparative setting, the Middle East's record of resisting imperialism is not the worst. First, nearly all of South Asia, East and Southeast Asia, and Africa was colonized by the Europeans during the nineteenth century. Only Japan, Thailand, China and Ethiopia avoided

---

9   Lewis (2002):151-152.

direct colonization during this period, though Ethiopia and much of China were colonized during the 1930s. Moreover, given its proximity to Europe, the Middle East came early and directly in the path of European imperial ambitions. It is also the case that Europe's colonial appetite in the Middle East was stimulated by the historical legacy of the region. Not a few thought of the new colonization as the resumption of the Crusade against old adversaries. Under the circumstances, it is significant that much of this region managed to avoid direct colonization during the nineteenth century.

Uncurious Ottomans

There is even less support for Lewis's charge that Middle Eastern societies responded too slowly to Western threats, especially when we compare their responses with the record of East Asian societies.[10]

First, consider Lewis's charge that the Muslims showed little curiosity about the West. He attributes this failing to Muslim bigotry that frowned upon contacts with the infidels.[11] This is a curious charge against "a world civilization" that Lewis admits was "polyethnic, multiracial, international, one might even say intercontinental."[12] It also seems strange that the Ottomans, and other Middle Eastern states before them, were quite happy to take their Christian and Jewish subjects into employment – as high officials, diplomats, physicians and bankers – traded with the Europeans, bought arms and borrowed money from them, and yet, somehow, loathed learning anything from the same 'infidels.' In addition, Muslim philosophers, historians and travelers have left several very valuable accounts of non-Islamic societies. Among others, Al-Biruni's monumental study of India remains without a rival for its encyclopedic coverage, objectivity, and sympathy for its subject. Clearly, Lewis has fallen prey to the Orientalist temptation. When

---

10 Unlike the Islamicate world, China, Korea and, after an early period of openness, Japan, pursued a policy of minimal contacts with Western nations. After 1760, China restricted all foreign trade to one port, Canton, where foreigners were permitted to reside only during the trading season, from October to March. Starting in 1637, Korea banned all contacts with foreigners except the Chinese, a policy that earned it the reputation of the Hermit Kingdom. In the same year, Japan's trading contacts with Western nations were restricted to one annual visit by a Dutch ship to the tiny island of Deshima. China did not open additional ports to foreign trade until after its defeat in the Opium Wars (1840-1842); the Japanese ended their isolation, under American pressure, in 1850; and Korea did not open its doors to Western nations until 1882. William H. McNeill, *The Rise of the West* (Chicago: University of Chicago Press, 1991): 643-648; Jonathan D. Spence, *The Search for Modern China* (New York: W. W. Norton and Co., 1999): 121.

11 Lewis (2002): chapter 2.

12 Lewis (2002): 6.

something demands a carefully researched explanation, an understanding of material and social conditions, he prefers to pin it on some cultural propensity of Islamicate societies.

Lewis is little aware how his book is littered with contradictions. If the Muslims were not a little curious about developments in the West, it is odd that the oldest map of the Americas, prepared by a Turkish admiral and cartographer, Piri Reis, in 1513, is also the most accurate map from the sixteenth century.[13] In addition, Muslims were writing accounts of their travels to Europe from an early date. Lewis refers to no fewer than ten such accounts, nearly all of them written by Ottomans, spanning the period from 1665 to 1840. One of them, Ratib Effendi, who was in Vienna from 1791 to 1792, left a report that "ran to 245 manuscript folios, ten times or more than ten times those of his predecessors, and it goes into immense detail, primarily on military matters, but also, to quite a considerable extent, on civil affairs."[14] Diplomatic contacts provide another indicator of the early Ottoman interest and involvement in the affairs of European states. Between 1703 and 1774, the Ottomans signed sixty-eight treaties or agreements with sovereign, mostly European states.[15] Since each treaty must have involved at least one diplomatic exchange, it would be difficult to accuse the Ottomans of neglecting diplomatic contacts with Europe.

Was there a failure of vision, as Lewis claims, in the Ottoman decision not to challenge Portuguese hegemony in the Indian Ocean in the sixteenth century? Despite some early warnings from elder statesmen, they chose to concentrate their war efforts on acquiring territory in Europe, which they saw as "the principal battleground between Islam and Europe, the rival faiths competing for enlightenment – and mastery – of the world."[16] First, we can scarcely blame the Ottomans for not anticipating that the Portuguese incursion would translate some 250 years later into a broader and more serious European challenge to their power. It is doubtful if this was because

---

13 Gregory McIntosh, *The Piri Reis Map of Europe* (Athens, GA.: University of Georgia Press, 2000). Lewis (2002: 37) gives the impression that the Ottomans made little use of the Piri Reis map; they deposited the map in the Topkapi Palace in Istanbul, "where it remained, unconsulted and unknown" until it was discovered in 1929. There is no basis for this assertion. In fact, Reis prepared two maps of the world, one in 1513 and another in 1528; besides these he drew many other charts and maps that were assembled into a book, *Kitab-i-Behriye* (Book of the Sea), which was made available in two editions. See Gregory McIntosh, "A Tale of Two Admirals," *Mercator's World: The Magazine of Maps, Atlases, Globes, and Charts* (May-June 2000).

14 Lewis (2002): 27.

15 Donald Quataert, *The Ottoman Empire, 1700-1922* (Cambridge: Cambridge University Press, 2000): 75.

16 Lewis (2002): 15.

the Ottomans lacked the ability to launch an adequate response to a maritime challenge. Departing from their own tradition of land warfare, the Ottomans, starting in the fifteenth century, had built a powerful navy and created a seaborne empire in the eastern Mediterranean, the Black Sea and the Red Sea. If the Ottomans chose to concentrate their resources on land wars in Central Europe rather than challenge Portuguese hegemony in the Indian Ocean, this was not the result of religious zealotry. It reflected the balance of class interests in the Ottoman political structure. In an Empire that had traditionally been land-based, the interests of the landowning classes prevailed against commercial interests that looked to the Indian Ocean for their livelihood. Although the decision not to contest the Portuguese presence in the Indian Ocean in the sixteenth century proved to be fateful, that policy was rational for the Ottomans.[17]

A Military Decline?

Several Orientalists – Lewis amongst them[18] – have argued that the military decline of the Ottoman Empire became irreversible after its second failed siege of Vienna in 1683, or perhaps earlier, after its naval defeat at Lepanto in 1571. In an earlier work, Lewis claimed that "the Ottomans found it more and more difficult to keep up with the rapidly advancing Western technological innovations, and in the course of the eighteenth century the Ottoman Empire, itself far ahead of the Islamic world, fell decisively behind Europe in virtually all arts of war."[19]

Jonathan Grant has convincingly questioned this thesis of an early and inexorable decline. The Ottomans occupied the third tier in the hierarchy of military technology, behind innovators and exporters, at the beginning of the fifteenth century; they could reproduce the latest military technology with the help of foreign expertise but they never graduated into export or introduced any significant innovations. The Ottomans succeeded in maintaining this relative position, through two waves of technology diffusion, until

---

17 Andrew C. Hess, "The Evolution of the Ottoman Seabourne Empire in the Age of the Oceanic Discoveries, 1453-1525," in Felipe Fernández-Armesto, ed., *The Global Opportunity* (Brookfield, VT: Variorum, 1995): 218. It is unlikely that the Ottomans faced any insuperable barrier to the adoption of the new naval technology; the North Africans managed to do this toward the end of the sixteenth century [Hess (1995): 222].

18 Lewis (2002): 151.

19 Bernard Lewis, *The Muslim Discovery of Europe* (New York: W. W. Norton, 1982): 226.

the early nineteenth century. However, they failed to keep up with the third wave of technology diffusion, based upon the technology of the industrial revolution, which began in the mid-nineteenth century. The Ottomans fell below their third-tier status only toward the end of the nineteenth century, when they became totally dependent on imported weaponry.[20]

If we put together the evidence made available by Lewis, it becomes clear that the Ottomans were not slow in recognizing the institutional superiority enjoyed by Europe's military.[21] A debate about the causes of Ottoman weakness began after the Treaty of Carlowitz in 1699, growing more intense over time. A document from the early seventeenth century recognized that "it was no longer sufficient, as in the past, to adopt Western weapons. It was also necessary to adopt Western training, structures, and tactics for their effective use." The Ottomans began to dispatch special envoys to European capitals "with instructions to observe and to learn and, more particularly, to report on anything that might be useful to the Muslim state in coping with its difficulties and confronting its enemies." Several of these envoys wrote reports, occasionally quite extensive and detailed, on their European visits, and these reports had an important impact on thinking in Ottoman circles. The first mathematical school for the military was founded in 1734, and a second one followed in the 1770s.

While the Ottomans generally kept up with advances in military technology, at least into the first decades of the nineteenth century, they took longer to introduce supporting organizational changes. As a result, the first serious attempts at modernizing the army did not begin until the late eighteenth century, during the reign of Selim III, who sought to bypass the problems of reforming the existing military corps by recruiting and training a new European-style army. Although, he had raised a modern army of nearly twenty-five thousand by 1806, he had to abandon his efforts in the face of resistance from the ulama and a Janissary rebellion. He took up this task again in 1826 after disbanding the Janissary corps, and in two years, the new Ottoman army included seventy-five thousand regular troops. Simultaneously, the Ottomans introduced reforms in the bureaucracy; they

---

20 Jonathan Grant, "Rethinking the Ottoman "Decline": Military Technology Diffusion in the Ottoman Empire, Fifteenth to Eighteenth Centuries," *Journal of World History* 10, 1 (1999):179-201.
21 Lewis (2002): 20, 25-29.

also reformed land-tenure policies with the objective of raising revenues.[22] Yet these efforts at modernizing the Ottoman military – quite early by most standards – failed to avert the progressive fragmentation and eventual demise of the Ottoman Empire at the end of World War I. One might join Hodgson in thinking that this was inevitable, that agrarian societies in Asia and Africa could not modernize fast enough in the face of the ever-increasing economic and military power of the modern Western nation-states.[23] Perhaps, this assessment is too fatalistic. Among others, the Russians modernized in time to save their Empire.

A comparison of the Ottoman and Russian experiences at modernization reveals several extraneous factors that undermined the Ottoman initiatives. The Ottoman Empire, which straddled three continents, lacked the compactness that might have made its territories more defensible. In addition, the Ottoman Turks, the ethnic core of the Ottoman Empire, made up less than a third of its population and occupied an even smaller part of its territories. Finally, the nationalist ideas emanating from Europe found fertile ground in the Ottoman Empire, which had organized its religious minorities into autonomous religious communities. Starting in the nineteenth century, the Ottomans faced one nationalist insurrection after another in the Balkans, each backed by one or more European powers, until the last of these territories broke free by the early decades of the twentieth century. In as much as these insurrections reduced the revenues of the Empire and diverted its resources to war, they delayed the modernization of the military and economy. Finally, during World War I, the British and the French divested the Empire of all its Arab territories.

The Egyptian program to modernize its military, which began in 1815 under the leadership of Muhammad Ali, was more ambitious and more successful. It was part of an integrated program of modernization and industrial development financed through state ownership of lands, development of new export crops, and state-owned monopolies over the marketing of the major agricultural products. In 1831, Egypt's Europeanized army consisted of one hundred thousand officers and men, and two years later, after conquering

---

22 Roger Owen, *The Middle East in the World Economy, 1800-1914* (London: I. B. Tauris, 1993): 58, and, J. C. Hurewitz, "The Beginnings of Military Modernization in the Middle East: A Comparative Analysis," *Middle East Journal* 22 (1968): 2:149.
23 Lewis (2002), of course, argues that the modernization did not go far enough because of fundamental flaws in Islamicate institutions; we will return to this argument.

Syria, it was penetrating deep into Anatolia when its advance was halted by Russian naval intervention. The major European powers intervened again in 1839 – all of them but the French – to stop the Egyptians from advancing upon Istanbul.[24] They forced the Egyptians to withdraw, give up their acquisitions in Syria and Arabia, reduce their military force to eighteen thousand, and implement the Anglo-Ottoman Commercial Convention, which required the lowering of tariffs to three percent and the dismantling of all state monopolies.[25] By depriving Egypt of its revenues and dramatically reducing the military's demand for its manufactures, these measures abruptly terminated the career of the earliest and most ambitious program to build a modern, industrial society in the Periphery.

Lewis faults the Ottomans and Egyptians for seeking to build a modern industrial economy. He thinks it odd that these countries "tried to catch up with Europe by building factories, principally to equip and clothe their armies."[26] All too often, the military has provided the markets and the impetus for pushing through a program of early industrialization. In fact, the Ottomans and Egyptians were leading the way. Of course, Lewis thinks that the Ottomans should have been working harder to remedy their cultural deficiencies, especially their less-than-enthusiastic appreciation for European harmonies.

Industrial Failure – But Why?

Lewis declares that the industrialization programs launched by the Ottomans and Egypt "failed, and most of the early factories became derelict."[27] These programs were doomed from the outset because their promoters lacked a proper regard for time, measurement, harmonies, secularism, and women's rights – values that underpin Western industrial success.

We must correct these jaundiced observations. Far from being a failure, the Egyptian "program of industrialization and military expansion," according to Immanuel Wallerstein, "seriously undermined the Ottoman Empire and

---

24 The Egyptian superiority during the Syrian campaigns was quite decisive; they won easy victories even when they were outnumbered two to one. David Ralston, *Importing the European Army* (Chicago: University of Chicago Press, 1990): 89.

25 Hurewitz (1968): 145-48.

26 Lewis (2002): 46-47.

27 Lewis (2002): 145-148.

almost established a powerful state in the Middle East capable eventually of playing a major role in the interstate system."[28] Muhammad Ali's fiscal and economic reforms, between 1805 and 1847, brought about a more than nine fold increase in government revenues.[29] At their height in the 1830s, Egypt's state monopolies had made investments worth $12 million and employed thirty thousand workers in a broad range of industries that included found-ries, textiles, paper, chemicals, shipyards, glassware, and arsenals.[30] By the early 1830s, Egyptian arsenals and naval yards had acquired the ability to "produce appreciable amounts of warships, guns and munitions," elevat-ing Egypt "to a major regional power."[31] Naturally, these developments in Egypt were raising concerns in British official circles. A report submitted to the British foreign office in 1837 sounded the appropriate note: "A manu-facturing country Egypt never can become – or at least for ages."[32] Three years later, when Istanbul was within the grasp of Muhammad Ali's forces, a coalition of European powers intervened to roll back his gains, downsize his military, and dismantle his state monopolies. These measures success-fully reversed the Periphery's first industrial revolution.

The Ottoman program of industrialization was similarly constrained by the jealousy of Western powers. Forced by the Unequal Treaties to limit their import tariffs to less than three percent, the Ottomans were unable to pro-tect their manufactures or raise revenues for investments in development projects. In addition, the Anglo-Turkish Commercial Convention of 1839 forced them to dismantle all state monopolies, dealing another blow to their fiscal autonomy. It speaks to the determination of the Ottomans that they sought to launch an industrial revolution despite their adverse fiscal circumstances. In the decade starting in 1841, the Ottomans had set up to the west of Istanbul a complex of state-owned industries that included spinning and weaving mills, a foundry, steam-operated machine works, and a boatyard for the construction of small steamships. In the words of Edward Clark: "In variety as well as in number, in planning, in investment, and in attention given to internal sources of raw materials these manufac-

---

28 Immanuel Wallerstein, *Unthinking Social Science: The Limits of Nineteenth Century Paradigms* (London: Polity Press, 1991): 14.

29 Helen Anne B. Rivlin, *The Agricultural Policy of Muhammad Ali in Egypt* (Cambridge: Harvard University Press, 1961), 120.

30 M. Shahid Alam, *Poverty from the Wealth of Nations* (Houndmills: Macmillan, 2000):115

31 John Dunn, "Egypt's Nineteenth-Century Armaments Industry," *The Journal of Military History* 61 (1997): 2:236.

32 L. S. Stavrianos, *Global Rift: The Third World Comes of Age* (New York: William Morrow, 1981), 218.

turing enterprises far surpassed the scope of all previous efforts and mark this period as unique in Ottoman history."[33] Several foreign observers saw in the Istanbul industrial complex the potential to evolve into "a Turkish Manchester and Leeds, a Turkish Birmingham and Sheffield," all wrapped in one.[34] Similar projects were initiated in several other parts of the Empire. However, once the Crimean War started, the Ottomans were strapped for funds, and they abandoned most of these industrial projects. Thus ended another bold experiment in industrialization, early even by European standards, but whose failure was linked to the loss of Ottoman fiscal sovereignty.

It's in Their Culture

Lewis blames the political, economic and military failures of the Middle East over the past half a millennium on their culture. He identifies a whole slew of problematic cultural traits, but singles out two for special attention: the mixing of religion and politics and the unequal treatment of women, unbelievers and slaves. Moreover, he insists that these are Islamic flaws.

Lewis argues that secularism constitutes a great divide between Islamdom and the West: the West always had it and Islamdom never did. Secularism, as the separation of church and state, "is, in a profound sense, Christian." Its origins go back to Jesus – his injunction to give God *and* Caesar, each, their due – and to the early history of Christianity when, as a persecuted minority, they developed an independent Church with its "own laws and courts, its own hierarchy and chain of authority." The Church is unique, setting Christian Europe apart from anything that went before and from its competitors. In particular, the Muslims never created an "institution corresponding to, or even *remotely* resembling, the Church in Christendom (emphasis added)."[35]

These claims about a secular Christendom and theocratic Islamicate societies are problematic. Lewis rests his case upon two propositions. First, he contrasts the presence of the Church in Christendom against its absence in Islamdom. Second, he works on the presumption that the existence of a

---

33 Edward Clark, "The Ottoman Industrial Revolution," *International Journal of Middle East Studies* 5, 1 (1974): 67.
34 Clark (1974): 68.
35 Lewis (2002): 96.

Church, a hierarchical religious organization separate from the state, necessarily implies a separation between religion and political authority. For the most part, these claims are contestable.

The absence of an Islamic Church does not mean that Islamicate societies did not develop a separation between religion and the state. Admittedly, there existed a fusion between the state and religion in early Islamdom; the Prophet and the first four Caliphs combined religious and mundane authority in their persons. In addition, most Islamic thinkers have maintained that the ideal Islamic state must be guided by the Qur'an and the Prophet's Sunnah. The Islamic practice in the centuries following the pious Caliphs, however, departed quite sharply from the canonical model as well as the theory.

In one of his numerous attempts at distortion, Lewis asserts that the Islamic "pietists" retreated into "radical opposition or quietist withdrawal" when they failed to impose "ecclesiastical constraints on political and military authority."[36] This is only part of the picture. Many pietists turned vigorously to scholarship. Independently of state authority and without state funding, they developed the Islamic sciences, which included the Traditions of the Prophet, biographies of the Prophet and his companions, Arabic grammar, and theology. Most significantly, these pious scholars elaborated several competing systems of Islamic laws – regulating every aspect of individual, social, and business life – on the premise that legislative authority was vested in the consensus of the pious scholars or, in the case of Shi'ites, in the rulings of the imams. The state had executive powers but it possessed no legislative authority. In effect, Islamdom had evolved not only separate political and religious institutions, but it detached the legislative function from the state. It was the pious scholars – with their competing schools of jurisprudence – who constituted the informal legislatures of Islamdom, long before these institutions had evolved in Europe.[37]

Lewis's second proposition – that separation between religion and political authority flows from the presence of a Church – is equally dubious. If the

---

36 Lewis (2002): 99.
37 Lapidus writes that since the middle of the tenth century, "Muslim states were fully differentiated political bodies without any intrinsic religious character, though they were officially loyal to Islam and committed to its defense." Ira Lapidus, *A History of Islamic Societies* (Cambridge: Cambridge University Press, 1988): 364.

Church commands power over people's lives, it becomes a rival of the state. It does not matter if it exercises this power directly – or indirectly, by using the state for its own ends. In time, after Christianity became the official religion of the Roman state, it used the power of the state to eliminate or marginalize all competing religions; it gained the exclusive right to define all religious dogma and rituals; it acquired properties, privileges and exclusive control over education; it expanded its legislative control over different spheres of society. In time, since the Church and state recruited their higher personnel from the same classes, the two developed an identity of class interests. In other words, although the Church and state remained organizationally distinct, each mixed religion and politics.

The adoption of Christianity as its official creed led the Roman state, hitherto tolerant of all religious communities, to inaugurate a regime of growing intolerance toward other religions, and even toward any dissent within Christianity. As Daniel Schowalter says, "By the end of the fourth century, both anti-pagan and anti-Jewish legislation would serve as licenses for the increasing number of acts of vandalism and violent destruction directed against pagan and Jewish places of worship carried out by Christian mobs, often at the instigation of the local clergy."[38] Although the practice of Judaism was not banned, by the end of the fourth century c.e., a variety of decrees prohibited conversion to Judaism, Jewish ownership of non-Jewish slaves, and marriage between Jews and Christians, and Jews were excluded from most imperial offices.[39] In dogma, theology, legislation and practice, the Church and state crafted a regime that suppressed paganism and marginalized all other non-Christian forms of worship.

The modernization of Islamic societies, Lewis insists, has been plagued by another set of cultural barriers – namely, the inferior status of unbelievers, slaves and, especially, women. Not that these groups labored under greater handicaps than their counterparts in Europe, but their unequal status was "sacrosanct" in that they "were seen as part of the structure of Islam, buttressed by revelation, by the precept and practice of the Prophet, and by the classical and scriptural history of the Islamic community." As a result, these

---

38 Daniel L. Schowalter, "Churches in the Context: The Jesus Movement in the Roman World," in: Michael D. Coogan, ed., *The Oxford History of the Biblical World* (New York: Oxford University Press, 1998): 570.
39 Schowalter (1998): 582-583.

three inequalities have endured; they were not challenged even by the radical Islamic movements that arose from time to time to protest social and economic inequalities.[40]

These claims are problematic for several reasons. First, they lack historicity. Implicitly, Lewis' reading of European history inverts the causation between economic development and social equality. He believes that Europeans developed because they *first* created a more egalitarian society, a necessary basis for rapid progress. This shows a curious indifference to chronology. While Europe was establishing global capitalist empires, it was conducting the Inquisition, expelling the Moors and Jews from Spain, waging unending religious wars, burning witches, and conceded few legal rights to women. In addition, the Europeans introduced systems of slavery in the Americas that would be abolished only after the 1860s. In Russia, serfdom remained the basis of the economy at least until the 1860s. The equality Lewis speaks of began to arrive in slow increments at the beginning of the nineteenth century. It was a byproduct of the industrial revolution, not its precursor.

In comparison with Europe, Islamdom was not less egalitarian. Having spent more than fifty years studying the history of the Middle East, it is a bit surprising that "the doyen of Middle Eastern studies" is unaware of at least a few challenges to the 'inferior' status of women or unbelievers. In the early centuries, there were at least three groups – the Kharijis, the Qarmatians and the Sufis – that did not accept the legal interpretations of the four traditional schools of Islamic law as sacrosanct. Instead, they looked for inspiration to the Qur'anic precepts on the moral and spiritual equality of men and women, claiming that the early applications of these precepts were time-bound. The Kharijis and Qarmatians rejected concubinage and child marriage, and the Qarmatians went further in rejecting polygamy and the veil. In a similar spirit, the Sufis welcomed women travelers on the spiritual path, permitting women "to give a central place in their lives to their spiritual vocation."[41] In sixteenth-century India, the Mughal emperor Akbar abolished the *jizyah* (the poll tax imposed by Islamic law on all non-Muslims), banned child marriage, and repealed a law that forced Islam on prisoners of war.[42]

---

40 Lewis (2002): 83-84.

41 Leila Ahmed, *Women and Gender in Islam* (New Haven: Yale University Press, 1992): 66-67.

42 Ahrar Ahmad, *Islam and Democracy: Text, Traditions, History* (Black Hills State University, Fall 2001, mimeo): 25.

The "most profound single difference" between Islamdom and the West, however, concerns the status of women. In particular, Lewis argues that Islam permits polygamy and concubinage and that the Christian Churches prohibit it.[43] Once again, Lewis is exaggerating the differences. In nearly all societies, not excluding the Western, men of wealth and power have always had access to multiple sexual partners, although within different legal frameworks. Islam gave equal rights to all the free sexual partners of men as well as to their children. The West, driven by a concern for primogeniture, adopted an opposite solution by vesting all the rights in a man's primary sexual partner and her offspring. All the other sexual partners – a man's mistresses – and their children had no legal rights.[44] Arguably, Europe's mistresses may have preferred the advantages of Islamic law.

Lewis's emphasis on polygamy and concubinage might lead one to conclude that these were very common in Islamdom. In fact, both were quite rare outside the highest circles of the ruling class. Among others, this is attested by European visitors to eighteenth-century Aleppo and nineteenth-century Cairo. A study of documents relating to two thousands estates in seventeenth-century Turkey could identify only twenty cases of polygamy. The practice of concubinage was most likely more rare.[45]

As if this validated his claims about the "striking contrasts" in women's status in Europe and Islamdom, Lewis reports how Muslim visitors were startled to see European men curtsying to women in public places.[46] Once the bowing and curtsying are done, we need to compare the property rights enjoyed by women in Europe and Islamdom, a quite reliable index of the social power of women inside the household and outside. On this score, too, the Muslim woman held the upper hand until quite recently. Unlike her European counterpart, a married Muslim woman could own property, and she enjoyed exclusive rights to income from her property as well as the wages she earned. In Britain, the most advanced country in Europe, married women did not acquire the right to own property until 1882.

---

43 Lewis (2002): 66.
44 Marshall G. S. Hodgson, "Cultural Patterning in Islamdom and the Occident," in *Rethinking World History*, ed. Edmund Burke III (Cambridge: Cambridge University Press, 1993): 155.
45 Ahmed (1992): 107-108.
46 Lewis (2002): 65.

Their superior property gave considerable advantages to Muslim women. If she was a woman of independent means, she could initiate a divorce or craft a marriage contract that prevented her husband from taking another wife. Muslim women often engaged in trade, buying and selling property, lending money, or renting out stores. They created *waqfs*, charitable foundations financed by earnings from property, which they also administered. A small number of women distinguished themselves as scholars of the religious sciences. Women in the early nineteenth century attended al-Azhar, the leading university in the Islamic world. Ahmed concludes that Muslim "women were not, after all, the passive creatures, wholly without material resources or legal rights, that the Western world once imagined them to be."[47]

What Went Wrong?

Why have so many Jewish scholars and columnists, in recent decades, taken culturalist positions on the history and conflicts of the Middle East, blaming the historical difficulties of the region on its religious and cultural heritage?

In happier times, before the Zionists developed a proprietary interest in Palestine, European Jews often took the least bigoted positions in the field of Oriental studies. These pro-Islamic Jews "were among the first who attempted to present Islam to European readers as Muslims themselves see it and to stress, to recognize, and indeed sometimes to romanticize the merits and achievements of Muslim civilization in its great days."[48] At a time when most Orientalists took Muhammad for a scheming imposter, equated Islam with fanaticism, wrote that the Qur'an was a crude and incoherent text, and declared that the Arabs were incapable of abstract thought, a growing number of Jewish scholars often took opposite positions. They accepted the sincerity of Muhammad's mission, described Arabs as "Jews on horseback," lauded Islam as an evolving faith that was more democratic than other religions, and debunked Orientalist claims about the contrast between a static Islamdom and a dynamic West.[49] It would appear that these Jews were anti-Orientalists long before Edward Said.

---

47 Ahmed (1992): 111.
48 Bernard Lewis, "The Pro-Islamic Jews," in: *Islam in History: Ideas, People, and Events in the Middle East* (Chicago: Open Court, 1993): 12.
49 Martin Kramer, ed., *The Jewish Discovery of Islam* (Tel Aviv: The Moshe Dayan Center for Middle Eastern and African Studies, 1999), 1-48; www.martinkramer.org/pages/ 899528/index.htm

There were several motives behind these contrarian positions. Even as the Jews began to enter the European mainstream, starting in the nineteenth century, they were still outsiders, having only recently emerged from the confinement of ghettos, and it would be scarcely surprising if they were seeking to maintain their distinctiveness by emphasizing and identifying with the achievements of another Semitic people, the Arabs. In celebrating Arab civilization, these Jewish scholars were sending a non-too-subtle message that Arabs often excelled Europeans in many fields of human endeavor, and that Europe was building upon Islamicate achievements in science and philosophy. In addition, the Jewish scholars' discussions of religious and racial tolerance in Islamdom, toward Jews in particular, may have offered hope that such tolerance was attainable in Europe too. The discussions may also have been an invitation to Europeans to incorporate religious and racial tolerance in their standards of civilization.

Yet this early anti-Orientalism of Jewish scholars would not survive the logic of the Zionist movement. Since the Zionists sought to create a colonial-settler state in Arab Palestine, they understood quite well that this would lead to conflicts with the Palestinians, whom they planned to drive out of their homes, and with the neighboring Arab states who would be forced to respond to the Zionist occupation of the Arab heartland. This could only be achieved if the Zionist state could gain the support of Western powers, and to secure this, the Zionists early offered to become an outpost of Western powers against the Arabs. As the Zionists mobilized support amongst Jewish constituents in the West, it was inevitable that the European Jews' attraction for Islam was not going to endure. In fact, it would be replaced by a bitter contest, one in which the Jews, as junior partners of Western imperialists, would seek to deepen the Orientalist project in the service of the West. Bernard Lewis played a leading part in this Jewish reorientation. Indeed, in the words of one camp-follower, he "came to personify the post-war shift from a sympathetic to a critical posture."[50]

Ironically, this shift occurred when many Orientalists had begun to shed their Christian prejudice against Islam, even making amends for the excesses of their forebears. Another factor aiding this shift toward a less polemical Orientalism was the entry of a growing number of Arabs, both

---

50 Kramer (1999).

Muslim and Christian, into the field of Middle Eastern studies. The most visible upshot of these divergent trends was a polarization of the field of Middle Eastern studies into two opposing camps.[51] One camp, consisting mostly of Christians and Muslims, has sought to bring greater objectivity to their study of Islam and Islamicate societies. They seek to locate Islamicate societies in their historical context, arguing that Islamicate responses to Western challenges have been diverse and evolving over time: they do not derive from an innate hostility to the West or some unchanging Islamic mindset. The second camp, led mostly by Jews, has reverted to Orientalism's original mission of subordinating knowledge to Western power, now filtered through the prism of Zionist interests. This Zionist Orientalism has assiduously sought to paint Islam and Islamicate societies as innately hostile to the West, modernism, democracy, tolerance, scientific advance and women's rights.

This Zionist camp has been led for more than fifty years by Bernard Lewis, who has enjoyed an intimate relationship with power that would be the envy of the most distinguished Orientalists of an earlier generation. He has been strongly supported by a contingent of able lieutenants, whose ranks have included the likes of Elie Kedourie, David Pryce-Jones, Raphael Patai, Bat Ye'or, Daniel Pipes and Martin Kramer. There are many foot soldiers, too, who have provided distinguished service to this new Orientalism. And no compendium of these foot soldiers would be complete without the names of Thomas Friedman, Martin Peretz, Norman Podhoretz, Charles Krauthammer, William Kristol and Judith Miller.

In my mind's eye, I try to visualize an encounter between this distinguished crowd and some of their eminent predecessors like Hienrich Heine, Abraham Geiger, Gustav Weil, Franz Rosenthal and the great Ignaz Goldziher. What would these pro-Islamic Jews have to say to their descendants, whose scholarship demeans and denigrates the societies they study? Would Geiger and Goldziher embrace Lewis and Kedourie, or would they be repelled by the latter's new brand of Zionist Orientalism?

---

51 For a recent evaluation of the conflict between the two camps, see Richard Bernstein, "Experts on Islam Pointing Fingers at One Another," *New York Times* (3 November 2001), sec. A, 13.

CHAPTER TWO

A Clash of Civilizations? Nonsense[1]

"O mankind! Lo! We have created you male and female, and have made you nations and tribes that ye may know one another."
—Qur'an: 49:13

March 2002

Every system of social inequalities conceived in violence must maintain itself by less violent means if it is to endure. Once they are in place, the inequalities must be preserved by social constructs that obscure the mechanisms that reproduce them. In the medieval past, religion formed a central component of such social constructs, but in modern capitalist economies, this task falls to the social sciences. At its highest levels – in the universities, think tanks and the media – the social science orthodoxy occupies a more central place in society than the priestly class ever did. In modern societies, the ideological task has grown more demanding, since the subordinate classes are better educated, better connected with each other, and, in democracies, they could overthrow the system with a vote.

These remarks create an appropriate context for examining Samuel Huntington's thesis of the "clash of civilizations," first offered in an essay and later, following its grand reception, developed into a sizeable book.[2] Huntington's thesis serves to obfuscate the global system

1   This paper first appeared in *The Journal of the Historical Society* 2, 3-4 (Summer/Fall 2002): 379-96.
2   Samuel P. Huntington, "The Clash of Civilizations?" *Foreign Affairs* 72, 3 (1993): 22-49; and *The Clash of Civilizations: Remaking of world order* (New York: Simon and Schuster: 1997). Senghaas (1998: 127) notes that the "title of the article included a question mark, whether seriously or rhetorically intended. In the subsequent book, the clash of civilizations, however, became the very definition of the new order of world policy in the 21st century. No question mark any more!" Dieter Senghaas, "A Clash of Civilizations: An Idée Fixe?" *Journal of Peace Research* 35, 1 (January 1998): 127-32.

of inequalities in power, technology and income that has divided the world into a Core and Periphery – rich and poor countries – for more than two hundred years. The immense popularity of the Huntington thesis among Western intellectuals and policy pundits suggests that it is indeed fulfilling an important ideological function.[3]

The Thesis Dissected

Huntington's thesis of a new era in global politics dominated by a "clash of civilizations" – starting in the 1990s – is embedded in a historiography of global conflicts that is breath-taking in its simplicity.[4] In the first period of human history, starting from the earliest times down to 1500 CE, "contacts between civilizations were intermittent or nonexistent."[5] This conception of minimal contacts, at least among civilizations in the Eastern hemisphere, has no basis in reality; the history of mankind since quite early times has been one of nearly continuous contacts – via trade, migrations, wars and transmission of diseases – amongst all major civilizations in the eastern hemisphere. Even the Greeks understood this quite well; they visualized the world as an *oikoumenikos* that included all the peoples in the inhabited parts of the earth. In Huntington's scheme, this period of isolation is followed by a "multipolar international system," extending from 1500 to 1945 and defined by interaction, competition, wars between Western states, and wars waged by the West against other civilizations. Once again, at the global level, it would appear that the central phenomenon of this period was the rise, expansion and global dominance of capitalism, a set of violent processes, which divided the world into a dominant Core and a subjugated Periphery. The most enduring – and the most deadly – conflicts during this period occurred between the Core and Periphery.

In Huntington's analysis, the end of the Second World War heralded a new period in global politics, the Cold War, dominated by the clash of ideologies between "mostly wealthy" societies, led by the United States, and a group of "somewhat poorer" communist societies led by the Soviet Union. Once

---

3   A quick search in google.com, showed 12,600 citations, which included both "Samuel Huntington" and "clash of civiliza-
    tions."
4   Huntington (1997): 20, 21 and 28.
5   Huntington (1997): 21.

again, the attempt at obfuscation should be obvious. First, the communist countries were not "somewhat" but significantly poorer than the developed countries. A substantial and growing gap divided the communist countries of Eastern Europe from the developed countries; and the Asian communist countries lagged by a still greater margin. More importantly, we must see the clash of ideologies during the Cold War for what it was: a clash between the interests of the Core and the Periphery. The Cold War marked a new phase in an old conflict. It was a clash between the Core and a *segment* of the Periphery, which had broken away from the global capitalist system. Similarly, and contrary to Huntington's claims, the end of the Cold War did not change the fundamental reality of a world divided between the Core and the Periphery. It only terminated the socialist development of a recalcitrant segment of the Periphery, and reintegrated it into the global capitalist system. The post-Cold War period also led to the dismantling of developmental states in most Third World countries. If the post-War era marks a new phase in global capitalism, this stems from a new unity in the ranks of the Core countries, which has given them a degree of control over global economic arrangements they have never exercised before. It was during this period that the Core countries created a world government of sorts, in the guise of IMF, World Bank and WTO. Since the end of the Cold War, this triad has succeeded in squeezing the whole world into a straightjacket, designed by and for the advantage of the Core countries.

Huntington summarily dismisses conflicts between the rich and poor countries. Such conflicts are unlikely because the poor countries "lack the political unity, economic power, and military capability to challenge the rich countries."[6] Ironically, this contradicts Huntington's own thesis of the "clash of civilizations" which warns of clashes between the West, on one side, and Islam and China, both of which would easily qualify as poor countries.[7] Huntington's position runs into a variety of other problems. He asserts that poor countries do not pose a threat because they "lack political unity" and "military capability." Why, then, is Huntington so obsessed about a "clash of civilizations" between the West and an Islamicate world that is fragmented

---

6 Huntington (1997): 32-33.
7 Even after decades of rapid growth, China's per capita income in US dollars – for this is what matters when measuring purchasing power on world markets – was $780 in 1999, compared to $30,600 for the United States. On an average, the Islamicate countries had lower per capita incomes than China. World Bank, *World Development Report, 2000/2001* (NY: Oxford University Press, 2001): 274-5.

into some 50 countries, nearly all quite poor? Moreover, China and India, two still poor countries, each with a population greater than that of the entire West, already constitute a significant and growing economic challenge to the West. Finally, the United States now worries a great deal about the ability of some small *and* poor countries – what it calls "rogue states" – to threaten its interests and security. Indeed, the Pentagon now invokes threats from these "rogue states" to justify the large appropriations on the nuclear defense shield.

A closer examination of the "civilizations" in Huntington's "clash of civilizations" reveals that this is mostly a clash of races.[8] Although Huntington does not explain what defines a civilization, what lies at its core, or how it preserves this core over time, he is quite clear about its correlates. People define their identity in terms of characteristics such as ancestry, religion, language, values and institutions.[9] However, it is "ancestry" (alternatively, "blood" and "race") that dominates all other characteristics. We can identify a dominant "race" for all but one of the civilizations on Huntington's list: the Western (Germanic), Orthodox (Slavic), Latin American (mostly Mestizo), Sinic (yellow), Japanese (Japanese), African (black), Indian (brown) and the Caribbean (black). Islamicate civilization is the one exception. On the other hand, the correlation between civilization and religion is quite a bit weaker. The Western, Orthodox, Caribbean and Latin American civilizations are *all* Christian; but the Japanese and Sinic civilizations are not defined by *any* religion, as we commonly understand the term.

An examination of the empirical relation between civilizations and states creates a different kind of problem for the Huntington thesis. Of the six major civilizations – the Western, Orthodox, Islamicate, Indian, Sinic, and Japanese – the last three are identical or nearly identical with a state. In other words, India, China and Japan are civilizations *and* states. In addition, two core states – the United States and Russia – contain a third and a half of the total populations of the civilizations to which they belong, leading some to treat these countries as synonymous with the Western and Orthodox civilizations. In the presence of such strong overlaps between civilizations

---

8   Senghaas (1998: 127-8) remarks that although "Huntington places civilizations at the center of attention, very little can be learned about them."
9   Huntington (1997): 21, 42, 126.

and states, one could easily construe an inter-state conflict over interests – say, between the United States and China, or China and Russia – as a clash of civilizations.

Are clashes between civilizations inevitable? According to Huntington, these conflicts have deep roots in human psyche. People define themselves by identifying with "cultural groups: tribes, ethnic groups, religious communities, nations, and, at the broadest level, civilizations." We deepen our identity by differentiating "our" group from other groups. "We know who we are only when we know who we are not and often *only* when we know whom we are against (emphasis added)."[10] Our deeply felt need for identity leads inevitably to cultural conflicts. This two-part thesis lies at the core of Huntington's book. We need to identify with groups, and our group identity battens on hatred of other identities. There are several problems with this thesis. The identification with groups will not always generate conflicts; this will depend on the groups with which we identify. We can define ourselves by identifying with the family, village, tribe, guild, trade union, college, town, profession or club; but we do not necessarily seek to reinforce our attachment to one primary group by hatred of other primary groups. No reason, rooted in our psyche, explains why a commitment to secondary groups, such as nation, race or civilization must supersede our identification with primary groups. Our devotion to secondary groups is socially constructed; we prefer to satisfy our existential need for self-definition by socialization with smaller groups. Similarly, *if* it is human to hate, as Huntington asserts, then surely we would prefer to direct this 'hatred' at our primary rivals in business, politics, sports or the work place.[11]

The obsession with nation, race and civilization assumes prominence only when we view the world from the perspective of modern European history. During the past two thousand years – and perhaps longer – empires have ranked as the most common, enduring and powerful system of governance across the world. More often than not, these empires embraced peoples of diverse ethnicities, religions and even races. In India, home to many rich and

---

10 The quotes in this paragraph are from Huntington (1997): 21. On page 20, Huntington also approvingly quotes this passage from Michael Dibdin's novel, *Dead Lagoon*, "Unless we hate what we are not, we cannot love what we are." In another passage, Huntington (1997: 130) asserts, "For self-definition and motivation people need enemies: competitors in business, rivals in achievement, opponents in politics."

11 Huntington (1997):130.

well-defined ethnic cultures, ethnic identities only infrequently motivated the politics of state formation.[12] An Indian identity, defined by consciousness of differences from – and hatred of – Others, was never very strong until the British conquest stimulated it. Indians did not trouble to name their continent: the Greeks and, later, the Muslims named it for them.

Huntington attributes civilizational conflicts to cultural differences per se, asserting that the conflicts between Islam and the Christian West "flow from the nature of the two religions and the civilizations based on them (emphasis added)." In addition, the conflict between these two great civilizations is "fundamental" and "will continue to define their relations in the future as it has defined them for the past fourteen centuries."[13] What then are the core ideas or tendencies within these civilizations, which pit them against each other? Huntington flags several sources of conflicts between Islam and Christianity: Western secularism collides with Islam's insistence on combining religion and politics; their religions refuse to accommodate other gods; their universalistic claims collide; and their missionaries compete for converts. It is possible to contest each of these claims.

Huntington regards the West and Islam as absolutes: each has a singular and determinate "nature," given at its conception and invariant over time and place. It follows that their differences also are absolute; the two religions are irreconcilable. All this ignores a great deal of history. For instance, the separation between the state and church is a quite recent development that began its career with the founding of United States. In Britain today, the Queen is not only the head of the state, she is also the head of the officially established Anglican Church. On the other hand, the autonomy that Islamicate empires generally offered to protected non-Islamic communities is generally not available under the secular Western democracies. The Ottoman Empire allowed various Christian denominations to administer their religious laws and religious and educational institutions, and even granted them the power to raise taxes to meet their expenses.

The nature of Christian and Islamic claims to universalism and, more importantly, the means employed to achieve them, are historically deter-

12 The weakness of ethnic consciousness in most of Asia and Africa proved a great advantage to the colonizing Europeans: the colonists could hire Asian and African soldiers to conquer their own peoples.
13 Huntington (1997): 210-12.

mined. They have evolved with time, though not always in the direction of greater tolerance. In the medieval past, the Catholic Church viewed Islam as a false religion, which it tried to extirpate by force. For many centuries, this exclusivist vision mobilized waves of Crusaders to wage wars against the Muslims in Spain, the Levant, North Africa and the Balkans. In general, Christian rulers did not tolerate an Islamic presence in territories it conquered from Muslims. In sixteenth century Spain, the Muslims had to choose between conversion and expulsion from their ancestral homes. Moreover, starting in the sixteenth century when the Protestant reformation fractured the religious unity of Western Europe, the Christians waged incessant wars against each other, which, at their height, were far more deadly than any wars fought between Christian Europe and Islamicate societies. In time, however, Christians learned to live with their differences, since the alternative was too costly. In the past two hundred years, the West has not fought any major war that had its roots in religious differences between Catholics and Protestants. Currently, Christianity does not define Western Europe anymore, although it remains a strong element in the identity and politics of the United States. However, Islamicate societies have moved in the opposite direction over the past two centuries, and away from the tolerance mandated by their religion. Faced with the growing marginalization of Islamicate societies, the erosion of their power and institutions, the new Islamic movements have become less tolerant of their own differences as well as other religions. Indeed, the Israeli-Palestinian conflict has increasingly led Muslims to frame their struggle in religious terms, and employ new forms of violence not sanctioned by their religion.

Huntington has more weapons in his armory. "Differences in material interests," he argues, "can be negotiated and often settled by compromise in a way cultural issues cannot."[14] Recent history suggests that the distinction may not be so categorical, since the savage wars the Europeans have fought in modern times were mostly about conflicts of power and material interests. He also overstates the claim that cultural differences are immune to negotiation. The Islamic empires extended a considerable amount of religious and cultural autonomy to non-Islamic communities in their territory. The Ottoman Empire encouraged non-Muslims to organize themselves

---

14 Huntington (1997): 130.

into *millets*, autonomous communities with the power to regulate their lives according to their own religious laws. In sixteenth century India, the Moghul emperor, Akbar, abolished the *jizya*, an Islamic tax levied on non-Muslims in lieu of military service; he even tried to launch a syncretic religion that would be acceptable to Hindus and Muslims alike. More generally, the Hindus and Muslims in India evolved a common language of discourse – Urdu – a common dress, common forms of address, and a considerable degree of respect for each other's festivals and holy places.

Later, Huntington appears to negate his own thesis – that most conflicts have their source in cultural differences – when he describes the genesis of civilizational conflicts.[15] He argues that these "fault line wars" originate in the usual sources – conflicts over people, territory, resources, and the anarchy of states; religion enters into these conflicts only later as the primary rivals mobilize support among the larger population. "As violence |in fault-line wars| increases, the initial issues at stake tend to get redefined more exclusively as "us" against "them" and group cohesion and commitment are enhanced. Political leaders expand and deepen their appeals to ethnic and religious loyalties, and civilization consciousness strengthens in relation to other identities."[16] This analysis of fault-line wars contradicts Huntington's thesis of the primacy of cultural factors in "civilizational" conflicts.

Finally, Huntington fails to explain the timing of what he thinks were civilizational clashes in the 1990s. He states that "social-economic modernization" caused these clashes.[17] First, modernization created dislocation and alienation, which, in turn, increased the need for more "meaningful identities." Second, as modernization increased the points of contact between civilizations, growing awareness of their differences created stronger civilizational identities. Third, economic growth in Asia and population growth in Islamicate societies have revitalized cultural identities in these societies. These explanations fail on several counts. First, there is no evidence that modernization peaked or accelerated across all civilizations in the 1990s. If it did not, it is hard to see how modernization could have caused the clashes

---

15 Huntington (1997): 266.
16 We find a specific example of this in Huntington's (1997: 269) comments on the Bosnian conflict. On the one hand, he claims that this was a fault-line war. On the other hand, he acknowledges that "Bosnian Muslims were highly secular in their outlook, viewed themselves as Europeans, and were the strongest supporters of a multicultural Bosnian society and state."
17 Huntington (1997): ch. 3 and 4.

of the 1990s. Second, if modernization caused these clashes, they should be emanating from East Asia, not Islamicate societies, as Huntington claims. Third, if population growth causes cultural resurgence, Africa, which has been growing faster than Islamicate societies, should have taken the lead in these clashes. Since population in Latin America too has been growing rapidly since the 1900s, they should have exploded in civilizational clashes much earlier.

The Evidence

There are two sets of propositions that are central to Huntington's thesis of the clash of civilizations: one relates to such clashes generally, another to claims about the greater propensity of Islamicate societies to get into clashes. Not surprisingly, for a theory that is so flawed in its conception, these propositions do not stand up to the evidence.

The Huntington thesis claims that since 1989 – and before 1945 – two states were more likely to engage in wars if they belong to different civilizations; it was only during the Cold War, between 1945 and 1989, that the competition between two rival ideologies, capitalism and communism, suppressed this propensity. Huntington devotes 367 pages to developing this thesis, but the supporting evidence remains selective and mostly anecdotal. Did he really believe that his thesis about clashes would persuade by its intuition, rooted, as it is, in the existential need for cultural identity, drawing sustenance from a steady diet of loathing for other peoples? Perhaps, he knew all along that ideologies succeed by appealing to interests, not evidence.

Although his thesis of a "clash of civilizations" after 1989 lends itself to quantification, Huntington does not exploit this possibility.[18] He offers one statistic on ethnic conflicts, which shows that slightly less than half of such conflicts in 1993 involved groups from different civilizations, and it is not very helpful. If he wishes to establish a break in the pattern of conflicts after 1989, he needs to compare the trends before and after this date. Jonathan Fox has undertaken such a comparison, and his findings contradict Huntington's thesis.[19] He observed a modest *decline* in inter-civilization conflicts – com-

---

18 Huntington (1997): 37.
19 Jonathan Fox, "Two Civilizations and Ethnic Conflict: Islam and the West," *Journal of Peace Research* 38, 4 (2000): 459-72.

pared to conflicts within the boundaries of a civilization – as we move from the Cold War (1945-1989) to the post-Cold War period (1990-1998).

Alternatively, we might test Huntington's thesis about the clash of civilizations by exploring if the probability of conflicts rises with cultural differences in the post-Cold War period. For this, we would need to control for other factors that affect conflicts. In their study of international conflicts, Henderson and Tucker identify three such factors, in addition to differences in civilization: distance between the countries, the presence of democracy, and an index of power capabilities.[20] Once Henderson and Tucker introduce controls for these influences, they find that cultural factors had no visible impact on the probability of wars during the post-Cold War years. Again, Huntington's thesis of the clash of civilizations falls short.

Although the period before 1945 offers fertile ground for testing his thesis, Huntington shows little interest in this period. In his 1993 paper, however, he claims that over the centuries "differences among civilizations have generated the most prolonged and the most violent conflicts."[21] Again, history does not support this conclusion. Of 18 major wars fought by great powers between 1600 and 1945, only six involved states from two or more civilizations, and the deadliest, which caused millions of deaths, were fought among Western states.[22] When Henderson and Tucker examined international wars between 1816 and 1945, with controls for other influences, they found that the probability of conflicts between two states was *greater* if they belonged to the *same* civilization – the opposite of what Huntington predicts.

Huntington asserts that culture, not geography, forms the basis of cooperation among nations. In the military field, he cites the example of NATO as the most successful example of such cooperation.[23] He forgets that NATO is a vestige of the Cold War. It was created to defeat the Soviet Union, and not a few have questioned its utility in the post-Cold War era. More significantly, during the 35 years that preceded its formation, the countries that

---

20 Errol A. Henderson and Richard Tucker, "Clear and Present Strangers: The Clash of Civilizations and International Conflict," *International Studies Quarterly* 45 (2001): 317-38. We might add another factor to this list: the length of borders a country shares with countries from a different civilization.

21 Huntington (1993): 25.

22 These data are from Jack Levy, *War in the Modern Great Power System, 1495-1975* (Lexington, KY: University Press of Kentucky, 1983), quoted in Charles Tilly, *Coercion, Capital and European States, 990-1990* (Oxford: Basil Blackwell, 1990): 165-66. Major wars are those with at least 100,000 battle-deaths.

23 Huntington (1997): 130-35.

are at the core of NATO had fought the two bloodiest wars in human history. In the same spirit, Huntington offers the European Union as the greatest success in economic cooperation, which he attributes to the common culture of its members.[24] While a connection may exist between culture and economic cooperation, Huntington's conclusion fails on several counts. First, this cooperation was motivated from its outset by the threat of economic competition from the United States, another *Western* country, and no one has proposed turning the European Union into an Atlantic Union. The success of economic cooperation has better prospects among neighbors at similarly advanced levels of development than among those who share only a common culture. In the fifty years before the Second World War, Europeans were not clamoring for the creation of a customs union; even after 1950, the Europeans proceeded slowly, taking nearly fifty years, to weld their disparate economies into an economic union. Further complicating matters, the European Union has begun to open its doors to several countries in Eastern Europe, with Orthodox majorities.

Other examples of organizations that span several civilizations receive little attention or respect in Huntington's analysis. Thus, he sneeringly dismisses ASEAN as "an example of the limits" of such organizations,[25] and yet ASEAN has enjoyed demonstrable success over its relatively short existence. Founded in 1967 to promote regional security, ASEAN moved towards the creation of a customs union in 1977 and a free-trade area in 1992. In recent years, ASEAN has expanded its membership from the original five to ten countries, and is already very close to achieving its goal of creating a free-trade area. In November 2001, ASEAN and China signed an agreement to create the world's largest free-trade area within 10 years.[26] Outside of the developed countries, the creation of a free-trade area has moved fastest amongst countries with diverse cultures.

Now consider the accusations about the "bloody borders" of Islamicate societies. Huntington asserts that Muslims "have problems living peaceably with their neighbors," and "in the 1990s they have been far more involved in intergroup violence than the people of any other civilization."[27] In support,

---

24 Huntington (1997): 131.
25 Huntington (1997): 132.
26 http://www.forbes.com/newswire/2001/11/06/rtr415466.html
27 Huntington (1997): 256-57.

he presents various bits of data from 1992-1994 purporting to show that Muslims were disproportionately engaged in wars with other civilizations. A more careful examination of the data tells a different story. Surveying ethnic conflicts, Fox found that Islamicate societies were involved in 23.2 percent of all inter-civilizational conflicts between 1945 and 1989, and 24.7 percent of these conflicts during 1990 to 1998.[28] First, we do not observe a dramatic rise in the Islamicate world's share of conflicts since the end of the Cold War. Second, the Islamicate world's share of conflicts is quite close to their share of the world population.

Islamicate societies appear to have bloodier borders because they have a proportionately larger share of inter-civilizational borders. The Islamicate world stretches from Senegal, Morocco and Bosnia in the West to Sinjiang, Indonesia and Mindanao in the East. This geographic sweep across the Afro-Eurasian landmass brings Islamicate societies into contact – both close and extensive – with the African, Western, Orthodox, Hindu and Buddhist civilizations. If we add up all these borders – inter-country and intra-country borders – the share of Islamicate societies might well exceed the combined share of all other civilizations. All this should help to place observations about Islam's "bloody borders" in a less prejudicial perspective.

September 11 and the "Clash"

September 11 will remain a day inscribed in infamy. But does it mark the first strike in a clash of civilizations – predicted by our sage political scientist?

Samuel Huntington prevaricates, but he appears to stick to his guns. In an interview, he declared that the attacks "were not a clash of civilizations but a blow by a fanatical group on civilized societies in general."[29] So, it is *not* an attack on United States, or its policies, but an attack on "civilized societies in general," often a synonym for the West. Other voices were more forthright, declaring that this *is* a clash of civilizations.[30] Should we accept this

---

28 Fox (2001): 464.

29 John Vinocur, "Taboos Are Put to Test in West's Views of Islam," *International Herald Tribune* (October 9, 2001). www.iht. com/ articles/35046.html (accessed January 1, 2002). This is also the official position of the government of the United States.

30 Robert S. Wistrich, "It Is a Clash of Civilizations," *Jerusalem Post* (October 19, 2001); and March Erikson, "It Is a "Clash of Civilizations"," *Asia Times* (November 28, 2001).

reading of September 11 as an attack on the West, and part of an unfolding war between the West and Islamicate societies? In my judgment, even the most elementary facts show that this thesis is indefensible.

The events of September 11 mark an escalation in attacks of a similar nature. The history of such attacks – starting with the 1983 attacks on US interests in Lebanon, winding through more attacks on US embassies, US military facilities, US officials and US citizens in Kuwait, Saudi Arabia, Yemen, Britain, Germany, Tanzania and Kenya, and leading up to their culmination in the attacks of September 11 – reveals two unpleasant facts. In nearly all cases, the target of these attacks was unmistakably the United States.[31] In nearly every case, these attacks were carried out by Arabs, on Arab soil at first, then in non-Arab countries, and, eventually, to attacks on US soil. In the 1980s, the attackers were mostly Lebanese and Palestinians. Later, Egyptians and Saudis joined them.

This history establishes that the attackers were not waging war against "all civilized societies in general", but against *one* in particular – the United States – with less than one-third of the population of the West. They were not waging war against the West, or the freedom, democracy and pluralism of Western societies. The attacks were primarily aimed at military and official targets, with the Lockerbie crash and the two attacks on WTC as notable exceptions. Equally important, nearly all the attackers were of Arab ethnicity. We must reject Huntington's reading of the attacks of September 11, which, like previous attacks, had a specific target – the United States. Even if we regard the attackers as representative of all Arab societies – a questionable assumption – this only pits one-sixth of Islamdom against less than one-third of the West. This is not exactly a clash between two civilizations. Instead, it points to deep tensions between a specific country, the United States, and the Arab world – and to US policies in the Middle East, which have mediated the relations between the two.

Concluding Remarks

Why has the Huntington thesis dominated public discourse in the West despite its weak theoretical foundations, the lack of empirical support for

---

31 John Moore, "The Evolution of Islamic Terrorism: An Overview." www.pbc. org.wgbh/pages/frontline/shows/target/etc/modern.html (accessed November 11, 2001).

its most important predictions, and its frequent descent to espousal of hatred as the necessary basis of cultural identity?

This question may be answered with a story from Mulla Nasruddin, an enigmatic character in the Sufi folklore of the Islamicate world, at once funny and unpredictable, but always revealing. On one occasion, the Mulla borrowed a large cooking pot from his neighbor. When he returned the pot a few days later, he placed a smaller pot inside the larger one. His neighbor reminded the Mulla that he had borrowed only one pot, to which the Mulla replied, "Oh that's a baby pot. While your pot was with me, it gave birth to a baby." The neighbor asked no further questions. Several days later, the Mulla borrowed another pot from the same neighbor. This time, however, he chose not to return it. When the neighbor asked for his pot, the Mulla explained that he could not have it – the pot had died. Visibly upset, the neighbor expostulated, "Do you take me for a fool. Pots don't die." The Mulla answered: "If it could have a baby, why can't it die?"

This story illuminates an important aspect of the nature of ideologies; although there are other ways of reading the Mulla's antics. Our acceptance of narratives, even quite ridiculous ones, depends on how well they serve our interests – individual and collective ones. Not a few of the stories social scientists have constructed about race, climate, culture, civilizations, free markets and free trade, although thickly interwoven with logic, rhetoric, mathematics and statistics, are equally ridiculous, if only they could be seen in their true colors. Nevertheless, they endure so long as they serve powerful interests. They endure because these powerful interests can employ a legion of scholars who willingly – though often unwittingly – trade the prestige of their scholarship for a good job, good pay, and the accolades of their bosses.

Huntington's "clash" conjures up images of Islamic vandals attacking cherished Western values: freedom, democracy and secularism. It tells us, we are in a conflict with an age-old adversary: it is *our* Crusade against *their* Jihad. Once we hijack these images, we succeed in obscuring the real issues about the system of global inequities and the structural violence it has perpetrated daily, routinely, for more than two hundred years. It obscures questions about America's foreign policy in the Middle East and about the 'blowback' from that policy. It mobilizes the approval ratings, which then allow us to deal with the 'blowback' with more violence. If the Huntington thesis prevails, the twenty-first century will return the West and Islamdom to the twelfth century, when they fought wars in the name of religion. Only this time it is likely to be much worse for both antagonists.

CHAPTER THREE

The War Against Global Terrorism

One day Mulla Nasruddin went to his neighbor – known to be a mean sort of fellow – to report a problem. "Sir," he explained, "your ox has gored my cow and killed her after she refused his amorous advances." His neighbor interrupted, "So what has that got to do with me? Should a man be held responsible for what an animal does." The Mulla answered cheekily, "Thank you, Sir. It was my ox that gored your cow."[1]

January 2005

In current American demonology, terrorism occupies the position once held by communism. It is the indisputable evil of our times, the gravest threat to our freedoms, a menace to all civilized societies.

Indeed, soon after the hijackers struck the Twin Towers and the Pentagon, the United States chose to invest its prestige and a considerable portion of its military resources in a 'war against terrorism.' We have been told that this is a war against a new kind of enemy, elusive, sinister, evil. The new enemy is tougher too and will be harder to beat than communism. This war may last for several generations. It is going to be a war without end.

Oddly, few Americans are baffled by the notion of a 'war against terrorism.' However reprehensible, terrorism is a tactic, not a goal or ideology. America's erstwhile adversary, communism, offered a vision of a classless society to supersede capitalist exploitation; it had its ideologues, its economics, its analysis of world history, and it mapped out a trajectory for reaching its goal. But terrorism is a tactic, a weapon, perhaps one of many, in the enemy's arsenal. Who is this enemy that

---

1   Adapted from Idries Shah: *The Pleasantries of the Incredible Mulla Nasruddin* (Penguin Books: 1993).

dares to wield this weapon against the United States? What are his griev-ances? What are his goals?

Why is there such unwillingness to examine this enemy, to look it in the eye? It would appear that terrorism is a necessary ploy, useful to US capital in the present stage of its relative decline. It is useful precisely because of what it has done best: strike terror in Americans. Riding on this wave of terror, US capital can easily railroad Americans into supporting wars, it can waste their life and limb to boost its sagging fortunes, and bury an already castrated democracy under the cover of 'grave threats' to national security. Is it just possible that the primary purpose of the 'war against terrorism' is to fuel more terrorist attacks, to continually renew the fear and panic created by 9-11, so that Americans feel secure in the knowledge that their government daily wages a global war to protect them from terrorism? And if their nation is at war against terrorist, why should they complain if they have to give up some of their liberties?

Some have argued – and most Muslims are convinced of this – that the war against terrorism is a cover for waging war against Islamicate societies, a war for their oil resources, the fuel that drives the global economy. Others have insisted, with Israelis and American Zionists taking the lead in this, that Islam is a grave threat to 'liberal democracy,' that is, to the institutions and mores that underpin the global capitalist system. Could it be that the revival of political Islam is the greatest anti-systemic force to emerge since the demise of communism?

Yet the United States dares not name this enemy. Is this because the United States seeks victory in this war by pitting the 'good Muslims,' who coop-erate with American goals, against the 'bad Muslims,' who place Islam at the center of their political identity? This is the Oslo model applied to the entire Islamicate world: to use the nationalists, secularists, dictators, and monarchists in the Islamicate world to wage all-out war against their own people, the militants, the Islamists. Once started, at very little cost, the United States can manipulate this war to its advantage.

In waging war against terrorism, the United States has catapulted a very small group of Islamists who use terrorist methods into a world-historical force. Non-state terrorism, hitherto an occasional irritant in world affairs, now occupies the center stage of global politics. Suddenly, it has become the grand metaphor for framing global, regional and sub-national conflicts. Given all this talk, it is unlikely that we can go wrong if we use this metaphor as an entry point for our analysis of global capitalism at the present juncture.

Defining the Beast

Consider the official definitions of terrorism advanced by the three US agencies that have the responsibility for fighting it:[2]

> *FBI.* "The unlawful use of force or violence against persons or property to intimidate or coerce a government, the civilian population, or any segment thereof, in furtherance of political or social objectives."

> *Department of Defense* (DoD). "The calculated use of violence or the threat of violence to inculcate fear, intended to coerce or intimidate governments or societies as to the pursuit of goals that are generally political, religious or ideological.

> *Department of State* (DoS). "Premeditated, politically motivated violence perpetrated against noncombatant targets by subnational or clandestine agents, usually intended to influence an audience."

Surprisingly, the FBI and DoD definitions do not exclude states from terrorist acts. Indeed, they do not identify the agents who engage in terror. They only describe what these agents *do*: they "intimidate or coerce a government, the civilian population, or any segment thereof," or "coerce or intimidate governments or societies." Only the DoS with its reference to "subnational or clandestine agents" appears to restrict terrorism to non-state agents. In principle, under the first two definitions, the United States is free to level terrorist charges against other states.

In practice, the United States has directed the charge of terrorism primarily against non-state actors. In the few cases when this charge has been brought against states, this is not because they have terrorized their own citizens. Instead, these are countries that have refused to cooperate with the strategic plans of the United States or Israel. In alternative parlance,

---

2   David J. Whittaker, ed., *The terrorism reader* (London and New York: Routledge, 2001): 3.

they are also described as 'rogue states.' At one time or another, this list has included Iran, Iraq, Libya, Syria, Sudan, North Korea and Cuba.

The official definitions are unanimous in identifying "violence" and "force" as the markers of terrorism; the second definition also includes the "threat of violence." In other words, terrorism is defined by the use of means that are violent in and of themselves; this has the advantage of excluding actions that are visibly non-violent but which generate violent consequences, whatever the scale of the suffering or horror they produce. Violence and the threat of violence are indispensable ingredients of terror.

There is ambiguity in the official US definitions about the proximate targets of terrorism. The DoD does not identify a target, while the FBI does not specify whether the "persons and property" targeted belong to the private, official or military domain. Only the DoS restricts the targets to "noncombatants."[3] However, the category is quite generous. It only *excludes* those segments of the military that are actively engaged in military hostilities. It appears that America's enemies are offered very few legitimate targets.

Finally, the US agencies define the goals of terrorism with the broadest possible brush. In his goals, the terrorist is not different from other political actors: his goals are "political, religious or ideological." The terrorist seeks to influence an audience, whether it is the government, society or some segment of society. The message is clear: no "political, religious or ideological" goals can be supported by violence.

In the official US definitions, the terrorists are state or non-state actors who engage in, or threaten violent actions, that produce harm to property or persons – 'noncombatants,' in one formulation – for political ends. Alternatively, terrorism is defined by four ingredients. It involves agents who may be state or non-state actors. The agents employ means that are violent in and of themselves, or threaten the use of such violence. The means are violent if they result in harm to property or persons – 'noncombatants,' in one formulation. Finally, their goals are political.

Consider a quaint implication of the official US definitions of terrorism. First, the Boston Tea Party must be deemed an act of 'terrorism.' This act of protest violated British law; it destroyed property; and its intent was to

---

3   US Department of State, *Patterns of global terrorism, 1993.* <www.fas.org/ irp/ threat/terror_93/intro.html>

"intimidate or coerce" the British government. A *fortiori*, according to the official US definitions, the founding fathers, who led an armed insurrection against the lawful authority of the British in the Americas, would also appear to be 'terrorists.' It is an anomaly that is little noted.

Clearly, then, the official US definitions of terrorism seek to de-legitimize nearly all forms of violence in the service of *any* political goals. Since it is much harder to criminalize legitimate political goals that are hostile to its interests, the United States seeks to restrict the legitimate instruments available for pursuing those goals. Under conditions of deep asymmetry, where violent resistance may be the only effective way to combat the aggression of one state against another state or against non-state actors, the attempt to confine resistance to non-violent activities is to render it sterile. If this also indicts America's founding fathers as 'terrorists,' an imperialist power was never hurt by embarrassments or inconsistencies.

The official US definitions of terrorism also suffer from the opposite problem: they fall short in their coverage of terrorism. This is because terrorism can only occur through the use of means that are violent *per se*. If non-state actors infected with AIDS were to enter a country legally and engage in random acts of love-making, eventually producing an epidemic of AIDS, they could not be described as terrorists under the US definitions. In general, the spread of pathogens, whether through water, food, air, syringes, blankets or love-making, cannot be charged with terrorism. In all these cases, no inherently violent act is required to spread the pathogens.

The problems for the conduct of US administrations are worse when we switch to state actors in the American definition of terrorism. Unlike the non-state actors who engage in terrorism as a means of resistance, the United States has employed terrorism to defend economic interests that would be hard to defend on moral grounds. Through much of its history, the United States has employed state terrorism against its own civilian population, mostly native Americans and blacks.[4] The United States decimated the native population by displacing them from their lands, by killing off their buffalo herds, and, occasionally, by spreading epidemics to their communities. Once this task was nearly completed, by the end of the nine-

---

4 Churchill Ward, *A little matter of genocide* (San Francisco: City Light Books, 1998).

teenth century, the expansion of American power was extended beyond its border by wars of aggression, by support for murderous foreign governments, covert activities, assassinations, and, more recently, economic sanctions.[5] In an objective evaluation of global terrorism over the past two centuries, the United States may well emerge as one of the leading *sources* of state terrorism.

Defining Violence

The mainstream American discourse on non-state terrorism, led by the government and corporate media, creates the impression that non-state terrorism is (a) a particularly odious form of violence and (b) it accounts for a large proportion of all violent acts.[6] In order to evaluate the first charge it is necessary to examine the nature of *all* violent actions.

In ordinary political discourse, violence is equated with violent means that produce violent consequences. Consider two indisputable acts of violence: bombs dropped on a city block full of people or a sniper's bullet tearing through a child's head. In both cases, the means employed are regarded as violent: dropping a bomb and firing a bullet. The consequences of these violent acts too are violent: destruction, maiming and death. In addition, the connection between the two is transparent. In the language of politics, then, violence is defined by three ingredients: violent means, violent effects, and a direct connection between the two.

Consider a different kind of action: the privatization of water in one of the poorest of poor countries, Niger. The government of Niger has introduced this policy under duress in order to qualify for additional loans from the International Monetary Fund. Once this privatization takes effect, forcing the poorest Nigeriens to use contaminated water, many of them will eventually fall sick and die. Perhaps, eventually tens of thousands will die. Compare these deaths from privatization of water – deaths that follow with certainty, though with some delay – with the instantaneous civilian deaths produced by bombs dropped on military targets in civilian areas. Is there

---

5   Fredereck H. Gareau, *State terrorism and the United States* (London: Zed Books, 2004) and William Blum, *Rogue state: A guide to the world's only superpower* (Boston: Common Courage Press, 2000).

6   Over a much longer period, the Israeli establishment too has achieved similar success in focusing attention on the non-state terrorism of the Palestinians, although the scale of this violence pales in comparison to the violence directed by the Israeli government and society against Palestinians.

a moral difference between these actions because the means employed in the second case was in itself violent, that is, normally associated with violent consequences?

It is often argued that the civilians deaths in the two cases of violence just examined are unintentional, and, hence cannot be equated with actions which deliberately produce civilian deaths. The distinction between the two types of deaths – one produced intentionally and another unintentionally – is rarely absolute. It hinges on knowledge and probabilities.

Consider two scenarios. In one, John murders Matt for his money; he uses the money for a surgery that saves his mother's life. In a second scenario, John steals money that he knows Peter has been saving for a surgery that will save his life. John uses the stolen money to buy a racing car. In the first case, John deliberately kills Matt. In the second case, John steals money that he *knows* will cause Peter's death. What is the moral distinction between Matt's murder and Peter's 'unintentional' but certain death? Indeed, in the present comparison, the murder is less wanton than the 'unintentional' death. John kills Matt in order to save his mother's life; there is a trade-off between two lives here. In the second case, John knowingly causes Peter's death in order to buy a racing car.

In a moral universe, then, violence would encompass *all* acts, processes or structures that produce violent consequences, that is, death or debility for living things. It does not matter if these acts, processes or structures are violent or non-violent, and legal or illegal. What should matter is that they are known to produce, with reasonably certainty, consequences that are violent. Once we distinguish between the means and effects, it is easy to see that a violent act may not always or necessarily produce violent consequences. Consider a bomb dropped on an uninhabited desert. On the other hand, all too frequently, legal and nonviolent actions produce devastating effects on human societies.

This discussion suggests a taxonomy of violence that points to its bewildering variety. This taxonomy would embrace the following ingredients: (a) the agents of violence may be state or non-state actors; (b) they employ instruments that are violent (actual or threatened) or non-violent, and legal or illegal; (c) the proximate targets of violence may be humans, animals or property; (d) these targets may pertain to state or non-state sectors of society; (e) the violent impact of the instruments, both direct and indirect, may include shorter human lives, maiming of humans, or threats thereof; (f) the agent's goals may be political, pecuniary or nihilistic; and (g) the political goals may be legitimate or illegitimate. There are many different ways in which these ingredients, including their components, may be combined. A simple permutation of these ingredients suggests that violence may take many different forms.

Consider how these ingredients may be used to define one violent act, *viz.* the successful efforts of the US auto industry to block the introduction of seat belts in cars. (a) The agents are non-state actors. (b) They use non-violent instruments, including false information and bribes, to persuade lawmakers to block laws making seat belts mandatory in cars. (c) Although these instruments are illegal, they are disguised or covered up. (d) The proximate targets are all users of cars, who are overwhelmingly civilians. (e) The blocking of seat belts causes thousands of avoidable deaths and injuries from traffic accidents. (f) The auto industry has two goals: avoid lower profits from reduced car sales (a pecuniary goal) and defeat the collective power of consumer advocacy (a political goal).

Once again, considered *morally*, the actions of the auto industry – blocking the inclusion of seat belts in cars – are comparable to a recognizably violent act: say, a bomb thrown in a crowded railway station by non-state actors demanding civil rights for a persecuted minority. The auto industry uses illegal means to block a law, an action that they *know* will cause thousands of deaths and injuries annually. The terrorists also use illegal means – throwing a bomb – to kill a few people randomly. In both cases, the deaths are randomly distributed. On the other hand, the auto industry *causes* thousands of deaths and tens of thousands of injuries; the terrorists kill a few. Morally, the auto industry is more blameworthy: they kill many more people than the terrorists.

Yet most people feel a stronger moral outrage over a few deaths caused by terrorist bombs than they do over thousands of avoidable auto deaths. In part, this is because the terrorists use violent means, and people have been 'trained' to focus their outrage on violent means, not violent consequences. It is also the case that the media will not report on the actions, legal or illegal, of the auto industry to block seat belt laws. In addition, when reporting traffic fatalities, the same media will fail to point out that the fatalities could have been avoided if the cars were equipped with seat belts. Most importantly, we are 'trained' to think that because the avoidable traffic deaths are random, they are also unintentional. The auto industry may not know *who* will die in the absence of seat belts, but they do know with certainty that *some* will die.

The moral difference between terrorism and the 'innocuous' lobbying of the auto industry exists only in the imagination of the public. It should be emphasized, however, that this imagination is politically constructed: it does not exist or emerge naturally. In fact, the way in which the public perceives and thinks about these matters is carefully cultivated – through schools, entertainment and the media – by the corporate classes and their intellectual underlings. They cannot allow our moral faculties to remain unsullied by their interests. It would be too dangerous to leave the members of the public free and actively engaged in arriving at their own, independent judgments about what is morally outrageous.

Violence, Terrorism and Deaths

Consider a selective list of violent actions, processes and structures – violent in the way that we define the term – and the deaths they are estimated to produce.

In 2003, Sub-Saharan Africa, with a population of 703 million, had an average life expectancy at birth of 46 years. On the other hand, the nearly billion people in the High Income Countries had a life expectancy of 78. If this is an attainable standard for everyone in today's world – and why not – the scale of avoidable deaths in Sub-Saharan Africa alone is colossal. Collectively, we are running a system of global inequalities that shortens *lives* in Sub-Saharan Africa by 32 years. Altogether, our global system – created and sustained by wars, conquests, terror and genocide – destroys 22.5 billion years of human life in Sub-Saharan Africa alone. In the Low Income Countries, with a population of 2.3 billion in the same year, the loss is considerably greater at 46 billion years.[7]

7   The data in this paragraph are from The World Bank, *World development report, 2005* (New York: Oxford University Press, 2004): 256-7.

The tobacco corporations are one of the biggest killers in the world today. In the United States alone, 400,000 deaths result from tobacco use every year, or one out of every five deaths.[8] Recently, researchers at the Harvard School of Public Health estimated that, globally, smoking caused 4.83 million premature deaths in 2000. Of these, 2.41 million deaths occurred in developing countries.[9] Many of these deaths could have been avoided with a complete ban on cigarette advertising and better-funded campaigns against tobacco use.

Traffic accidents are another big source of deaths. Globally, they cause 1.17 million deaths and many more serious injuries every year.[10] Most of these deaths occur in developing countries, and most of the dead are pedestrians. According to a report of the World Health Organization, "poorly maintained public transport" explained between 60 and 70 percent of traffic deaths in the developing countries.[11] Arguably, a significant fraction of these deaths occur due to the negligence of society: its failure to provide better roads, better public transport, better policing of roads, and stricter laws against drunken driving.

In August 1990, after Iraq invaded Kuwait, the Security Council voted to impose sanctions against Iraq: the most comprehensive ever imposed against any country in modern times. Although Iraq withdrew its forces from Kuwait in February 1991, the sanctions were not lifted till May 2003, only after US forces had occupied Baghdad. The oil-for-food program, which offered partial relief from these sanctions, came into effect in late 1997. Several independent sources have offered estimates of the massive Iraqi deaths caused by these sanctions. According to one UNICEF report, "if the substantial reduction in child mortality throughout Iraq during the 1980s had continued through the 1990s, there would have been half a million fewer deaths of children under-five in the country as a whole during the eight year period 1991 to 1998."[12] Under the sanctions, Iraqi children were dying at the rate of more than 5,000 every month. Arguably, most of these deaths could have been avoided in the absence of the US-imposed sanctions against Iraq.

---

8 "Tobacco use: United States, 1900-1999," *Oncology*, 13, 12 (December 1999).<www.cancernetwork.com/journals/oncology/o99912d.htm>

9 "Smoking kills 5 million a year," *BBC News* <http://news.bbc.co.uk/2/hi/ health/3099936.stm>

10 FIA Foundation, "Road accidents a 9-11 tragedy every day."<www. fiafoundation.com/media/press_releases/pr_ 11022003.html>

11 "$100bn cost of million road deaths," *CNN News*.<www.archives.cnn.com/ 2002/WORLD/europe/08/28/health.crash>

12 UNICEF, "Iraq survey shows 'humanitarian emergency," August 12, 1999. <www.unicef.org/newsline/99pr29.htm>

Now consider the death toll from the deadliest non-state terrorist attacks ever, those of September 11, 2001. Altogether, these attacks killed 2752 people.[13] This includes the dead in the World Trade Center, the Pentagon and the passengers in the four hijacked planes. This toll – although grisly by any metric – is far fewer than the Iraqi children killed *every month* by the sanctions against Iraq over nearly fourteen years.

Finally, consider the statistics on the global casualties – both dead and injured – from *all* non-state terrorist attacks between 1998 and 2003, as reported by the US State Department. The total yearly casualties for these years were: 6694 (1998), 755 (1999), 1192 (2000), 5806 (2001), 3072 (2002) and 4271 (2003).[14] On an average, the yearly casualties between 1998 and 2003 were 3737. Once again, the annual casualties – both dead and injured – from global terrorism is well below the toll of Iraqi children who were dying every month during the 1990s.

A Paradox

This presents a paradox. Non-state terrorist acts, as recorded by the US agencies, account for a very small fraction of global human losses inflicted by all violent acts, processes and structures. In addition, we have argued that on moral grounds, there is little to choose between terrorism and certain legal actions which knowingly produce deaths, even horrible deaths. Yet, since September 11, 2001 the United States has been obsessed with non-state terrorism, a miniscule source of global violence.

This demands an explanation. Why does terrorism – now, as it has in the past – evoke such strong reactions from governments when its human costs are so small relative to the scale of avoidable deaths caused by other forms of violence? We also need to understand why the reactions now, especially after 9-11, are so much stronger than in the past.

The state exists by virtue of its monopoly or near-monopoly over violence; it alone is legally empowered to arrest, punish, incarcerate or kill people. This is a necessary monopoly. Without it, the state could be challenged by any

---

13 Phil Hirschkorn, "New York reduces death toll by 40," October 29, 2003. <www.cnn.com/2003/US/Northeast/10/29/wtc.deaths/>

14 US Department of State, *Pattern of Global Terrorism*, June 22, 3004.< www.state.gov/s/ct/rls/pgtrpt/2003/33777.htm>

group that could organize sufficient violence to oppose or coerce the state. If such challenges could be mounted quickly and frequently, society is likely to descend into anarchy.

In order to maintain this monopoly, the state seeks to de-legitimize the use of violence by all non-state actors. This includes violent crimes as well as terrorism – violence that has a political tag. However, violent crimes are a much less serious matter than terrorism. Crimes, even when they violate the state's monopoly over violence, do not seek to alter the behavior of the state; they do not challenge the state itself. Terrorism is a different matter. It uses violence to challenge the state, its authority to fashion the social order. And that is unacceptable.

Terrorism challenges the state at another level. The state claims its right to exist through its success in protecting its citizens against violence of other states and non-state agents. This is its *raison d'etre*. Terrorism seeks to create the perception that the state cannot protect its citizens, although violent crimes also produce the same effect. This explains why terrorists choose to engage in random and sensational violence; this multiplies its impact on perceptions about the failure of the state.

In some cases, the state or government may respond to terrorist acts with opportunism. A government that abridges rights or wages wars, actions that lack popular support, it may seek to create that support by sensation-alizing terrorist acts in order to magnify their impact on the insecurity of the public. Indeed ambitious leaders may be tempted to go beyond this: they may fabricate or stage terrorist acts.

While the state seeks tirelessly to outlaw the use of violent means, it does not routinely seek to de-legitimize violent outcomes when they are pro-duced by non-violent means. This is not surprising. As the instrument and ally of the governing classes, the state will not rule against the legitimacy of processes – most importantly, the workings of the markets – that the ruling classes use to appropriate wealth. Instead, these processes are given legal protection, glorified, and their violent consequences camouflaged or explained away. Only under persistent pressures from below does the state occasionally rule against the legitimacy of non-violent processes which produce violent results.

Sources of Non-State Terrorism

Once we identify the essential ingredients of terrorism (according to the official definition), it is not too difficult to see what motivates non-state actors to engage in terrorism.

What are these essential ingredients? They consist of violent instruments directed – by state or non-state actors – against civilians in order to achieve political ends. When non-state actors engage in such violence, we will assume that they seek to alter the behavior of one or more states.

The non-state actors may choose violent instruments for several reasons. First, non-violent instruments may not be available; this happens when these actors confront a tyranny that blocks the channels of political action and negotiation. Alternatively, even when these channels are available, the non-state actors may prefer to use violent instruments because they perceive this to be more effective. Among other things, the violence may gain publicity for their cause; by provoking retaliation, it may gain new converts to their cause; or they may want to move faster on their demands than the people they represent. Finally, they may pursue terrorism, together with political action, in order to warn the government that if they close the political track they will face more terrorism.

In the past century, terrorist tactics have been employed by at least three distinct groups of non-state actors. Terrorist tactics have been used by liberation movements against foreign occupations, among other places, in Ireland, Kenya, Algeria, Palestine (by the Palestinians), South Africa and Lebanon. Separatist groups too have turned to terrorism; one recalls the Basques in Spain, the Irish in Northern Ireland, the Moros in Philippines, the Kashmiris in India, the Kurds in Turkey, and the Tamils in Sri Lanka. A third category of terrorism emanates from fringe revolutionary groups, with little or no chance of achieving their objectives. In the era of the Cold War, this category has included the Bader Meinhoff (Germany), the Red Brigade (Italy), the Red Army (Japan), and the Symbionese Liberation Army (US).

In their choice of instruments, any rational non-state actor will weigh the effectiveness – the benefits and costs – of both violent and non-violent instruments. It appears that technological changes over the past two centuries – especially those affecting travel, communication, and the portability of destructive power – have increased the array of violent instruments avail-able to non-state actors; in addition, there has occurred a nearly parallel increase in the availability of large targets vulnerable to terrorist acts. Yet, we do not detect, over this period, any rising trend towards the use of ter-rorist acts by non-state actors. This may be due to an increase in the power of the state – fuelled by the same technological changes – to monitor and stop the violent actions of non-state actors.

However, once the non-state actors decide to embrace a violent death for themselves, once they are ready to weaponize their own deaths, this changes the calculus of violent actions. Faced with a non-state actor who is ready to die, the state loses its power of deterrence over him, since deter-rence is effective only *if* the non-state actor expects to survive his terrorist act. Once the state's power of deterrence is neutralized by his decision to accept death, the non-state actor has a wide range of instruments and tar-gets he can choose from. Potentially, he can choose his instruments and targets to produce large numbers of casualties. In other words, it is a psy-chic factor – the readiness of some non-state actors to kill themselves in executing their mission – that has elevated the risks of politically motivated violence against the United States.

Global Non-State Terrorism

Who are the non-state actors that have targeted Americans at home and abroad over the past two decades, and why?

If we accept the official accounts of 9-11, the identity of these non-state actors in most cases is clear enough: they are Muslims, mostly Arab Muslims. Indeed, the 19 young men who mounted the attacks of 9-11 were all Arabs. We also know that al-Qaida and its affiliated groups consist of Muslims – mainly but not exclusively Arabs – drawn from nearly every coun-try in the Islamicate world.

What is the significance of the terrorist attacks mounted by mainly Arab non-state actors against American interests, attacks that have been magni-fied since 9-11 into the most serious threat to American power since the end of the Cold War? Are these attacks from Islamicate militants cut from the same cloth as the anti-colonial struggles of the past, which, in several cases, used terrorism as one of their weapons?

In some ways, the American dominance over much of the Islamicate world is comparable to the colonial occupations of the past. Since the 1950s, the United States has been the hegemonic power in the Islamicate world, perpetuating, directing, modifying and manipulating the system of Arab and Islamicate states inherited from the colonial period. Today, the United States occupies Iraq and Afghanistan, and Israel (with US support) occupies Palestine and parts of Syria. In addition, the United States maintains a military presence in Pakistan, Turkey, Saudi Arabia, Afghanistan, Jordan, Kuwait, Qatar, Uzbekistan, Kyrgyzstan, Oman, Sharjah, etc. The American ambassador in many Muslim countries today exercises powers comparable in many ways to those enjoyed by colonial governors in British Africa.

Conversely, the al-Qaida sees itself – and is seen by many in the Islamicate world – as the vanguard of the Islamicate resistance against US-Israel's virtual occupation of the Islamicate world, an occupation that has been maintained through wars, sanctions, covert operations, and carefully cultivated local surrogates, consisting of monarchies, one-party tyrannies and military dictatorships.

At this point, the question that presents itself with force is this: If we are indeed witnessing an Islamicate resistance against US-Israeli occupation of the Islamicate world why haven't the Islamists – or Islamicate nationalists – directed their attacks against America's local surrogates? The anti-imperialist struggles of the past – even in the Islamicate world – were directed almost exclusively against the foreign powers *inside* the colonies, not in their home bases.

More pertinently, the Iranian groups who opposed the Pahlavi tyranny – seen as a surrogate of the United States by most Iranians – did not carry their anti-imperialist struggle to the United States. Instead, the Iranians directed their armed resistance and, in time, mass movement squarely against their country's repressive regime. It is not as if the Shah of Iran was soft on the opposition; indeed, his regime was one of the most repressive in the Third World. In addition, there is the Afghan resistance to the Soviet occupation of their country during the 1980s. Although led by Islamic fighters, the Afghans did not attack Soviet targets outside Afghanistan.

The Arabs too have faced local tyrannies – supported with arms, training and intelligence by the Americans and Israelis – during much of the post-War period. Yet, the Arab Islamist opposition has failed to overthrow any of these tyrannies over the past 50 years. Why? This is a tantalizing puzzle. There have been a few Islamist insurrections – in Syria, Iraq, Egypt and Algeria – but, with the exception of the Algerian insurrection, they were quickly suppressed never to cause trouble again. What are the social and economic conditions that have produced such enduring tyrannies in nearly every Arab country?

This is not the place to examine this question in any depth; it would be difficult to offer the answers in a few brush strokes. Still some circumstances about the history of this region, as well as the external conditions it has faced, point towards a weak national consciousness. The same conditions have also weakened their civil society.

Nearly all the Eastern Arab states were carved out of the Ottoman Empire during or soon after the First World War; they were British or French protectorates thrust into existence as monarchies. While this overrode the old Islamic unity and also fragmented a slowly emerging Arab identity, there was little national consciousness to form the basis of any of these new states. This made it easier for the monarchies – or the dictatorships that succeeded some of them – to fragment these societies along tribal lines, to destroy or weaken their established religious classes, and establish their power around tribal or sectarian cliques that were quite willing to kill in order to perpetuate their rule.

To this injury was added a grievous insult. This was the insertion of an alien Jewish-Ashkenazi state in Palestine, an imperialist prodigy, which proclaimed its arrival by defeating the rag-tag armies of the new Arab protectorates and cleansing much of Palestine of its Arab inhabitants. In their infancy, the malformed Arab states faced an expansionist colonial-settler state, just when such states were being dismantled in Africa. More humiliations followed, in 1956, with the first Israeli occupation of the Sinai, and in 1967, when the two leading Arab states, strongly nationalist, were brought low by the Israeli army in six days. These repeated humiliations gave the Arab regimes an excuse, in the cause of retrieving Arab honor, to complete the stifling of all forms of political dissent in their societies.

Many of the new Arab states were also oil-rich. At first, with one exception, all of these states were monarchies or, more accurately, family-run fiefs. How likely was it that these oil-rich monarchies were going to evolve into democracies? Their oil revenues freed these monarchies from the need to tax their populations. If they did not have to tax their subjects, why consult them? Indeed, in most cases, the monarchies had enough oil revenues to pamper their small populations with unheard of luxuries. In turn, the people were happy to trade these luxuries for their rights.

Their oil-wealth created another enduring problem for the Arabs. In order to acquire a firm handle over the oil resources of the region, the United States decided to work with Israel and the friendly oil-rich states in the region to defeat the Arab nationalists. Under this partnership, the United States encouraged the oil-rich states in their policy of tyranny, a convenient arrangement for both parties. By arranging their relations with a few royal families, the United States has for decades extracted handsome dividends from the region's oil resources. Aside from a single interruption, the oil fiefdoms have kept the oil flowing from their wells, used the proceeds to buy US weaponry, offered their largesse to US corporations, and recycled the rest to American banks. The Saudis alone hold nearly a trillion dollars in American assets. They have cared little to develop their own economies or their region.

Over time, America's partnership with Israel too paid off handsomely. After suffering a third defeat in 1973 – a near-victory that turned into a near-calamitous defeat – the Egyptians lost nerve. In 1978, at Camp David, they sought accommodation with the United States and Israel, leaving Israel free to pursue its hegemonic designs in the region. This marked the beginning of a sea-change in the dynamic of Arab societies. The historical task of opposing pro-American Arab tyrannies – both conservative and secular – would now pass from the Arab nationalists to the Islamists.

Once the Islamists took the lead, even the secular Arab states sought external sponsorship to counter their loss of legitimacy. The United States, Israel and the Arab regimes now became strategic partners, working secretly and openly to stifle and defeat the Islamists. The rising political repression forced the Islamists to go underground; quite a few left their countries. In the 1980s, they were encouraged to wage Jihad in far away places – Afghanistan, Bosnia, Kashmir and Chechnya.

This pan-Islamic Jihad marks a turning point in Islamist consciousness. Young Muslims from across the Muslim world were thrown together, away from their homes, in what they believed was a war for the defense of the Ummah. Perhaps, this was the first time in their history that Muslims of diverse ethnicities had gathered *as* Muslims to fight in defense of Islamicate lands. This deepened their sense of unity and their commitment to Islam. In time – vitalized by the success in reversing the Soviet invasion of Afghanistan – this experience encouraged radical tendencies in the Islamist movement. Back home from the wars in Afghanistan, Bosnia, Kashmir and Chechnya, when the Islamist opposition raised its head, it was armed and ready to employ violence to achieve its aims. Few had expected that this violence would be directed against the United States – even in its home territory. And this demands an explanation.

The Jihadist experience had produced a revolutionary vanguard without a popular base. Only in Algeria, during the late 1980s, massive public protests had forced an Arab regime to agree to hold elections. However, when the prospect of an Islamist victory loomed in 1992, the elections were cancelled. A civil war ensued. The Islamists lost the civil war because their popular base was not ready for armed resistance, and the state security apparatus remained loyal to the Algerian autocrats. No Arab society came even close to mounting the protests that occurred in Algeria. The writing on the wall was clear. Currently, Arab societies are unwilling to assume the risks necessary to change their autocratic governments. The Islamist movements had not yet grown a backbone.

Unable to carry the people with them, some Islamicate militants – led by al-Qaida – turned to shortcuts. They decided to attack US interests in the Islamicate world, even if it involved attacking civilians. These attacks had multiple objectives. The militants expected to rally the Muslims by demonstrating that the United States was vulnerable; with determination, the Muslims could strike at American interests in the Islamicate world. In response to these attacks, the United States and Israel would work more openly with the Arab regimes. Increasingly, they would be seen as American and Israeli lackeys. Finally, al-Qaida had also been planning attacks inside the United States, hoping that this would sting it into directly attacking the Islamicate world. In turn, al-Qaida was expecting the American attacks to mobilize the Islamicate world from Mauritania to Indonesia to overthrow their local tyrannies.

At least, this was the theory behind the attacks of 9-11. A prescient theory it was. This was also the gleam in the eye of the Neoconservatives; a 'galvanizing event' was what they wanted.[15] On September 11, 2001, the al-Qaida handed the Neoconservatives their Pearl Harbor. Instantly, Washington had launched a war against terrorism. After occupying Afghanistan, America was dreaming of redrawing old British-drawn maps of the Middle East. In the name of democratizing the Arab world – the civilizing mission of the twenty-first century – the Arab world would be balkanized, fragmented into ethnic and sectarian micro-states, 'democracies' allied to and dependent for their survival on the United States and Israel. Under this plan, the occupation of Iraq is the first stage in the march to an American Empire.

Concluding Remarks

It is a great travesty of our times that the United States, regarded by many in the Third World as a leading practitioner of state terrorism, now seeks to legitimize its imperialist ambitions in the name of defending the West against the terrorism of non-state actors.

It is true that non-state terrorism is a problem for the United States. If we wish to make any progress in analyzing the present spurt of non-state terrorism, two basic facts must be recognized. First, that its primary targets are the United States and Israel, its chief ally in the Middle East. Second, the agents of this terrorism have their provenance primarily in the Arab societies of the Middle East. The etiology of this terrorism – as well as its rationale – can be discovered primarily in the asymmetric relationship between these two sets of actors: the United States and Israel on one side, and the Arab and Islamicate societies on the other. On one side are two of the most

15 David Fitts, "Those Who Don't Remember History," *Ace Weekly* (April 10, 2003): <www.aceweekly.com/Backissues_ACE-Weekly/2003/030410/cover_story030410.html>

powerful states today; on the other a people repressed by their own governments, tyrannies supported by the United States. If only briefly, this essay
sets out the fundamentals of this relationship that have produced non-state
terrorism as one of many responses to the massive state terrorism of the
United States and Israel against Palestinians and Iraqis.

The American 'war against terrorism' is a cover under which at least three
forces are operating. On the one hand, this war allows the United States
to flex its already powerful military muscle to warn potential rivals against
challenging American hegemony. At another level, the American war against
the Islamicate countries is an old-style imperialist war for control over their
oil resources. Israel too enters into this equation in complex ways. The
American invasion of the Islamicate heartland feeds into Israeli plans to
fragment the present Arab states into smaller units, micro-states based on
religious, ethnic, sectarian and tribal identities, some of which can only
survive as clients of Israel. In defeat and victory, the United States will be
tempted to move in this direction.

Ironically, the American war against Islamicate societies also meets the
expectations of militant Islamists. They expect that the American invasion of Afghanistan and Iraq – and, in time, its extension to other countries
– will win more converts to the armed Islamicate resistance, destabilize the
American surrogates in the region, and eventually help them to achieve
their three-fold objective. The Islamists are seeking to force an American
withdrawal from the region, to overthrow the surrogate regimes in the
Islamicate world, and to create a core Islamic state embracing the Arab
heartland. On a realistic evaluation, it appears unlikely that the Islamists
can reach these objectives any time soon.

It should be noted, however, that the Islamicate resistance is likely to gain
strength from a growing demographic momentum. The Islamicate population, nearly a fourth of the world total, continues to grow faster than the rest
of the world population. It cannot be prudent for the United States and Israel
to press against so large a mass of people, inhabiting lands that stretch
across two continents – Africa and Asia – and establishing a growing presence in a third – Europe. It would appear that any effort to defeat, balkanize,
and humiliate so large a mass of population may consume resources which
may further undermine US competitiveness in the global economy. In the

unlikely event that the United States attains its goals quickly, it may prove to be a pyrrhic victory.

It is unlikely that a defeated – and impoverished – Islamicate world will shrink into a comatose state. At least, this is the prognosis if one takes a hard look at the struggles that the Palestinians, Bosnians, Chechens, Moros and Iraqis have put up against formidable odds. The historical memory of the Islamicate peoples – as the US-Israeli alliance pushes them against the wall – will continue to generate countervailing actions until a tolerably just equilibrium is established. However, it would be naive to rule out a catastrophic scenario. As the Islamicate resistance intensifies, the US-Israeli alliance will be tempted to seek victory through nuclear and biological warfare. It would appear that those who think this is doable and acceptable are in the ascendant – at least for now.

CHAPTER FOUR

Is There An Islamic Problem?

"Thus We have appointed you a Middle Nation, that ye may be witnesses against mankind, and that the Messenger may be a witness against you."
—Qur'an: 2:143[1]

January 2002

It has become fashionable after September 11, 2001, to excoriate Islam – the religion and civilization – as the source of the problems facing the Muslims. The air is thick with theories that identify Islam as the single greatest obstacle to the modernization of Islamicate societies. Oddly, after derailing modernization, that same Islam now fuels the rage over the absence of modernity in Islamicate societies.

In a recent essay, Pervez Hoodbhoy, a physicist and activist from Pakistan, argues that a deadening obscurantism has paralyzed Islamicate civilization since the twelfth century. Muslims can end this sustained paralysis, he writes, only if they decide to replace Islam with secular humanism.[2] Perhaps unknowingly, Hoodbhoy echoes a common Orientalist fallacy, which speaks of an early decline in the vitality of Islamicate civilization. It is fitting that we take a closer look at this thesis and see if we can quickly lay it to rest.

There is a touching irony in Hoodbhoy's thesis – not intended by him, I think. He concludes, a bit pompously, that secular humanism *"alone* offers the hope of providing everybody on this globe with the right to life, liberty and the pursuit of happiness (emphasis added)." Hoodbhoy's faith

---

1 *The Glorious Qur'an: Arabic Text and English Rendering, Text and Explanatory Translation by* Mohammad M. Pickthall (Des Plaines, IL.: Library of Islam, 1994). All quotes from the Qur'an refer to this translation.
2 Pervez Hoodbhoy "Muslims and the West after September 11," *Dawn,* December 10 and 11, 2001.

is touching. It is also a bit ironic, given that he opens his essay by acknowledging that the United States – as he puts it, the "Grand Exorcist" – is busy pursuing its own "happiness" by "exacting blood revenge" for September 11. In blatant disregard of its founding principles, the Grand Exorcist has for decades – two hundred years, in the Western hemisphere – worked feverishly to deny basic human rights to more than three-fourths of humanity.

No doubt, there are Americans who cringe at actions of their government that undermine freedoms abroad. Sadly, they are too few to have made much difference. In the 1970s, many Americans marched against the war their country was waging against the Vietnamese, but that – skeptics will remind us – did not happen until American boys started coming home in body bags. Americans have shed few tears for the two million Vietnamese, including half a million children, killed in their own country by the US war machine.

During an ascendancy that now spans at least two hundred years, the West has done little to forge a single humanity that embraces all the peoples of the world. For the most part, Western thinkers have pursued their humanist ideals within the paradigms of race and tribe. With few exceptions, the Enlightenment thinkers refused to share their humanity with Africans, Amerindians, Aborigines or Asians. Racism was germane to the thinking of the leading Western humanists, not excluding the great Montesquieu, Hume, Kant and Jefferson.[3] Even as they glorified 'man,' they saw little that was wrong in colonialism, slavery or the massacres of 'uncivilized tribes,' 'barbarians' and 'savages.' Europe's dream of reason did not produce sweetness and light for Amerindians, Africans, Asians or the 'outsiders' in Europe itself.

A Matter of Timing

I will turn directly to Hoodbhoy's Orientalist thesis on the decline of Islamicate societies: his rejection of Islam hinges on this theory.

First, he is quite wrong about the timing of this decline. He claims that Islam lost its creative élan in the thirteenth century, a result of the twin blows dealt by the 'ulama – the jurisprudents and theologians of Islam – and

---

3 Emmanuel Eze, *Race and Enlightenment: A Reader* (Blackwell: 2000).

the Mongols. This suggests that Hoodbhoy has been raised on a rather pure diet of Orientalism and its falsification of Islamicate history.

Hoodbhoy employs graphic imagery in presenting his ideas. Islam was "choked" in the twelfth century by the "vice-like grip of orthodoxy" created by the anti-rationalism of Ghazali, whom he describes, incorrectly, as a "cleric." He also refers to the "trauma" of the thirteenth century. Presumably, he is referring to the Mongol destruction of Baghdad in 1258.

Bernard Lewis, the dean of the post-war generation of Zionist Orientalists – and, probably, an important source of Hoodbhoy's inspiration – places the Islamicate decline even earlier. Although "signs of decadence are visible even earlier," he declares that by the eleventh century "the world of Islam was in a state of *manifest* decay (emphasis added)."[4] He accomplishes this *tour de force* – establishing the early decline of the Islamicate world – by equating Islamicate civilization with Arab power.

It is odd that after its "manifest decay," Islamicate power, barring the reversal in Spain, continued to expand for several more centuries. In the Levant, the Muslims contained the repeated onslaughts of the Crusaders over two centuries, finally expelling them in 1291. The Ottomans expanded into the Balkans, taking Constantinople in 1453, and twice laid siege to Vienna, the second time in 1683. In the West, the Berbers extended Islamicate power into Sub-Saharan Africa. Perhaps most importantly, once the Turks and Mongols entered Islam, Islamicate power extended deep into Central Asia, up the Volga River, beyond the Tarim Basin, and past the Hindu Kush into the plains of North India. In addition, Arab and Persian traders were seeding Islamicate communities in East Africa, southern India, and the islands of the Indonesian archipelago.

Marshall Hodgson has challenged the Orientalist canard about an early decline of Islamicate civilization in The Venture of Islam (1974), a deep, sweeping and multi-faceted account of the history and civilization of Islamicate societies. He has written that, "in its own setting, the age of the sixteenth and seventeenth centuries was one of the greatest in Islamdom's history. The artistic, philosophic, and social power and creativeness of the age can be

---

4   Bernard Lewis, "The Arabs in Eclipse," in: Carlo M. Cippola, ed., *The Economic Decline of Empires* (London: Methuen, 1970): 102.

symbolized in the spaciousness, purity – and overwhelming magnificence of the Tâj Mahal at Agra. In some sense there was a great florescence."[5] The Isfahan School of philosophy, founded by Mulla Sadra (d. 1640), is now recognized by Western authorities as a major philosophical movement.[6]

Scientific activity in the Islamicate world did not face sudden death either. George Saliba, a leading historian of Islamicate science, extends the Islamicate golden age to the fifteenth century.[7] Soon after their conquest of much of the central Islamicate lands, the Mongols turned their energies to rebuilding the societies they had destroyed. In fact, several of them took up earnestly the patronage of the arts and sciences, and major observatories were being set up as late as the fifteenth century. The astronomical tables computed at these observatories, together with the work of Ibn-Shatir (d. 1375), a time-keeper in the central mosque of Damascus, were passed on to Europe, and are believed to have contributed to the Copernican Revolution. Western debt to Islamicate sciences – in the fields of mathematics, optics, astronomy and medicine – may turn out to be deeper yet, once historians take up the research into these connections more seriously.

If there was a falling off in the scientific output of Islamicate societies after the eleventh century, this was compensated by growing activity in a variety of other human endeavors, including historiography, poetry, architecture, painting and – in Iran – philosophy. Given this, it is a bit silly to scapegoat Ghazali for "choking" Islam with his "vice-like grip" of orthodoxy. In fact, Ghazali was a major philosopher in his own right whose philosophical skepticism anticipated Descartes and Kant; but unlike them, he turned to spiritual empiricism to transcend his doubts. Ghazali attacked the heterodox Isma'ilis and the heretical tendencies among Muslims who delved in Greek metaphysics. He was not opposed to logic, mathematics or the sciences.

Rise of Western Europe

If it was not in the eleventh or twelfth centuries, when did the decline of Islamicate societies become manifest? We must look for the beginnings of this process, as well as its source, not so much in Islamicate societies

---

5   Marshall G. S. Hodgson, *The Venture of Islam*, Volume 3 (Chicago: University of Chicago Press, 1974): 14.

6   Henry Corbin, *History of Islamic Philosophy* (London: Kegan Paul, 1993).

7   George Saliba, *A History of Arabic Astronomy* (New York University Press: 1994): 7.

as in Western Europe. It was Western Europe that gathered speed and moved ahead of *all* other societies, starting in the fifteenth century. In turn, the ascendancy of the West produced decline and decay in nearly all non-Western societies, not only those in the Islamicate world.

Western Europe's ascendancy began with its lead in two critical areas, gunnery and shipping, starting in the fifteenth century. The West Europeans did not invent gunpowder and cannons; both are Chinese inventions that were carried to Europe and the Middle East by the invading Mongols in the thirteenth century. However, the constantly warring Europeans soon took the lead – because of their more decentralized polity – in improving gunpowder weaponry; this included lighter cannons and handguns. At the same time, the Western Europeans were building sturdier ships to negotiate the stormy Baltic Sea and the Atlantic Ocean. In the fifteenth century, when the Western Europeans mounted their light cannons on their sturdy ships, this combination proved deadly against the galleys of the Mediterranean and the flimsier ships of the generally calm Indian Ocean. Luck also favored Europe. In 1433, the Chinese not only withdrew their maritime presence from the Indian Ocean, they scrapped their fleet of superior ships. This was a fateful measure. If the Chinese had continued their maritime explorations, they would have challenged the European entry into the Indian Ocean. It is even likely that they would be 'discovering' Europe, instead of the other way around.

This superiority in gunnery and shipping launched Atlantic Europe, through deepening cycles of cumulative causation, on the path of global ascendancy. Its first dividend was the 'discovery' of the Americas, perhaps the greatest resource windfall ever received by any society. This was quickly followed by the European passage into the Indian Ocean, which led to a growing monopoly over the trade of the Indian Ocean, easily the world's richest trading area. In addition, America's gold and silver gave an economically backward Europe the means for entering into the trade of the Indian Ocean. In the long run, Europe's command of the high seas produced vast new sources of wealth through plunder, trade, shipping, banking and overseas investments; and, in turn, the growth of shipping and commerce stimulated manufactures. When some of this new wealth was used to support universities and academies, it produced a growing interest in philosophy, mathematics and the sciences. Directly and indirectly, these advances contributed to Europe's military technology, which, in turn, expanded their overseas empires and brought still greater profits. By the beginning of the nineteenth century – in India before that – these developments had come to a head. Europe was ready to start its project of dismantling Islamicate empires and states in the Mediterranean and the Indian Ocean.

Why did the Islamicate – or other Asian and African – polities fail to resist this growing European thrust? The Eurocentric narratives insist that Europe's ascendancy since the sixteenth century is not new. It was only the latest expression, now played out on the global stage, of the superiority that Europe has always enjoyed over other civilizations; and it owes this superiority to its rationality, individualism, vigor, enterprise, curiosity and love of freedom. These perennial tendencies are gifts of divine Providence, a superior biological endowment, a diverse and more generous topography, or a more invigorating climate. In blaming Ghazali – read Islam – for the decline of Islamicate societies, Hoodbhoy is buying into the Weberian version of this Eurocentric narrative, which identifies Western ascendancy with the greater rationality promoted by Protestantism.

A historical narrative – one that is rooted in cumulative processes, contingencies, conjunctures, contradictions, accidents and unintended consequences – tells a different story. The colonization of the Americas, the growing control over the trade of the Indian Ocean, the mercantilist rivalries and incessant wars among European states – produced by the anarchy of their decentralized political system – accelerated the dynamic of historical change in Europe, allowing it to outpace the more centralized, mostly land-based empires of the Middle East, India and China. In the long run, the Netherlands, Britain, France and the United States slowly built upon their successes in commerce, shipping, the arts of warfare, state-formation and manufactures to develop into centers of capitalist production, which drew their economic strength from an alliance between capital and the state.

Globally, the growth of these centers of capitalist production – the Core of the world economy – produced, simultaneously, their opposite and complement, an underdeveloped Periphery, dominated by capital from the Core and restructured to supply raw materials – in some cases, labor – to the Core countries. In most cases, the loss of sovereignty preceded or accompanied a country's incorporation into the Periphery. With the solitary exception of Japan, the leading Core countries converted the non-White countries into outright colonies or forced them to sign open-door treaties, which gave preferential treatment to Core capital. However, most countries of European ethnicity in the Periphery – for reasons of geopolitics and heritage – retained much of their sovereignty. These countries exercised various degrees of sovereign control over their economic policies to promote indigenous capital and technology. In the long haul, some of them pulled out of the Periphery to join the Core.[8]

Quite a few historians and sociologists attribute the ascendancy of Western Europe to its greater rationality, a legacy thought to derive from its cultivation of Greek philosophy. This is spurious history and false sociology – two unavoidable ingredients of all Eurocentric thought. The truth is quite the opposite of this. The verdict of Ernest Gellner, a philosopher and social anthropologist, deserves to be quoted in full: "By various obvious criteria – universalism, scripturalism, spiritual egalitarianism, the extension of full participation in the sacred community not to one, or some, but to *all*, and the rational systematization of social life – Islam is, of the three great Western monotheisms, the closest to modernity."[9] The French sociologist, Maxine Rodinson, arrived at a similar conclusion when he examined the precepts of Islam in relation to the demands of a capitalist system.[10]

In addition, the standard claims about the rationality of modern Europe – even during the Enlightenment – are exaggerated. Several of the leading scientists of the seventeenth century – including Tycho Brahe, Galileo Galilei, Johannes Kepler and Pierre Gassendi – admired for their contributions to the development of modern physics and astronomy, held astrology in high esteem. Even Isaac Newton, perhaps the greatest scientist of modern times, devoted nearly two decades of his life to investigations in alchemy. A mere twelve percent of the books in Newton's personal library were on physics, astronomy and mathematics. On the contrary, not only were the leading philosopher-scientists of Islamicate societies opposed to astrology, so was Islamic orthodoxy.

---

8 M. Shahid Alam, *Poverty from the Wealth of Nations* (Houndmills, UK: Palgrave Macmillan, 2000).
9 Ernest Gellner, *Muslim Society* (Cambridge, UK: Cambridge University Press: 1981): 7.
10 Maxine Rodinson, *Islam and Capitalism* (Austin, TX: University of Texas Press: 1978).

Failing to Recoup the Losses

This brings us to the failure of Islamicate societies – a problem not shared by India or China – to mount an adequate recovery from the losses of the colonial epoch.

The European empires established in the nineteenth century did not last very long – as empires go. Their racist, exploitative, and sometimes geno-cidal policies fuelled vigorous anti-imperialist movements across much of Asia, Africa and the Caribbean. In time, the colonial powers got into two major brawls – better known as the two World Wars – accelerating their own demise. The First World War created an opening for the emergence of the world's first anti-capitalist regime in Russia; the Second World War did the same in China. In addition, the Second World War crystallized a new power structure, dominated by the United States and the Soviet Union, each opposed for different reasons to the old colonial empires. As the leading capitalist economy, the United States was jealous of the privileged access the colonial powers had to their colonies. The Soviet Union contested the capitalist powers by supporting radical and nationalist movements in the colonies. In other words, the conditions were ripe for the dismantling of colonial empires at the end of the Second World War.

The end of colonial era, however, did not herald a bright future for all subject populations. In particular, the Islamicate world that emerged from the colo-nial era was weak and fragmented. It lacked a core state; the colonial powers had splintered the Arabs into some twenty states, some of them little more than collections of oil wells; Britain and the United States had placed the oil-rich states under despotic monarchies; and the Zionists had established a Jewish state in nearly all of Palestine. In contrast, India and China were decidedly better off. The Indians entered the new era with great hopes. Only for the third time in their long history, the Hindus were in charge of a united India, the second largest country in the world that appeared poised to rise to the ranks of a great power. India was in capable hands too; its leaders were committed to democracy and keenly aware of the unique moment in their history. In addition, despite two centuries of colonial rule, the Indian econ-omy was mostly in the hands of indigenous capital. China too had emerged single and whole – but for the loss of Taiwan, Hong Kong and Macao –

having fought off a succession of imperialist powers and indigenous centrifugal forces. In 1948, after nearly a century of civil wars and the depredations of Europeans, Americans and Japanese, the long-suffering Chinese reconstituted their ancient Confucian state under new forms. The imperial house and the mandarins gave way to a communist party forged through decades of struggle against Chinese warlords and foreign imperialists.

The Islamicate world commanded at least three major empires in 1600: the Ottoman, Safavid and Mughal. At the time, and for several more decades, the Ottomans alone could stand up to the forces assembled by any combination of the leading European states. Yet none of the post-colonial Islamicate states could aspire to the power that belonged to these empires. Why had Islamicate societies failed to reconstitute their former power in the post-colonial period? It is important to answer this question, since this *political* failure lies at the root of the present troubles in the Islamicate world. The Orientalists who claim that the turbulence in the Islamicate world is born from a failure of modernity are inverting the order of causation.

As recently as 1750, Islamicate power stretched from Mauritania and the Balkans in the West to Indonesia and Mindanao in East Asia. However, this power lacked a demographic base. In the Balkans and India, the Ottomans and the Mughals ruled over non-Muslim majorities. Once nationalist consciousness gained ground as the principal basis of statehood, the Ottoman Empire lost its legitimacy, challenged first by its Christian population in Europe and later by Arab fellow Muslims who resented domination by the Ottoman Turks. In India, Hindu resentment against their Muslim rulers accelerated the dissolution of the Mughal Empire, and, later, the defeat of Muslim successor states in the face of British competition. Importantly, once these Islamicate Empires disintegrated, it would be nearly impossible to reconstitute them in the absence of a Muslim majority.

The Islamicate societies suffered from a second demographic handicap in their struggle against European imperialism. Once the Middle East had lost the momentum of an early start with the agricultural revolution, the population advantage shifted to China, India and Europe. While the population of Europe increased nearly six-fold between the start of the Common Era and 1800 CE, the population of the Nile-to-Oxus region had not quite doubled over the same period.[11] As a result, the total population of North Africa, Egypt, the Fertile Crescent and Arabia in 1800 was only modestly ahead of the population of France. In other words, these central Islamicate regions lacked both demographic weight and geographic depth – since this population was strung out along the Mediterranean coast and two river valleys – in its vital contest with expansionist European powers. Given this demographic disproportion, some Europeans dreamed of eradicating the Islamic character of North Africa and the Levant with a little help from colonial settlers.

The Islamicate states bordering the Mediterranean faced another handicap: they were only a few days' sail from Europe. This made them tempting targets for European capital and cupidity, mixed with some of the old Christian zeal for eradicating Islam. France, Britain, the Zionists and Italy took up this project successively. The French proceeded to colonize Algeria, Tunisia and Morocco, and quickly introduced white settlers with the aim of annexing these regions to France. The European powers dismantled the Egyptian effort to industrialize – initiated by Muhammad Ali Pasha in 1810 – after they intervened to block his march on Istanbul in 1839. When the Egyptians mobilized again in the 1870s to assert their independence, the British occupied Egypt in 1882. Taking advantage of the First World War, Britain and France occupied the Arab territories of the Ottoman Empire and carved them into several small states, with one slice going to the Zionists, as promised in the Balfour Declaration of 1917. Britain, France and Israel mounted another invasion of Egypt in 1956, roiled when Gamal Nasser nationalized the Suez Canal. Luckily, the United States was not too pleased over this European adventure, and the invasion was called off in a hurry.

This capsule history of the Middle East offers some sobering reflections for the Eurocentrists and their Muslim acolytes who attribute the backwardness of Islamicate societies to their religion and culture: to Islam's antipathy to science, rationality and modernity. Imagine just one counterfactual. Imagine if the Egyptian bid to industrialize had *not* been dismantled by the European powers. It is then likely that an industrialized Egypt would have become a catalyst for industrial transformation in other Middle Eastern countries. This thought experiment explains why the Europeans united

---

11 McEvedy, Colin and Richard Jones, *Atlas of world population history* (New York: Penguin Books, 1978): various tables.

to abort Muhammad Ali Pasha's industrial drive. An industrialized Middle East would have renewed the old threat of Islam to Europe.

On the other hand, the European powers showed little interest in blocking Japan's industrial drive initiated some sixty years after Egypt's. Japan succeeded because it was an archipelago tethered off the eastern edge of Asia, half a world away from Western Europe and separated from the United States by the vast Pacific Ocean. Of equal importance, Japan's mix of Shinto and Confucian culture did not set off alarms in the European psyche. Could Japan have pulled off its industrial coup if it had been a Muslim island anchored in the Eastern Mediterranean or even the Arabian Sea?

The impotence of Arabs in the post-colonial period goes back to three additional factors: Zionism, the old Christian vendetta against Islam, and oil. The Zionists founded their project on a confluence of Jewish and Western interests in the Middle East. The Zionists proposed to rid Europe of Jews if Europe would help them to establish a Jewish state in Palestine. In succession, Zionist ambitions combined with European Islamophobia to produce the Balfour Declaration of 1917, the dismantling of the Ottoman Empire, the vivisection of the former Ottoman territories in the Fertile Crescent, the creation of a Maronite-dominated mini-state in Lebanon, the British mandate over Palestine, and the creation of a Jewish colonial-settler state in Arab Palestine. Arab aspirations in the Fertile Crescent had been dealt a body blow from which it would be hard to recover. Had the Arabs of this region been free to realize their nationalist aspirations, most likely they would have created a single Arab state that might well have included – because of its religious significance – the Arabian Peninsula as well, or at least the Hejaz and the oil-rich Gulf coast.

In the meanwhile, the United States and Britain were negotiating arrangements in the Persian Gulf to ensure Western control over the richest oil reserves in the world. They decided to place the region under archaic, absolutist monarchies whose survival, against the rising tide of nationalism, would depend on the United States. As part of this plan, when a democratic movement overthrew the Iranian monarchy in 1953, the United States and Britain orchestrated a coup to re-instate the monarchy. In 1967, Israel inflicted a humiliating defeat on Egypt and Syria – leading to the occupation of Sinai, the Golan Heights, the West Bank and Gaza – virtually removing the

Arab nationalist challenge to Western control over Middle Eastern oil. The Middle East straightjacket was now securely in place.

While appreciating the global forces arrayed against them, it is disconcerting to watch the ease with which the Arabs, the peoples no less than their leaders, have slipped into the straitjacket prepared for them by the Western imperialists. In the final analysis, the historical verdict on the Arab national awakening is clear: it failed. While the leaders of the Arab nationalist movements created a discourse of Arab nationalism – a concept of nationhood founded on language and history – they failed to create a deep consciousness of Arab unity, one that would seek its goal in Arab political unity, in a single Arab statehood. Although Arab nationalists had gained power over Egypt, Syria and Iraq by the end of the 1950s, their failure to realize a political unity – apart from a short-lived union between Egypt and Syria – is testimony to the tenuous character of the Arab nationalist project. Not even the successive defeats inflicted by Israel on various combinations of Arab states – in 1948, 1956 and 1967 – could create the impetus for unity, the desire to restore Arab honor, or mobilize to face the massive threat that Israel posed to Arab security. Arab nationalism was mostly talk – rhetoric without substance.

The Iranian revolution of 1979 failed to loosen the Western stranglehold on the Middle East. On the contrary, by raising the specter of Islamist power in the region, this paved the way for an 'Arab' war against Iran – with funding from the Gulf Arabs, manpower from Egypt, and the blessings of Western powers – to contain the spread of the Islamist revolution to the Arab countries. In time, after the collapse of the Soviet Union, the corrupt Arab regimes formed a grand alliance – under the aegis of the United States and Israel – to control and repress their Islamist movements. In 1993, the Palestine Liberation Organization recognized Israel and agreed to police the Palestinians in return for municipal control over parts of the West Bank and Gaza. Syria and Libya chose to repress their Islamists without joining this alliance; as a result, the United States placed them in the limbo of 'rogue states.' When foolhardy Iraq dared to challenge this alliance in 1990, without the nerve to carry it to completion, it was bombed back to the Stone Age and crippled with comprehensive economic sanctions.

A new imperialism had descended on the Islamicate world in the 1990s. Its rules were clear. The United States would support despots in the Muslim states so long as they came to terms with Israel and kept a tight lid on political Islam. If any country dared to depart from the terms of this contract, it faced economic sanctions – and, if these did not work, war. When Iraq challenged this contract in 1990, it faced both endless war and crippling sanctions that have devastated its economy and caused more than a million deaths. Similarly, Algeria illustrates the fate awaiting a Muslim country if the Islamists seek to capture power – even through the democratic process.

This new imperialist contract explains why the 'democratization' of the 1990s bypassed much of the Islamicate world. Professor Hoodbhoy thinks otherwise. Instead of offering a historical analysis, rooted in the dynamics of global capitalism and the legacy of past conflicts between Europe and the Islamicate world, he joins the Orientalists in blaming the difficulties of the Islamicate world on Islam, the religion and civilization. His method is familiar – damnation by accusation, damnation by defining the essence of Islamicate societies. If Islam is obscurantist, anti-rationalist, fanatical, and misogynist, *then* we can explain the aversion of the Islamicate world towards modernity and democracy. The Orientalist has spoken: the case is closed.

Those who maintain that Islam is anti-democratic might gain from a short lesson in the modern history of constitutional movements in Islamicate countries. Muhammad Ali of Egypt appointed his first advisory council in 1824, consisting mostly of elected members. In 1881, the Egyptian nationalists succeeded in convening an elected parliament, but the British disbanded this when they occupied Egypt a year later. Tunisia had promulgated a constitution in 1860, setting up a Supreme Council purporting to limit the powers of the monarchy. However, the French suppressed this Council in 1864 when they discovered that it interfered with their ambitions in Tunisia. Turkey elected its first parliament in 1877 though it was dissolved a year later by the Caliph; a second parliament was convened in 1908. Iran's progress was more dramatic. It started with protests against the grant of a British tobacco monopoly in the 1890s, but this escalated into demands for a constitutional monarchy. In 1906, Iran's first elected parliament adopted a constitution limiting the powers of the monarchy and assumed the power to confirm the cabinet. However, this led to a struggle between the Qajar rulers and the constitutionalists. In 1911, with support from their Russian and British patrons, the Qajar monarch defeated the Constitutionalists and disbanded the parliament. The Constitutional movement persisted for two more decades, until the new Pahlavi dynasty, which rose to power with help from the British, suppressed it in 1931.

Compare these developments with the history of constitutional movements elsewhere, not excluding Europe, during the nineteenth century – and the world of Islam does not suffer from the comparison. Incredible as this appears to minds blinded by Eurocentric prejudice, Tunisia, Egypt and Iran were taking the lead in making the transition to constitutional monarchies. In recent decades too, democracy in the region has not been stifled by some essential incompatibility between democracy and Arab or Islamic traditions. Both directly and indirectly, oil, Israel and the old Western antipathy to Islam have been important factors derailing the normal evolution of these societies. Oil led to British and, later, US support for monarchies and dictatorships that suppressed the nationalist and democratic aspirations of their people. The insertion of Israel – an expansionist, colonial-settler state – into the region produced wars and tensions, which supported the creation of security states at the cost of civil society. More recently, the growth of an Islamist opposition has deepened Western support for repressive regimes in the region.

A US-Imposed Straightjacket

The US-imposed straightjacket has deepened the contradictions of global capitalism in the Islamicate world: a development that is pregnant with consequences that threaten to spin out of control.

During the Cold War, the dominant factions in many Third World countries competed with each other to win the US contract for repressing their radical and populist movements. As long as they did their job, these repressive regimes enjoyed a degree of autonomy in managing their economies. Taking advantage of this autonomy, many Third World countries implemented interventionist policies to develop indigenous capital and technology. A few of them in East Asia, those most favored by the United States, became showcases of capitalist success. When the Soviet Union collapsed in 1990, the United States terminated this Cold War contract. It was replaced by the

Washington Consensus, which called upon the countries in the Periphery to open up their economies to Core capital. The World Trade Organization was created to formalize the new arrangements, which were a great deal more comprehensive than the Open Door treaties imposed on nominally independent countries in the nineteenth century. The elites in the Periphery quickly got the message. Soon they were competing to open up their economies for takeover by multinational corporations.

The United States offered two versions of this new colonial contract. Countries in the non-Islamicate Periphery are generally encouraged to compete for the contract through the ballot box. In countries that have strong Islamist movements, this option is not available; their dictators and monarchs are employed to keep the lid on Islamist movements. The excuse for this two-track policy is flimsy. Western commentators argue that the Islamist parties will only use the ballot to abolish democracy once they gain an electoral majority. The real reason is Western nervousness over the Islamist's twin goals: introducing an Islamic social order and reversing the fragmentation and marginalization of Islamicate societies. Washington has decided that it will oppose and suppress the Islamists at all costs.

The US-Israeli siege of the Islamicate world is unlikely to deliver peace to the region. On the contrary, it has engendered contradictions that will only deepen over time. After the Israeli rout of the Arab armies in 1967, secular Arab nationalism stood discredited: not only had it failed to unite the Arabs to reclaim Palestine, it had lost more Arab lands to Israel. Having depleted their political capital and, therefore, the support of their people, the Arab regimes were now ready for deals with Washington and Tel Aviv. In 1973, with appropriate cash rewards from the US, Egypt made a separate peace with Israel. In abdicating its leadership of the Arab world, Egypt wrote the obituary of Arab nationalism. Only the Islamists could now assume the historic task of liberating and uniting the Arab world.

Although humiliated, the Arab regimes remained firmly ensconced in power. In large part, this was a gift of the new colonial contract. The United States encouraged the Arab regimes – with intelligence, technology and loans when needed – to compensate for their loss of legitimacy by tightening their repressive regimes. The turn around from a strident Arab nationalism to capitulation was quick, moving through abdication at Camp David, concessions at Oslo, normalization of ties with Israel, and the embrace of the Washington Consensus. On the domestic front, these regimes intensified the repression of their Islamist opposition. They banned the Islamist parties, removed the Islamists from leading positions in professional associations and trade unions, and eventually the leading Islamists were jailed, executed or hounded out of the country.

This repression of Islamists has produced two results. Nearly everywhere, the Arab regimes blocked Islamists who wished to work through the institutions of civil society, including political parties, professional associations, the media, courts and charities. This shifted the focus to radical Islamists, those who were willing to engage in violent actions – guerilla war, assassinations and terror – to gain their ends. However, even the radicals had little leeway under the repressive Arab regimes. Those who evaded capture or execution went underground or escaped to Afghanistan, Pakistan or the Western countries. At some point, some radical Islamists decided to change their strategy. They would target their problems at the source – and inflict damage on the United States. They decided to sting the United States into lifting its siege of Islamicate countries. Alternatively, they hoped to provoke wars – like the one in Afghanistan – on the chance that this would stir radicalism and revolutions against neocolonial surrogates in the Islamicate world.

There are powerful economic forces that affect this dynamic. I will mention one: the brain drain that has accelerated with the growing mobility of skilled workers. The range of deleterious economic and social effects produced by brain drain has received little attention from social scientists. Perhaps, the most talented members of the work force now migrate to developed countries. This drains the developing countries of their best doctors, engineers and scientists: an all too familiar phenomenon. In addition, the brain drain depletes a country of its leaders, activists, scholars, poets, and its conscience. Over the past two decades, this has greatly weakened the progressive forces in nearly all the countries of the Periphery.

Almost as damaging, the brain drain leaves a second layer of alienation in its wake. Those who succeed in leaving are only a fraction of those who *want* to leave and who, therefore, order their lives around the chance of leaving. As a result, the college graduates who stay at home – because they cannot yet leave – remain disconnected from their own societies. This has had a deadening effect on mechanisms for social change, deepening the vicious circle of poverty, social apathy and corruption.

All of this has slowly produced a coarsening of the Islamic discourse in some Islamicate countries. The brain drain has contributed to a growing lumpenization of the Islamist opposition. As more people from the middle classes exercise the exit option, the intellectual and political leadership of the Islamist movements has passed into the hands of persons who have little chance of taking the exit option. Increasingly, the Islamist leaders come from marginalized classes – including shopkeepers, clerks and self-employed workers – who are excluded from the exit option by their education in the vernaculars or religious schools. These Islamists are busy creating a militant Jihadi culture in Pakistan, Algeria, Indonesia and Afghanistan.

Giving Up 'False Notions'?

Pervez Hoodbhoy counsels Muslims to give up the 'false notions' of Islam.[12] On the contrary, Muslims alienated from their roots need to renounce false Orientalist narratives – of an Islam that has been misrepresented as irrational, misogynist, fatalist and fanatical.

Rational thinking did not begin with the Enlightenment. In fact, several Enlightenment thinkers turned to Islam to advance their own struggle against medieval obscurantism, the intolerance of an organized clergy, and the anti-rationalism of their own mystery religion. According to Bernard Lewis, "The image of Mohammed as a wise, tolerant, unmystical and undogmatic ruler became widespread in the period of the Enlightenment."[13] It is time for alienated Muslim intellectuals to tear the Orientalist veil that obscures their vision of Islam, re-enter the historical currents they have abandoned, create a deeper understanding of the dynamics of derailed Islamicate societies, and lead them into an Islamic vision of a world where all communities, ethnic and religious, race against each other "in doing good works."[14] After

---

12 The second part of Hoodbhoy's essay appeared under the title: "Time To Give Up False Notions."

13 *Islam and the West* (Oxford University Press: 1993): 90.

14 This refers to the following verse from the Qur'an: "For each We have appointed a divine law and a traced-out way. Had Allah willed He could have made you one community. But that He may try you by that which He hath given you (He hath made you as ye are). So vie one with another in good works. Unto Allah will ye return, and He will then inform you of that wherein ye differ." (5:48)."

more than eighty years of Kemalism, a military clique still calls the shots in secular Turkey, wages war against a fifth of its own population, trembles at the sight of women in scarves, and grovels to gain entry into the margins of European society. Do we want to litter the Islamicate landscape with yet more half-baked Turkeys?

The West too must overcome its false notions of the Islamicate world as the irreconcilable 'Other', the fundamental peril that must forever be opposed, fought against, bottled and besieged. If Islamicate societies appear to be a greater threat to the West than India or China, that is because the actions of Western powers, now and in the past, as well as the forces of history, geography and demography, have fragmented Islamicate societies and, so far, prevented them from reconstituting their center, their wholeness and history. Nearly a fourth of the world's peoples seek their identity and dignity, their place in this world and the next, within a stream of history that flows from the Qur'an. They want to live by ethical ideals that have produced the austere nobility of the Prophet's companions, an egalitarianism that elevated slaves to kingship, the juristic insights of Al Shafi'i and Abu Hanifa, the mystical flights of Al-Arabi and Rumi, the rationalism of Ibn Rushd and Ibn Tufail, the mathematics of Al-Khawarizmi and Khayyam, the scientific achievements of Ibn Sina and Al-Haytham, the sociological insights of Ibn Khaldun and Al-Biruni, the majesty of Al-Hambra and the Taj, the observatories of Samarqand and Maragha, the tolerance of Salahuddin and Akbar, and the poetry of Rumi, Hafiz, Ghalib and Iqbal. Once they regain their autonomy, dignity and integrity, the Islamicate societies can again produce another cultural efflorescence that draws upon the light, freshness and sweetness of the Qur'an. The Qur'anic impulse towards truth, justice, sincerity and beauty will find expression again, not in combat, but in a new Arabesque of creative minds and soulful hearts, intertwined with reason and mercy.

CHAPTER FIVE

How Different are Islamicate Societies?

"O mankind! Be careful of your duty to your Lord Who created you from a single soul and from it created its mate and from them twain hath spread abroad a multitude of men and women."
—Qur'an: 4:1

February 2002

There are two opposite visions that animate American scholarship on Islam and Islamicate societies. In the days, months and years ahead, a great deal will hinge on which of these visions informs American foreign policy.

One vision represents Islam – the religion and society – as an enemy that must be destroyed, or it will destroy the West. This is the camp of warriors, led, among others, by Bernard Lewis, Daniel Pipes, Charles Krauthammer and Martin Kramer. Their thinking is reductionist and ahistorical; they believe that Islam is fundamentally at odds with the core values of the West. These warriors urge the United States to confront this menace now and contain it militarily before it threatens Western dominance.

The second vision proposes that Islamicate societies are diverse, containing tendencies – religious, cultural and political – that pull in different directions. It argues that political Islam does not reject modernity; instead, it seeks to indigenize modernity, to give it a local habitation and a name. This is the diplomatic camp, led, among others, by John Esposito, Richard Bulliet and Bruce Lawrence. They believe in engaging Islamist movements, giving them a chance to run Islamicate societies since this will either discredit them or bring them into the political mainstream.

It is worth noting that, in the world of scholarship, the warriors are a minority. However, together with their neoconservative allies, they enjoy considerably greater political and media clout than the diplomatic camp. This clout had been increasing since the end of the Cold War. And now, after September 11, President Bush appears to be embracing their objective of waging pre-emptive wars against major Islamicate countries. At the present juncture, laden with tensions, it would be all too easy to start these wars; but, once started, they may be harder to stop.

I will review some of the charges leveled by the camp of warriors against Islamicate societies. Are Islamicate societies lagging in economic development; do they face a clear democracy deficit; and do they have "bloody borders," a phrase coined by Samuel Huntington? Contrary to popular perceptions, the evidence fails to support these charges.

Economic Development

The Islamicate world does face any number of serious problems: it would be foolish to deny this. What we need to determine is whether Islamicate countries have done worse or much worse than others with a comparable history in pursuing economic growth, promoting equality between the sexes, developing free institutions, and keeping the peace with its neighbors?

First, consider the question of economic development. Judging from their living standards in 1999, measured as per capita income in international dollars – taken from the World Development Report, 2000 – it does not appear that Muslims have done too badly.[1] In several paired comparisons, Iran holds its own against Venezuela, Malaysia is well ahead of Thailand, Egypt is modestly ahead of Ukraine, Turkey only slightly behind Russia, Pakistan a little behind – and Indonesia somewhat ahead – of India, Bangladesh is somewhat behind Vietnam, Tunisia is well ahead of Georgia and Armenia, and Jordan is significantly ahead of Nicaragua. It is important to note that some of the comparisons concede the historical advantage to the non-Islamicate countries that gained their independence earlier.

---

1   World Bank, World Development Report, 2000 (New York: Oxford University Press, 2000).

The results do not change if we base the comparisons on a broader human development index. In a ranking that includes 162 countries in 1999 – taken from the *Human Development Report*, 2000 – 22 Islamicate countries occupy ranks between 32 and 100.[2] Pakistan, Bangladesh and Sudan rank lower down the scale, but they are still ahead of several non-Islamicate countries in Africa. Notably, the Arab oil-rich countries are the leaders of the Islamicate pack. Incredibly, Saudi Arabia, the bastion of conservative Islam, spends 7.5 percent of its national income on public education; this places it in the same class as Norway and Finland.

The evidence does confirm the charge of a gender bias in Islamicate countries. Nearly half of them show gender bias in their development indices. We observe that 17 of the 36 Islamicate countries suffer a loss of rank as we move from a general index of human development to one that makes corrections for inequalities between sexes; both indices are available in the latest *Human Development Report*. These losses are highest for Saudi Arabia, Yemen, Oman, Sudan and Lebanon. Only Turkey improves its rank significantly, by four places.

The cultural determinism of the warriors extends to demographics. Observing the rapid growth of Islamicate population, they attribute this to a cultural resistance to birth control. Once again, an examination of the evidence quickly dispels this charge. Between 1970-75 and 1995-2000, nearly every Islamicate country experienced a decline in the total fertility rate: this is the number of childbirths per woman over her lifetime. In several, the decline was quite impressive. The fertility rates for 1995-2000 were 1.9 in Azerbaijan, 2.3 in Tunisia, 2.6 in Indonesia, 3.2 in Iran, 3.3 in Malaysia and Algeria, and 3.4 in Morocco and Egypt: compared to 3.3 and 3.6 for India and Philippines respectively. The Islamicate countries reached these low rates of fertility over shorter periods than Europe or Latin America.

Bloody Borders

We now turn to the matter about the "bloody borders" of Islamicate societies. In his book, *The Clash of Civilizations*, Samuel Huntington claims that "Muslim bellicosity and violence are late-twentieth century facts which

2 UNDP, *Human Development Report, 2000* (New York: Oxford University Press, 2000).

neither Muslims nor non-Muslims can deny."[3] In support of this thesis, he offers a list of inter-civilizational conflicts affecting Islamicate borders in the 1990s. He also provides some quantitative evidence purporting to show that Muslims had a disproportionate share in inter-civilizational conflicts during 1993-94.

A more careful examination of the data tells a different story. Jonathan Fox has shown that Islam was involved in 23.2 percent of all inter-civilizational conflicts between 1945 and 1989, and 24.7 percent of these conflicts during 1990 to 1998.[4] This is not too far above Islam's share in world population; nor do we observe any dramatic rise in this share since the end of the Cold War. It would appear that Huntington's claims of "Muslim bellicosity" do not qualify as facts.

In any case, we have to be careful when we talk about "bloody borders." A hard look at the geography of civilizations soon reveals that civilizational borders vary strikingly, and that the Islamicate share of such borders is disproportionately large. On the one hand, the geographic sweep of the Islamicate societies across the Afro-Eurasian landmass brings it into con- tact – both close and extensive – with the African, Western, Orthodox, Hindu and Buddhist civilizations. We must contend not only with borders between Islamicate and non-Islamicate countries. In addition, we must take account of the internal borders, between Muslim and non-Muslim populations within non-Islamicate countries. It is my impression that if we added up all of these borders, the Islamicate share of borders might well exceed the combined share of all other civilizations. These facts might help to place observations about Islam's "bloody borders" in a less prejudicial perspective.

The Democracy Deficit

Finally, there is the charge of a democracy deficit in the Islamicate world. Several warriors, including Samuel Huntington and Elie Kedourie, have theorized that this is because of an incompatibility between Islamic values and democratic institutions.[5]

---

3   Samuel P. Huntington, *The Clash of Civilizations and the Remaking of World Order* (New York: Simon and Schuster, 1996): 258.

4   Jonathan Fox, "Two Civilizations and Ethnic Conflict: Islam and the West," *Journal of Peace Research* 38, 4 (2000): 459-72.

5   Elie Kedourie, *Democracy and Arab Political Culture* (Washington, D.C.: Washington Institute of Near Eastern Policy, 1992).

The warriors find evidence of a democracy deficit in Islamicate countries in the latest global rankings on freedom and democracy provided by 'experts' at the Freedom House. It is questionable if we can evaluate such complex matters by examining snapshots of countries at any one point in time. There is a further problem with the Freedom House rankings: they are subjectively determined. Concerned about the biases this might introduce, the UNDP quickly discontinued their use in their annual *Human Development Report* after using them once.

The cultural determinism of Freedom House is on proud display in their most recent report. On the one hand, a quick review of the record reveals two waves of democratization, in the 1950s and 1990s, which point towards powerful international forces regulating these movements. The first wave accompanied the post-War dismantling of colonies; the second wave followed the end of the Cold War. If some countries, or block of countries, have not participated in these waves of democratization – or pseudo-democratizations for the most part – this is attributed to cultural flaws. Thus, the latest Freedom House report declares that "the *roots* of freedom and democracy are weakest" in the Middle East (emphasis added).

Nevertheless, let us take a closer look at the latest numbers provided by Freedom House. Their data for 2001 show that only 23 percent of the Islamicate countries have electoral democracies; the comparable numbers are 38 percent for Africa, 62 percent for Asian countries, 70 percent for post-Communist countries in Europe and the CIS, and 91 percent for the Americas. There are some revealing patterns *within* the class of Islamicate countries. Of the 16 Arab countries and six Central Asian Republics, not one is democratic. When we exclude these two groups from the Islamicate countries – about a fifth of world's Islamicate population – the proportion of democracies in the remaining Islamicate countries rises to 47 percent. In some cases, the Freedom House classifications are questionable. If we classify Iran and Malaysia as electoral democracies, the last number would go up to 59 percent, quite comparable to the ratio for Asian countries.

Is there any rationale for excluding the Arab and Central Asian countries from the Islamicate count? In fact there are several. Since the end of the Cold War, Western donors and multilateral institutions have used their financial leverage to encourage democratization in client countries. However, there is one significant exception to this. They have not applied these pressures on Islamicate countries – especially in the Arab world – where democratization is likely to bring the Islamists to power. On the contrary, the Arab despotisms – with the exception of the 'rogue states' – have received political, moral and intelligence support from Western powers in the repression of their mainly Islamist opposition.

There are other factors stacking the odds against democracy in the Arab world. Not the least of them is Israel, a colonial-settler state, increasingly seen by Muslims as the military fist of the United States in Zionist gloves. There is no other conflict in the post-War period, barring South African apartheid, which can match the Israel-Arab conflict in its durability or the way it has warped a whole region. The Israeli presence in the Arab heartland magnified the security imperative of the front-line Arab states, allowing them to build praetorian states with the capacity to suppress all forms of dissent.

In the Arab world, oil has been another negative factor. Of the sixteen Arab countries, nine are oil rich, and all but three of them have quite small indigenous populations. Their oil revenues and small populations have allowed most of these countries to exempt their citizens from paying taxes. That is one more strike against democracy: a citizenry that pays no taxes lacks the moral authority to demand representation.

In addition, eight Arab countries are monarchies, and six of them are oil-rich. The British created these oil monarchies, or – in the case of Saudi Arabia and Oman – supported and shored them through difficult times. Since the Second World War, these countries passed under the hegemony of the United States, which has worked through monarchies and dictatorships in the region.

The six Islamicate countries in Central Asia are former members of the defunct Soviet Union. Upon gaining independence, they have been ruled by former communist bosses backed by Moscow. Russia maintains a military presence in these countries, or has strong ties to their military, with the intent of sealing their southern borders against Islamist influence from Iran and Afghanistan. Russia is playing the same role in this region – opposing democratization – that the United States has played in the Arab world.

A Problem for the United States

If Islamicate societies are 'normal', why are they still a problem for the United States?

This problem is born of tensions between a great power, the United States, and a historical adversary, the Islamicate world. The United States enters into this contest with its vast power, Christian evangelism, the constraints of domestic lobbies, energy needs, and a vision of itself as a civilizing force. Islam enters the stage as a fractured, wounded civilization, humiliated by two centuries of Western domination, divided into ineffectual political units, without a core state, rich in oil resources it does not control, with a colonial settler state planted in its heartland that daily adds insults to its injuries. It appears that history has produced an explosive dialectic.

In its most recent convulsion, this dialectic has produced a decentralized, secretive and violent Islamist enemy that, unable to strike at its domestic tormentors, has decided to attack the United States, the most visible protagonist of the corrupt and repressive Islamicate regimes. Having destroyed their only safe haven in Afghanistan, and convinced that the Islamists who intend to perpetrate terror are still lurking in the shadows, the United States desperately searches for appropriate, accessible Islamicate targets.

The camp of the warriors offers easy targets to the United States in this unfolding dialectic. "It's the Islamic world, stupid. Just get rolling and take it out." In the present climate, this temptation will be hard to resist. It will be hard to resist because 9-11, with help from neoconservative commentators, has roused America's old penchant for evangelism, messianic faith and civilizing mission. If naively, Americans are also convinced of their overwhelming power to inflict damage without taking any losses.

Americans might perhaps take a leaf from Israel, its alter ego in the Middle East. Israel has long enjoyed incomparable military superiority over the Palestinians. It can rain down terror on the Palestinians at will, as it has for the past 56 years. However, Israel's unmatched military power has not brought it any closer to security or peace. In this contest, the greater responsibility for restraint rests upon the United States. It is the greatest power on earth, possessing greater degrees of freedom than the beleaguered Islamists do. In addition, American power is vested in the hands of Ivy League graduates, realists, sophisticates, men and women deeply acquainted with the modern world, who possess an understanding of the world that the extremist Islamists sorely lack. In this delicate hour, we must pray that the United States will act with restraint, will wield its power with responsibility, and that it will show the world that it is not only a great country, the greatest in the world: but it also cares for humane values.

CHAPTER SIX

On Islam: An Interview[1]

The interviewer, Cihan Aksan, is editor of State of Nature

October 2005

Q: *Islam as a religion holds within it a potent political force. Its message extends to the legal, economic and social organization of the Muslim community. Does this make it incompatible with secularism? Is secularism a deviation from the basic principles of Islam? Is it merely an idea imported from the West to which Islam can never relate? Or is there a place for a secular political order in Islamic countries?*

A: Secularism is an idea and a system of governance. The idea seeks to create a secular man who lives his life without reference to God. It believes in the sufficiency of reason as a guide to life. Conversely, it rejects the authority of religion, as a source of meaning and values. As a system of governance, secularism is a bit less ambitious. On the assumption that life divides into a public and a private sphere, each neatly separable, it seeks to exclude religion from the public sphere. The objective is to create a system of laws that does not favor any religion.

The conflict between Islam – any religion, for that matter – and secularism as an idea should be transparent. A Muslim lives his life with reference to God, His Book and His Prophet. A Muslim also reasons because God reasons with him. The Qur'an urges man to use his reason and experience to understand God, His creation and His Book, and based on this understanding to create a just society. The secular idea is not only incompatible with Islam. Indeed, they must oppose each other.

---

1 *State of Nature*, Autumn 2005. <http://www.stateofnature.org/onIslam1.html>

As a system of governance, secularism can be expansive or accommo-
dating. It can marginalize religion or give it greater sway over society. The
actual results depend on a variety of factors. Most importantly, perhaps,
it depends on the way the boundaries are drawn between the public and
private spheres. Is the public sphere large or small? For instance, does it
include education? Secondly, how rigorously does the state exclude religion from the public sphere? And what restrictions does it place on the
expression of religion in the private sphere?

One can imagine an extreme form of secular governance. In this case, the
public sphere is expansive – extending over education, media, laws of inheritance, relations between sexes, and modes of dress. It legislates religion
out of this large public sphere, taking positions which contradict religious
values. In addition, it inhibits the practice of religion even in traditionally
private spheres. Very likely, this will breed discontent if a majority or even
substantial segment of the population is religious. In the event, this form of
secularism will also be incompatible with democracy.

On the other hand, secularism can be minimalist. This is a secularism that
works within a limited public sphere, allows the democratic expression of
widely-held religious values in the public sphere, and even supports religious
organizations without discrimination in some activities (say, education or
charitable work) provided they contribute to public order and morality.
Indeed, variants of this minimalist secularism were the norm in most of
the Muslim Sultanates before they were destroyed or restructured, starting
in the nineteenth century, under the impact of Western power. If Muslim
countries had enjoyed a measure of democracy over the past decades, this
is the kind of secularism many of them would have produced.

In the face of colonial erosion of Islamic values and institutions – followed
by suppression of Islamic tendencies under corrupt and often militantly
secular governments – many Islamic thinkers seek to *recreate* Islamic societies. In several instances this re-Islamization is more ambitious than any
recent historical model. It proposes to reconstitute Islamicate societies
on the foundations of the Qur'an and the Sunnah. Some Islamic thinkers
believe that this cannot be achieved under democratic governance. Others
argue that democracy is compatible with Islam if its laws are subject to

oversight by a council of Islamic scholars. It would appear that Iran illustrates this second model.

Q: *Islam preserved much of the patriarchal nature of pre-Islamic society. In marriage, divorce, inheritance and other social relations the* Qur'an *appears to legitimize the unequal treatment of women. Is it possible to separate Islam and patriarchy? Can Islam ever promote gender equality? Is it open to gender reforms? Is the West using an ethnocentric perspective when it directs criticism at the status of women in Islam?*

A: Western imagination has been fertile at inventing projects for reforming the world, not least the world of Islam. This is their perennial cover for world domination: they are always engaged in 'civilizing' the people they exploit, enslave or exterminate. In the Islamic world, the white man has been championing women's rights since the late nineteenth century, even when they denied rights to their own women. Trapped inside the walls of harems, denied dignity in polygamous marriages, segregated, burqa-clad, or subjected to clitoral mutilation – the Islamic woman desperately awaits 'liberation' by white male warriors in shining armor. It would be a new departure – and unlikely – if the West stopped taking an imperialist or ethnocentric approach to the status of women in Islam.

It would appear that the premise of this set of questions is West-centric. They seem to accept Western standards in the field of women's rights. They accept Western criticisms of what goes under the name of patriarchy. They assume that the non-Islamic world has attained 'gender equality', that only Islam refuses to catch up. They appear to assume that gender equality – according to some mechanical calculus – is always desirable, or it is a value to be attained at all costs. They also ignore the fact that modern, capitalist society subjects women to new indignities, new forms of servitude, new pathologies, which may well be worse than the abuses of women in traditional societies.

An obsessive focus on women's rights emerges from the matrix of Western notions of individualism and freedom, values that quite nicely dovetail with the imperatives of capital. Are individualism and freedom the only values worth pursuing? In an Islamic society the rights of women, men and children must be seen as interlinked, and their relations to each other must be shaped by their need to support each other in creating a just, balanced and God-centered society.

Should society pursue Western ideas of individualism and rights even if they erode family values – values which recognize the primacy of male-female relationships, the raising of balanced children, and the care of the sick and elderly? Or should we expose the family to the merciless blast of market forces: let the market produce and deliver these 'family services'? What should we think of a market-driven set of rights if it led a majority of women to sacrifice marriage and motherhood for careers; if it persuaded men to jettison their duties as a father, son or brother? The West has accepted market-driven notions of 'rights' as supreme values. Should Muslims willy-nilly follow suit? Or should they seek greater justice in gender-relations within the matrix of their own system of values?

Q: *Islamic feminism advocates a re-reading of the* Qur'an *and the hadiths to find confirmation of gender equality. By confronting the traditional male interpretations of Islamic texts, it intends to demonstrate that patriarchal attitudes have distorted the principle of equality in Islam. But can feminist discourse be articulated within an Islamic framework? Is Islamic feminism in conflict with secular feminism? Is it more effective than secular feminism in the fight for the emancipation of women in Islamic countries?*

A: The feminist discourse is both a field of enquiry and a movement. As a field of enquiry, it seeks to understand how laws and institutions have been structured to 'advantage' men over women. As a movement, feminism seeks to dislodge these 'advantages' by seeking equality for women in the public and private spheres.

The feminists' understanding of male 'advantages' is not value-neutral. In general, they perceive *any* differentia in the legal or social positions of men and women as a male advantage, and the expression of superior male power. Generally, they do not seek to understand *if* these differentia have their origins in some other imperatives, whether they relate to differences between male and female biology, temperament or aptitudes; whether they seek to conserve the family as an institution; whether they support the pursuit of our spiritual vocations as men and women; or whether they contribute to public order. In other words, feminists regard 'equality' in all public and private spheres as an absolute value that pays no regard to other values.

I don't think that this secular feminist discourse can be accommodated within an Islamic framework. However, it appears to me that this discourse can be Islamized if a new understanding of the *differentia* between men and women in Islamic law is developed, one that pays close attention to Islamic values relating to spirituality, justice, family, and public order. This has to be an Islamic endeavor, led by men and women who bring a commitment to Islamic values.

Clearly, there is room for Muslim men and women to engage in a fresh reading of the Qur'an and Sunnah to begin to identify those *differentia* between the rights of men and women in Islamic legal systems that are not rooted in Islam's two canonical sources. These new understandings could then be used to enlarge the rights of women beyond what is accepted in the established schools of Islamic law.

There are several grounds for believing that a fresh reading of the Qur'an – in particular – holds out hope for bringing greater justice in the relations between men and women. In most Islamicate societies, the actual relations between men and women often reflect local customs – often tribal customs – that can be discredited by showing that they violate Islamic norms. In other cases, established *shar'iah* rulings on women's rights have been influenced by non-Islamic beliefs and practices. This is not hard to understand, since the gathering and codification of Prophetic traditions, during the first few centuries of Islamic history, occurred in a Middle Eastern milieu that was still saturated by pre-Islamic traditions of misogyny and the seclusion of women. Some of these spurious traditions, then, became sources of Islamic laws.

This creates an opportunity for serious work by leading Islamic scholars of impeccable integrity to undertake afresh the task of codification of the Prophetic traditions to screen out those traditions – on women, race, and governance, among others – which directly contradict the value systems enunciated in the Qur'an. In addition, through similar collective efforts, Islamic scholars should engage in *ijtihad* to translate Islamic notions of *eeman, taqwa, 'adl* and *ihsaan* into new proposals for ordering relations among

Muslims, the civil society and the state, and relations between Muslims and non-Muslims. This is a task that should be given the highest priority by the Ummah.

Q: In Samuel P. Huntington's "Clash of Civilizations?" we find the modern world defined by cultural conflicts, not ideological or economic ones. Seven or eight major civilizations are identified, but the confrontation between Islam and the West is placed centre stage. How can we interpret this culturalist approach to world politics? Is it an important thesis which describes a "new phase" in international relations? Or is it merely part of the attempt to find a new "Other" to justify US foreign policy in the aftermath of the Cold War?

A: Perhaps the most singular development over the three centuries following the voyages of Columbus and Vasco de Gama was the mobilization of the state and nation in the service of capital. This first happened in a small number of West European countries, giving their capital an enormous long-run advantage over other aggregates of capital. Backed by the resources of the state and nation, Portuguese, Spanish, and, later, Dutch, British and French capital gradually colonized much of the world. As their monopoly profits were ploughed back into shipping, ports, canals, manufactures, universities, libraries and scientific academies, these countries developed, grew rich, and built powerful armies. Eventually, starting in the nineteenth century, when these economies switched to fossil fuels, this new virtually inexhaustible source of energy gave a formidable boost to their developmental processes. Now they gained a growing economic, financial, technological and military lead over the rest of the world which would be unbeatable for a long time. They went out and colonized much of the rest of the world. The gap between these Western countries and the rest of the world grew, creating a bipolar global economy, consisting of a Center and its Periphery. Ever since, capital from the Center has sought to monopolize economic opportunities in the Periphery.

This global capitalist system suffered from several contradictions. First, there was the growing conflict between capitalists and the working classes at the Center. Karl Marx had predicted that as the working classes at the Center grew in size and consciousness, they would mobilize to overthrow capital and establish socialism. He expected this systemic change to be advanced by two additional contradictions in capitalism. Capitalist economies were subject to wide periodic swings, often creating very high levels of unemployment and misery in the working classes. This would deepen solidarity in the working classes. In addition, rivalry between national aggregates of capital for markets, resources, monopolies and territories would push them into wars. As the capitalist states bloodied themselves, this would create an opening for socialist revolutions.

Contrary to Karl Marx's prognosis, the Center did not experience a socialist transformation despite business cycles and two major internecine wars. Instead, the hegemony of the Center was challenged by the Periphery. In time, the expansion of capital from the Center into the Periphery – through force and the asymmetric action of markets – provoked a countervailing response from the Periphery. This took two forms: movements for national liberation and more radical movements which sought to overthrow capitalism in the Periphery. These dual developments were aided by internecine wars amongst the capitalist countries. In the midst of the conflict and chaos of World War I, the Bolsheviks seized power in Russia, and broke away from the world capitalist system to establish the world's first communist economy. This was followed during World War II by the establishment of another communist economy in China, the world's largest country. World War II also led to the dismantling of the major colonial empires and the emergence of dozens of newly independent but poor countries. Even as these countries sought to develop their own capitalist base, the Center strove to defeat their efforts with covert actions and occasional wars. At the same time, the United States began a military build-up – known as the Cold War – ostensibly to match the threat of global communism.

The Cold War ended rather suddenly with the collapse of the Soviet Union in 1990. The greatest single challenge to the global capitalist system had collapsed. This discredited both communism and socialism. It also led to the collapse of the developmental state, the concerted effort of former colonies to develop their economies with indigenous capital and technology. The IMF and the World Bank, with the help of a new set of global rules imposed by the WTO, took over the task of re-opening the Periphery for takeover by the Center. Nearly all countries in the Periphery were reduced to the status of 'open-door' economies; their governments had little control over their economic policies. Nevertheless, a few countries in the Periphery managed to preserve and develop their indigenous capitalist base. There were a few successes in the Far East: nurtured by the Center itself to combat the spread of communism. And then, there were China and India. With a third of the world's population, low wages, rapidly advancing skills, and vigorous indigenous capital, they would soon offer a growing challenge to the Center. Thus, in the very hour of its greatest triumph, the Center faced a broad-spectrum challenge to its economic dominance.

The collapse of communism was heralded by some as the 'end of history', as the final triumph of capitalism. No doubt the Center had triumphed, though it is a bit premature to say if this triumph is final. The Soviet collapse had another more ominous consequence. It had removed a powerful check on US imperial ambitions. The US was now the sole superpower, with a military budget nearly equal to that of the rest of the world. During the Cold War, the US had generally sought control through covert actions, foreign aid, propaganda and proxy wars; it engaged in direct military action only infrequently. Now it would be tempted to go down the path of naked imperialism.

The United States possessed absolute power: or so it seemed. A group of Republican hawks began formulating plans in the early 1990s to leverage this power, to make it enduring. These hawks – better known as the neoconservatives, most of whom were also close allies of Israel – were planning to use military power to prevent the emergence of any challenges to American dominance. They began to make the case for pre-emptive and preventive wars as an instrument of foreign policy. They started manufacturing threats of WMDs. Countries, mostly in the Middle East, that still resisted American dictate were categorized as rogue states. The neoconservatives had their eye on the oil fields in the Middle East, still the single greatest strategic prize in world history. If they could seize the oil spigot, they thought they could bend Europe, China, India and Japan to their will. After waiting out the presidency of Bill Clinton, the neoconservative hawks were back in power under President George Bush in 2000. They had their hands on the levers of power in the Defense Department. They waited for a galvanizing event to launch their plan. Without much delay, it arrived on September 11, 2001. It has already led to the occupation of Afghanistan and Iraq. More wars are planned against Syria and Iran and, in future rounds, against Pakistan and Saudi Arabia.

Samuel Huntington's thesis of a new era of 'civilizational clashes' is primarily an ideological cover for the wars that the US planned against the Periphery, starting in the 1990s, now that the Soviets were not around to check their ambitions. Since the Middle East was the primary target of US-Israeli imperial designs – because of its oil and Israeli ambition of balkanizing the region – American and Israeli ideologues emphasized the threat from Islamic societies. This was the 'rogue civilization' whose refusal to modernize, whose rejection of democracy, whose oppression of women, and whose terrorism posed the greatest threat to world order. Moreover, at the root of all these problems was an intransigent religion: Islam. This old enemy was now spawning new threats: Islamic fundamentalism, Islamo-fascism, and Islamic terrorism. The West now had an enemy that could arouse their old fears about Islam. It would now be easy to justify the wars planned against Iraq, Iran and Syria.

Q: *The intellectual history of political Islam is infused with the traditions of the Salafist or Wahhabi School and the Muslim Brotherhood, as well as the ideas of thinkers such as Abul A'la Maududi and Sayyid Qutb. But it is also framed by the political ideologies that inspired modern national liberation movements in the Third World, particularly Marxism-Leninism. Could it be that the political project is far more important than the religious one in defining the identity of Islamist groups? Is the religious message reduced to an instrument to articulate concerns over modern imperialism? Is this why Islamist groups receive considerable ideological support from left-wing thinkers in the West?*

A: The recent Western discourse on Islam speaks of political Islam as largely a phenomenon of the twentieth century that becomes visible with the formation of the Ikhwan-ul-Muslimeen in Egypt or the emergence of a Wahhabi state in Arabia. This is a myopic view of Islamic history.

In the first century of Islam, tribal, dynastic and personal rivalries were played out in the language of the proper qualifications of Islamic rulers or their legitimate functions. In the middle of the second Islamic century, the revolution that overthrew the Omayyads sought to establish a more egalitarian Islam that accorded equal treatment to Arab and non-Arab Muslims. Over the next few centuries, ethnic and tribal revolts against established states were justified in terms of various Shi'ite movements, always led by men who claimed descent from Ali and Fatima.

In recent centuries, the first movements of resistance against the Western invasion of Islamic lands were mobilized in the name of Islam. In Algeria, the Caucasus, Somalia and Libya, the resistance against Western invasions was led by tribal Islam under the leadership of Sufi Sheikhs. In Iran, starting in the late nineteenth century, the resistance was led by traditional 'ulama. In Arabia, a new puritanical Islam – later known as Wahhabism – sought to regenerate Islamic power purportedly by returning to the ways of the first Muslims.

These movements failed to stem the tide of Western imperialism. The West conquered Islamic lands, overthrew the Islamic order, marginalized Islamic courts and educational systems, and created a new learned class, schooled in European languages and convinced of the superiority of Western values. The liberation movements in Islamic countries were led by members of this new Westernized class, espousing ethnic nationalism over Islamic identity, and secular in their politics. Most of these new states were allied with the US. In the Arab world, a few states – important ones, like Egypt and Syria – were more radical and joined the Soviet camp. But nearly all of them failed to restore dignity or bring prosperity to their societies. The largest Muslim state, Pakistan, split in two after a civil war. The radical Arab states suffered humiliating defeats at the hands of the colonial-settler state of Israel. Iran was returned to repressive monarchy after a brief spell of democracy and sovereignty. Decolonization, nationalism, Westernization, secularism, socialism, monarchical Islam, and vast oil reserves had done little to reverse the fragmentation, decline and humiliation of the Islamic world.

The latest wave of political Islam is fundamentally a revolt against the ongoing humiliation of the Islamic world – against its political subjugation, against its humiliation in wars, and against the marginalization of Islam in the public sphere. This political Islam speaks the language of return to the vigor and purity of classical Islam. It is against the accommodations that Sufi Islam makes to populist cults of human intercession. It is equally against modernist Islam which often seeks to forge an Islam that is friendlier to Western values. It seeks to overthrow Western control over Islamicate polities as a prelude to creating Islamic unity. It fervently believes in Islamic solutions to all of life's challenges. It offers itself as an alternative to capitalism, consumerism and secularism.

It would be surprising if the Islamic revolt in a major section of the Periphery did not command the attention – and even sympathy – of leftist circles everywhere. This revolt has two dimensions. On the one hand, it is anti-imperialist. It clearly understands that US imperialism, in the post-war period, has held the Middle East in a tighter grip than any other region of the world. It understands clearly the role that oil and Israel play in this imperialist venture. It looks upon Israel not as a mere instrument of US imperial control over the Middle East. Instead, Israel is seen as an autonomous imperialist force – a racist, colonial-settler state – that partners with the US to deepen its own control over the Middle East. It understands how this partnership has divided, exploited, and distorted the political and economic evolution of this region. In this sense, the Islamic revolt is a movement for the liberation of Islamic lands, similar to earlier movements for national liberation and sovereignty.

There is of course the second dimension of the Islamic resistance – its Islamic symbols and aims – which raises concerns in Western Leftist circles. Do these Islamic symbols and aims constitute the true essence of this resistance? Or, have they been introduced to mobilize large masses of people, nearly a fourth of the world's population, in a struggle against the injustice of the neo-colonial order imposed on the Islamic world? It is clear that the success of the Islamic resistance will not lead to the establishment of a socialist order. But it will weaken and challenge, perhaps even overthrow, US-Israeli hegemony over the Middle East. This might also lead to the evacuation of American economic interests from the region.

Arguably, the evacuation of American capital from the Islamic world may cause deeper tremors than the exclusion of Western capital from China after the Communist revolution there. There are several reasons for this. The Islamic world today contains a somewhat larger share of the world's population than China did in 1948. Moreover, unlike China, the Islamic world occupies large swathes of territory stretching from West Africa to East Asia. Most importantly, US economic interests in the region – because of oil alone – are a great deal more weighty than Western interests in China in 1948. In other words, the Islamic resistance – whatever the ideology that motivates it – can potentially cause serious dislocations in the global capitalist order. That alone should arouse the interest of those leftists who see revolutionary opportunity in these dislocations.

Palestine

AND **Israel**

CHAPTER SEVEN

Israel and the Consequences of Uniqueness

"If you can look into the seeds of time,
And say which grain will grow and which will not,
Speak then to me."
—William Shakespeare, *Macbeth*, I, 3

October 2004

The creation of Israel has engendered deep and opposite emotions in Islamdom and the West; it has led to Arab wars against Israel and Israeli wars against Arabs; it has produced tensions that have poisoned relations between Islamdom and the United States, as the nearly unconditional backer of Israel's ambitions in the region; and, now, after the attacks of 9-11, the United States, with Israel urging and cheering from the sidelines, has launched a plan to impose a new imperialist order on the Islamicate countries. This essay seeks to show that the major features of the history of the Middle East over the past six decades – both internally and in its relations with the United States – have flowed in large part from the logic of the Zionist idea. This history could have been foretold: and indeed it was anticipated by the Zionist visionaries who founded Israel – as well as by others.

Claims of Normalcy

The Zionists claim that Israel is a 'normal' state, like India, Iraq or Indonesia. They equate their 'struggle' to establish a Jewish state in Palestine with the movements for national liberation in Asia, Africa and elsewhere during the twentieth century. The hostility of Islamicate peoples towards Israel, they assert, is motivated by Islamic anti-Semitism, a hatred of Jews implanted by Islam itself. In recent years, this hostility has also been explained as the result of an Arab or Islamicate envy of Israeli democracy.

We face a difficult choice here between Israeli and Arab normalcy. If Israeli statehood is normal, then it follows that there is perversity in the Islamicate opposition to it. On the other hand, if Israel is not a normal state – like India, Iraq or Indonesia – then we are justified in investigating this lack of normality and probing into its consequences. It may turn out that Islamicate hostility to Israel did not proceed from perversity but, instead, is a legitimate response to the 'unique'/abnormal conditions surrounding Israel's creation.

The Zionist claim to normalcy – that Israel belongs to the same species of states as India, Iraq or Indonesia – is based on two superficial similarities. First, Israel was created as an independent state out of Palestine, a British colony since 1917. Second, after 1945, some of the Jews in Palestine took up arms against the British to force them out of Palestine. On the basis of these partial truths, the Zionists claim that theirs was a nationalist movement aimed at 'liberating' Palestine from the British occupiers. Incidentally, the Palestinians are completely missing from this narrative about Jewish statehood in Palestine.

This claim is not tenable: one intransigent fact militates against it. The Jews who created the state of Israel in Palestine were not *indigenous* to Palestine. Indeed, more than 90 percent of them were settlers from Europe, having entered Palestine *after* its conquest by the British in 1917.[1] In the 1940s, Europe's persecuted Jews had a legitimate claim to our sympathy, but, as Europeans, they had no nationalist claim to statehood in Palestine. In other words, Israel is a 'unique' case of nation building.

---

1 The Zionist claim to Palestine is based on 'a historical connection:' the presence of Jews (more accurately, Hebrews) in ancient Palestine most of whom left after the second destruction of the temple in Jerusalem in 70 CE. This raises two questions. First, no system of laws or morality supports one people's (X) claim over lands inhabited by another people (Y) on the grounds of an *ancient* historical connection between X and the lands held by Y. Second, one has to ask: what is the connection of the Ashkenazi Jews, who founded Israel, to the ancient Hebrews? There is evidence that the Askenazis are descended mostly from the Khazars, a medieval Turkic people living in Southern Russia who had converted to Judaism in the eight century. Alternatively, if the Ashkenazi Jews originated in Palestine, they had lived in Europe for close to two thousand years – perhaps longer – during which marriages and conversion would have led to their biological assimilation into the gene pool of their host communities. The Zionist claim to Palestine is just as fantastic as a claim – thankfully, it has never been made – by Javanese Muslims to Spain because as Muslims they have a "historical connection" to Spain.

Sadly, the Jews of Europe did not have a nationalist claim to any part of Europe either. They did not constitute a majority in any of the territories which they shared with other Europeans. This was the unstated problem the 'nationalist' Jews confronted in Europe during the 1890s. The oppressed nations in Europe could stake a valid claim to sovereign statehood. Not so the Jews: they may have been a distinct people, and many of them were still oppressed, but they were not a nation. In order to become 'normal' – that is, in order to transform themselves into a European nation – the Jews of Europe would first have to create a Jewish majority in some part of Europe. This path of 'normalization,' however, was not open to European Jews. It would be opposed by all of Europe. Indeed, it would have amounted to courting disaster.

Nevertheless, there would be poetic justice in the creation of a Jewish state *in* Europe. After all, the Jews were a European people; the history of their continuous presence in Europe goes back to the time of the ancient Greeks. Since the Europeans Jews – as minorities – have historically faced perse-cution, and, under the Nazis, many Europeans participated in a fiendish attempt to exterminate them, one can argue that it was Europe's moral responsibility to accommodate the Jews as a nation inside Europe. The his-torical wrongs done to a segment of the European population should have been rectified *by* Europeans *inside* the geographical boundaries of Europe. At least, this might have been the right thing to do. But when has Europe shown magnanimity of this order?

A Unique Colonial Settler-State

Unable to stake a nationalist claim in Europe, those European Jews who sought 'normalization' as a nation had another idea. After all, this was the nineteenth century, the age of colonization and of settler-colonialism. If the British and the French could establish settler-colonies in Australia, New Zealand, South Africa and Algeria, among other places, why could not the Jews of Europe have their settler-colony in Palestine or anywhere else?

In its early stages, during the 1890s and 1900s, when the project to create a Jewish state was being broached in some Jewish circles of Europe, several locations for this state were considered. Although Palestine was his first choice, at various times Theodore Herzl, the founder of political Zionism, was willing to settle for Uganda or Madagascar. Earlier, others had scouted Surinam, Argentina, Missouri and New York! However, Palestine won easily. It would appeal to Jewish emotions associated with religious Zionism, and the Messianic Christians would support the idea of a Jewish return for their own eschatological reasons.

If political Zionism does not qualify as a movement for national liberation, was it a scheme for establishing a colonial-settler state? I will argue that it was, but with two differences that make Israel rather unique among states of this species. Unlike other colonial-settler states, Israel was not the creation of another state, a mother country, ethnically allied to it. Israel had no mother country. A Jewish state did not exist anywhere in Europe, one that could sponsor a Jewish settler-colony. Indeed the Zionist movement sought to create such a state; this would be its end point, not its point of departure. Secondly, there was an important difference between the other colonial-settlers and the Zionists in their goals. The former intended to expropriate the natives so that they could use them as cheap labor on the lands they would expropriate. In other words, they did not intend to expel the natives from their colonies. On the other hand, the Zionists intended to expropriate the Palestinians *and* expel them from Palestine. They wanted a Palestine without the Palestinians; this was their goal, not the serendipitous consequence of their settlement activity. In its conception, then, Zionism was a colonial-settler project with a difference.

This 'unique' project had several seminal consequences. First, in the absence of a Jewish mother country, the Zionists had to find a surrogate, a Western power that would use its military to implement their colonial-settler project. This would not be too hard to find. For more than two hundred years several Western powers – in league with Christian messianic groups – had worked on various schemes to persuade the Jews of Europe to establish a Jewish state in the Levant, a state that would serve as the staging post for their colonial ambitions in that region and farther east. Wisely, the Jews rejected these overtures, suspecting that that they were traps to get them out of Europe and into greater trouble.[2] However, the emergence of political Zionism in the late nineteenth century turned the tables. Starting in 1897, after the First Zionist Congress, the Zionists began courting the Powers to take on their cause.

---

2 Regina Sharif, *Non-Jewish Zionism, Its Roots in Western History* (London, Zed Books, 1983).

Their efforts were directed primarily at Britain, the greatest colonial power of that era. Success in this venture came twenty years later, when the British blessed the Zionist project in the Balfour Declaration of November 1917. This document stated that His Majesty's Government "view with favor the establishment in Palestine of a national home for the Jewish people, and will use their best endeavors to facilitate the achievement of this object..."[3] In fulfillment of this commitment, the British created the mandate (euphemism for colony) of Palestine. Under the terms of this mandate, duly approved by the Council of League of Nations in July 1922, the British administration in Palestine would work with the Zionist Organization to "secure the co-operation of all Jews who are willing to assist in the establishment of the Jewish national home."[4] Thanks to British support, the Zionist project was now in motion.

The Zionists converted the absence of a Jewish mother country into an advantage. Political Zionism appealed to the West for at least three reasons: messianic Christians saw the Jewish return as a prelude to the Second Coming; Western powers were eager to acquire control over the Middle East because of its strategic value; and the West was still animated by an antipathy to Islam and Islamdom. In September 1922, the US Congress passed a resolution endorsing the Balfour Declaration. When British support for the creation of a Jewish state wavered in the 1940s – coincidentally, just when British power was being superseded – the United States stepped into the breach, thanks to Jewish votes, money and influence in that country.[5] The Western sponsorship of Zionism would evoke historical memories in the Islamicate world. In time, many Muslims would come to see the creation of Israel as the return of the Crusaders, an escalation of Western Christendom's campaign to undermine their faith and civilization. This was a dynamic that contained the seeds of a clash of civilizations.

The goal of a Jewish state in Palestine with a Jewish population had an unavoidable corollary. As the Jews entered Palestine, the Palestinians would have to be 'transferred' out of Palestine. As early as 1895, Theodore

---

3   Lawrence Davidson, *America's Palestine: Popular and official perceptions from Balfour to Israeli statehood* (Gainesville, FL: University Press of Florida, 2001): 11

4   *Mandate for Palestine, July 24, 1922* (Internet Modern History Sourcebook). <www. fordham.edu/halsall/mod/1922mandate.html>

5   Lawrence Davidson, *America's Palestine: Popular and official perceptions from Balfour to Israeli statehood* (Gainesville, FL.: University of Florida Press, 2001): ch. 8.

Herzl had figured this out in an entry in his diary: "We shall try to spirit the penniless population across the border by procuring employment for it in the transit countries, while denying it any employment in our own country." Others took a more direct approach: "As soon as we have a big settlement here we'll seize the land, we'll become strong, and then we'll take care of the Left Bank. We'll expel them from there, too. Let them go back to the Arab countries."[6] At some point, when a dominant Jewish presence had been established in Palestine, and the Palestinians had departed or been marginalized, the British could end their mandate to make room for the emergence of a Jewish state in Palestine.

This plan ran into two problems. The Palestinians would not cooperate: they refused to leave and few landowners were willing to sell their lands to Jewish settlers. As a result, in 1948, the year that Israel was created, nearly all of Palestine's "penniless population" was still in place. In addition, more than fifty years after the launching of political Zionism, the Jewish settlers owned only seven percent of the lands in Palestine, not the best lands either. During the Second World War, the Zionists ran into a problem with the British too. In order to rally Arab support during the war, in 1939 the British decided to limit Jewish immigration into Palestine to 75,000 over the next five years. However, these problems would not derail the Zionist project. The Zionists would achieve under the fog of war what they had failed to achieve through money and discriminatory policies.

In cooperation with the British colonial authorities, the Zionists had been establishing since 1918 a parallel government in Palestine, consisting of a network of Jewish organizations that brought in Jewish settlers, acquired Palestinian lands, organized Jewish settlements, supported Jewish businesses, and established Jewish educational institutions. In addition, as early as 1920, the Zionists had set up the Haganah, a grass-roots military organization. Fifteen years later, the Haganah consisted of 10,000 mobilized men and 40,000 reservists, equipped with imported and locally manufactured weapons.[7] When the British refused to lift the restrictions on Jewish immigration after the war, the Jewish military organizations started a campaign of terror against them. Partly in response to this terror, the British

---

6   Nur Masalha, *Expulsion of the Palestinians* (Washington, D.C.: Institute for Palestine Studies, 1992): 9.

7   *Haganah* (Wikipedia). <http://en.wikipedia.org/wiki/Haganah>

announced their premature departure from Palestine before the conflict they had spawned could be resolved.

The Zionists found their opportunity in the British loss of nerve. On May 14, 1948, on the termination of the British mandate in Palestine, they declared the emergence of the Jewish state of Israel under a UN partition plan. Although the Jews in Palestine owned only seven percent of the land, the UN plan had assigned 55 percent of Palestine to Israel. The Palestinians and neighboring Arab states decided to resist the UN partition plan. But the ranks of the Palestinian resistance had been decimated before by the British, and the Arab armies were poorly equipped, poorly led, and their leaders lacked nerve and commitment. The Arab resistance was defeated. In the process, the Zionists occupied 78 percent of Palestine, and 800,000 Palestinians were expelled from their homes or fled under duress. Israel, Mark I, had arrived in the Middle East, a Jewish state in Palestine with only ten percent of its Palestinian population.

Israel Seeks Hegemony

The dynamic that brought Israel into existence, and no less the consequences it had already produced, indicate that Israel, Mark I, would be only the first stage in the unfolding of the Zionist project. A dialectic now existed, with Israel and its Western sponsors on one side and the Palestinians and the Islamicate world on the other, that would produce a widening circle of consequences.

The creation of Israel had thrown a spanner in the wheel of Islamicate history. In the aftermath of the First World War, the Western powers had dismantled the most powerful Islamicate state – indeed the Core Islamicate state – by instigating and supporting the still marginal forces of Arab nationalism. At the same time, even as they were using Arab nationalist feelings, they had made plans to fracture Arab unity by creating a multiplicity of Arab fiefdoms, each of them subject to Western powers. Adding insult to injury, the Western powers also worked with the Jews to establish a Jewish state in a segment of the Islamicate heartland. This restructuring of the Islamicate world by Western powers would not be easily swept under the rug of time. Indeed, the creation of Israel alone was pregnant with consequences, much of it yet to unfold.

Quite apart from Israeli ambitions in the region, the logic of the Israeli state would almost inevitably propel it to rapid demographic growth, military dominance and expansionism. At the time of its founding in 1949, Israel contained only 5.6 percent of the world's Jewish population.[8] In order to justify its creation as the world's only Jewish state, Israel would have to attract more Jews, perhaps even a majority of the world's Jews. Israel's small population – relative to that of its Arab neighbors – also demanded a rapid influx of Jewish settlers; more Jewish hands were needed to defend this Western rampart in the Arab world. Then there were the temptations of success: imagine what we can do if we brought a third or a half of the world's Jewish population into the region. The first large influx of Jews, doubling Israel's population over the next five years, came from the Arab countries. In large part, this was inevitable. The Arab Jews were migrating to greener pastures; Arab defeat in 1948 and the expulsion of Palestinians from their lands provoked hostility towards Jews in Arab countries; and Israel encouraged and facilitated their departure.[9]

In addition, given the very high educational levels of Jewish settlers (especially those drawn from Europe and the United States), the reparations from Germany, the financial contributions of world Jewry, and grants and loans from Western countries, Israel would soon acquire the characteristics of a developed country whose capabilities in science and technology would rival the best in the world. In itself, this enormous disparity between an advanced Israel and mostly backward Arab countries would tempt Israel to seek military solutions to its conflict with its Arab neighbors. Indeed, Israel had within a decade built a military that could defeat any combination of Arab states. Finally, Israel had acquired a nuclear arsenal by the late 1960s – with French technology – thus securing the Samson option against any potential Arab threat to its security.

At the same time, Israel would face hostility from Arab states that had gained independence under the aegis of Arab nationalism. This was inevitable. The creation of Israel was an affront to Islamicate peoples, in particular to Arabs. In Israel's victory, the Muslims had lost lands that had been

---

8   The world Jewish population in 1948 was around 11.5 million; in the same year, Jews in Israel numbered 650,000. *World Jewish Population* (Jewish Virtual Library). <www.jewishvirtuallibrary.org/jsource/History/worldpop.html>
9   When they had the option, Arab Jews preferred to migrate to Western countries; nearly all the Algerian Jews migrated to France.

Islamicate since the first century of Islamdom. Further, the Arabs feared that if Israel could consolidate itself, it would seek to dominate the region with new rounds of expansionary wars. In the climate of the Cold War, the Arab nationalist states had reasons to believe that they had a chance to roll back the insertion of Israel into Arab lands. In other words, the creation of Israel also charted, inevitably, a history of hostility between this state and its neighbors.

Whether in response to this Arab hostility or using it as an excuse – as some would argue – for deepening its assault on the Arabs, Israel would seek a new 'mother country' to replace Britain. This time, it would turn to the United States. It was a natural choice, given the preeminence of the United States, and its large and influential Jewish population. It would appear that American commitment to Israel was not strong at first, if measured by the volume of its military and economic assistance to Israel. Israel sought to change this by demonstrating its strategic value to the United States. This happened in 1967, when in a pre-emptive war it simultaneously defeated Egypt, Syria and Jordan. The defeat of Egypt and Syria, the two leading Arab nationalist states, both allied to the Soviet Union, persuaded the US to enter into a deeper partnership with Israel, one that would only grow with time, as Israel acquired greater influence over decision-making in the United States, and as US backing for Israel would create Islamicate hostility against the US.

Just as importantly, this second military defeat of the Arabs produced a new Israel. This was Israel, Mark II, now in occupation of 100 percent of the former British mandate of Palestine; this included the new territories of Gaza and the West Bank with 1.1 million Palestinians. Inevitably, Israeli ambitions rose to match the new opportunities created by the war of 1967. Immediately, plans were set in motion to make the occupation of the West Bank and Gaza permanent. Israel began to appropriate Palestinian lands in the occupied territories. It established fortified settlements all over the territories, in control of the main water reservoirs, and sitting on hilltops overlooking Palestinian villages.

After facing yet another defeat in 1973, Egypt broke ranks with the Arab states and recognized Israel in exchange for the return of the Sinai and an annual American subsidy. This capitulation of the core Arab country sounded the death knell of Arab nationalism; it was also the signal for Israel to expand its military operations. In June 1981 Israeli jets destroyed Iraq's nuclear reactor under construction in Osirak. A year later, it invaded Lebanon, occupied Western Beirut, laid siege to Palestinian refugee camps, and forced the exit of the Palestinian resistance from Lebanon. During the Israeli siege, the Phalangists, a Lebanese Christian militia allied to Israel, massacred 3000 Palestinian civilians in the refugee camps of Sabra and Shatilla.

At around the same time, in 1982, the World Zionist Organization, published a report in its official organ, Kivunim, urging Israel to annex the West Bank and Gaza, reoccupy Sinai, convert Jordan into a Palestinian state, expel all Palestinians west of the River Jordan, and split up the Arab states into ethnic and religious micro-states. Israel would dominate these micro-states by building garrisons on their borders, military outposts for projecting power over centers of Arab population. In addition, these states would be policed by local militias drawn from ethnic minorities in their population – like the Christian militia created by Israel in Southern Lebanon. Once executed, this plan would establish Israel as the dominant power in the Middle East, independent of the United States.[10] What this plan reveals is the reach of the dialectic inaugurated by the creation of Israel in 1948. In the 1980s, the World Zionist Organization was urging Israel to take steps to dominate the region on its own.

US Joins the War

The attacks of 9-11, the American invasion of Iraq, Israeli/American plans for attacking Iran's nuclear facilities, and American plans for restructuring the region, suggest that the dialectic that began with the rise of political Zionism may have entered a new, perhaps final phase.

There are several forces operating behind these developments, whose provenance – in various degrees – can be traced back to the pressures and inducements engendered by political Zionism. At many different levels, 9-11 is a riposte to political Zionism and its chief accomplice over the past 60 years, the United States. Islamicate anger over the insertion of a Jewish

---

10 Oded Yinon, "A strategy for Israel in the 1980s," *Kivunim, A Journal for Judaism and Zionism*; Issue No, 14--Winter, 5742, February 1982. <www.theunjustmedia.com/the%20zionist_plan_for_the_middle_east.htm>

state in their lands, the expulsion of Palestinians, Palestinian suffering under Israeli occupation in the West Bank and Gaza, Arab humiliation over repeated defeats at the hands of Israel, the dismantling of Arab nationalism following these defeats, Western support for repressive Arab states, the sanctions against Iraq, the stationing of American troops in the Arabian peninsula after the Gulf war, and the invasion of Iraq: all of them have contributed to the radicalization of a small segment of the Islamicate world, who, frustrated by the stupor of Muslims, have adopted terrorist tactics against their Western adversaries. The Islamic radicals see this as the only effective way in which they can leverage their small numbers into a credible response to Israel-American dominance over the region.

The post-911 shift in America's policy towards the Middle East, calling for a redrawing of the map of the region, owes much to two forces long in the making. On the one hand, there are the Christian evangelists in the United States, who have grown in tandem with Israel and its victories over the Arabs; they see the ingathering of Jews in Israel as a necessary prelude to the Second Coming. As the largest voting bloc in the Republican Party, they have pressed the United States to offer its unconditional support to right-wing parties within Israel. The Zionists have not only welcomed this support but worked to deepen their alliance with the Evangelists.

The second group of actors – small but influential – are the neoconservatives in the Bush administration who have for long, but especially since the early 1990s, urged the United States to use its military dominance to prevent the emergence of a rival power. Many of the most influential neoconservatives, both inside and outside the Bush administration, are Jews (but so are some of the most articulate members of the left in America) who have been involved with right-wing Zionist think tanks in the United States and Israel. Some of these neoconservatives were advising the Netanyahu government in 1996 to make "a clean break" from the Oslo Agreement.[11] After 9-11, the same neoconservatives became the principal intellectual backers of America's invasion of Iraq and the larger plan to restructure the Middle East. Could this represent the belated unfolding of an amended *Kivunim* plan?

---

11 *A clean break: A new strategy for securing the realm* (Jerusalem: Institute for Advanced Strategic and Political Studies, 1996). <www.israeleconomy.org/strat1.htm>

At least for now, Israel is taking a back seat in these developments. Instead of seeking to restructure the region on its own, Israeli interests appear to be well-served by Americans taking the lead. A major Arab state is in ruins and inching towards civil war and dismemberment. At the end of this process an independent Kurdistan might well emerge as the first Israeli client state in the region. When this process can be repeated in Syria, Iran and Saudi Arabia, perhaps there will be other micro-states in the region which will depend for their survival on Israeli protection.

The attacks of September 11, 2001, like the decision of the Young Turks in October 1914 to enter the First World War against the Allied Powers, mark a new historical turning point for the relations between the West and the Islamicate world. The Turkish entry in the war offered Britain the opportunity to settle the age-old Middle Eastern question. It invaded the Middle East to dismantle the Ottoman Empire, and laid the foundations of a Jewish state and a system of colonies and client states in the region. Now, after 9-11, the United States enters the region, in strategic partnership with Israel, to restructure the region. This is a pre-emptive restructuring before the anti-imperialist forces in the region gain ascendancy.

At this point, there are few who are predicting with any confidence what will be the benefits and costs of this attempted restructuring: or what will be its unintended outcomes. The law of unintended consequences works surreptitiously, always hidden from the gaze of the strong whose power and hubris blind them to the resilience and force of the human spirit. It is unlikely that even the most prescient Zionists had foreseen in 1948 – after they had created a Jewish state with a 90 percent Jewish population – that the Palestinians would still be around some fifty-seven years later, causing existential anxiety, and still raising questions about the legitimacy of Israel as it is presently constituted. Incidentally, Israel too was an unintended consequence of Hitler's plan to exterminate the Jews. There would have been no Israel without the Jews who fled the anti-Semitic horrors unleashed by the Nazis in Europe.

In mounting their terrorist attack on the United States, the Islamist radicals were not expecting to sting the US into reversing its policies towards the Islamicate world. It seems more likely that what the United States did was what these radicals wanted it to do – to invade the Islamicate heart-

lands. The Islamists expect to turn this into a broader war against the United States, a war that would be fought on Islamicate territory. It is likely that the United States will deliver this too with an attack on Syria or Iran. Prodded by the evangelists, the neoconservative ideologues and Israel, the Bush administration is eager to take on this challenge. These strategic partners expect to use the 'war against terrorism' to restructure the Islamicate world, 'modernize' Islam, defeat the Islamists, and create a new and deeper system of clientage. The Islamists expect to defeat the United States on their home turf, a repeat – they like to think – of their defeat of the Soviets in Afghanistan. At this point, it is hard to predict where the chips will fall – or what unintended consequences this will produce for the United States, Israel and the Islamicate world.

Avoiding Disaster

The consequences that have flowed from the creation of Israel could have been foreseen – and indeed they were foreseen by the leading Zionists. Even if the Zionists wanted nothing else, Israel could not be a mere safe haven for Europe's persecuted Jews. Israel would inevitably evolve into a powerful, expansionist state, and seek to manipulate, control and nullify the tragic consequences to which its existence had given birth. Israeli success in this contest too was inevitable.

However, Israeli success is not built on irreversible foundations, unlike the march of the English settlers in North America. As Israel has succeeded, as it has become more powerful, it has also pressed harder against the irrepressible human spirit of the Palestinians, the Arabs, and the Muslims at large. The harder Israel and the United States push against the mass of Palestinians, Arabs and Muslims, the deeper the reactions it evokes from this great mass of humanity – in humiliation, anger and the will to reclaim its dignity. Now, this dialectic has propelled the United States directly into this spiraling contest. Together, the actions of these two great powers will continue to evoke growing heat from the great mass against which they are rubbing ever harder.

Is it possible that the ascendancy of the United States and Israel over the Middle East is now being undermined by their own seemingly unstoppable successes? Already, in the attacks of 9-11, the wars against Iraq and

Afghanistan, and the excesses of the war against terrorism, we can witness some of the unintended – and adverse – consequences this dialectic has now produced for the United States. Israel too creates new long-term risks to its security with every success it encounters in its war against the Arabs. Is this dialectic of escalation unstoppable? If it is not stopped, it could eventually produce a great arc of conflict stretching from Morocco to Mindanao and Kenya to Kazakhstan. Instead of producing a new system of clientage, American and Israeli ambition could well produce a devastating disruption in the supplies of oil from the Middle East.

A generation ago, in Vietnam, the United States found itself in a situation that was painful but the cost of withdrawal seemed worse. Nevertheless, a point was soon reached when the United States was forced into withdrawal. In hindsight, we can all agree that withdrawal was not the catastrophe most argued it would be. Vietnam would be free from wars, and free also to recover from the ravages of the war. Yet, the predicted fall of dominoes never occurred.

In Iraq, the United States has now placed itself in a similar situation. A withdrawal now appears costly, but a delay is likely to make withdrawal even costlier. Vietnam was not embedded in a system of states to which it was deeply connected by ties of religion, history and ethnicity. Iraq is different. The longer the United States remains in Iraq, the deeper will be the reverberations its presence will produce in the region as well as the wider Islamic world. An Iraqi withdrawal, combined with real American willingness to restrain Israel, could help to pull the Middle East and the world from the brink of a catastrophe.

But that is like wishing for the moon!

CHAPTER EIGHT

A Colonizing Project Built on Lies

"We should there form a portion of a rampart of Europe against Asia, an outpost of civilization as opposed to barbarism. We should as a neutral State remain in contact with all Europe, which would have to guarantee our existence."
—Theodore Herzl (1896)[1]

"To make Palestine as Jewish as England is English."
—Chaim Weizman (1919)[2]

"We Jews have nothing in common with what is denoted 'the East' and we thank God for it."
—Ze'ev Jabotinsky[3]

April 2002

It is not an easy life when it must be lived, defended, justified everyday, every hour, before the world, before the bar of one's own conscience, with lies, cover-ups, deceptions and sophistry.

This has been the particular burden of Zionists as they conceived their plan for creating a Jewish colonial-settler state in Palestine; as they went about executing this plan on the backs of imperialists powers with wars, massacres and ethnic cleansing; as they have continued to dispossess the Palestinians of the last fragments of their rights and legacy whose Canaanite roots are more ancient than Isaiah, Ezekiel, David and Moses.

---

1 Theodore Herzl, *The Jewish State* (1896):http://www.geocities.com/Vienna/ 6640/zion/ judenstaadt.html.
2 Avi Shlaim, *The Iron Wall: Israel and the Arab World* (New York: W. W. Norton and Company, 2001): 8
3 Shlaim (2001): 12.

In the colonial epoch, when Europeans were the 'master race' – and from that exalted position, enslaved and 'improved' the lesser breeds of Asia and Africa – the Zionists had an easy time with their narrative of lies. They wanted to possess Palestine so that they could create a state that would belong exclusively to European Jewry. In order to possess Palestine, they knew that they would have to dispossess the Palestinians. They wanted a Palestine without Palestinians.

In that era of racist discourse, this was not a hard sell. It is true that the Jews were not given entry into the club of Europe's master races. Still, they were a biblical people, and it was from their 'chosen seed' that Jesus had sprung. In Europe's hierarchy of races and peoples, the Jews occupied a position well above the Arab inhabitants of Palestine. The Jews were Israelites, children of Jacob, "born of the spirit," while the Arabs were "born of the flesh," Ishmaelites – children of Hagar, the slave woman.[4]

This was the tenor of the Zionist sales pitch. The Jews are a biblical people, an ancient people, the original and only inhabitants of Palestine, who had preserved their traditions and (implausibly) their racial purity through more than two thousand years of co-habitation and co-mingling in Europe. They are a people without a land, living in exile from the land promised to them by the God of the Jews and Christians. They must now end this exile by returning to Palestine, a land once flowing with milk and honey, but which had declined since their departure into a wilderness, a desert now inhabited by wild Bedouin tribes, nondescript aborigines of no account.

All this was cleverly captured in the deceptive slogan, first coined by Israel Zangwill in 1897, "A land without a people for a people without a land."[5] This became a leading slogan of the Zionist movement. Unlike other colonialists, who justified their conquests with empty pieties about improving the natives, the Zionist settlers would improve the land, since there were no people in Palestine to be improved. After the fact, Israel would justify itself with the claim that it had made the deserts bloom. These Zionist 'blooms' – Jewish settlements – sprouted on lands which only recently had supported Palestinian life – Palestinian homes and villages. To this day, Zionist propagandists bill Israel as a land-improvement scheme.

---

4   Galatians, 4: 28-30.

5   Norman Finkelstein, *Image and Reality of the Israel-Palestine Conflict* (New York: Verso, 1995): 95.

When it was pointed out that Palestine was not empty, that it had close to a million inhabitants, the Zionists pressed two claims, one mythical and one secular. The land was theirs because Yahweh had promised it to them. Since Yahweh, later, also turned out to be the God of the Christians, this argument carried a lot of weight with Christians, who were unhappy about Turkish control over Biblical lands. In the words of Henry Cabot Lodge, a senator from Massachusetts during the 1920s, Turkish control over the holy lands was "one of the great blots on the face of civilization, which ought to be erased."[6]

A secular version of this narrative was also available. The Jews had a historical right to Palestine because they had once lived there; the adjective "historical" carries nearly the same weight for the secular that "divine" does for the faithful. The logic was quaint. No one would ever dream of pressing this claim in a court of law. Who has the greater individual or national claim, under any system of laws, to a land: those who *had* ruled it for a short time, and that too more than two thousand years ago; or those who hold it now and have held it continuously for thousands of years. But logic did not matter. In this case, those pressing the claims had an affinity with the Europeans, and the opposite party was a barbarous, savage race. Of course, no one asked if those who asserted the right to 'return' were in fact the descendants of those who had left.

With these weighty arguments, not to mention their financial and political assets, the Zionists handily won the support of the two leading imperialist powers. In 1917 Britain pledged to create a national home for the Jews in Palestine; the US Congress followed suit in 1922. After this, the Palestinians did not have a chance. The Zionist project could only have failed if it did not find takers among the Jews. It appeared at first that the Palestinians were in luck. Most Jewish emigrants from Europe preferred greener pastures in the Americas to the first Zionist settlements in Palestine.

Quaintly, Hitler changed all that. Once the Nazis began their persecution of Jews in the mid-1930s, Jewish emigration to Palestine, which had been a trickle before, turned into a flood. When the Palestinians resisted the colonization of their country, they were brutally suppressed by British and Jewish

6   Kathleen Christison, *Perceptions of Palestine* (Berkeley, CA: University of California, 1999): 37.

forces. In 1948, the United Nations, under pressure from the United States, approved a plan to partition Palestine between Jews and Palestinians. It gave 55 percent of historic Palestine to Israel, including most of the coastline and the best agricultural lands, though Jews made up only 31 percent of the population and owned less than 7 percent of the land. The Palestinians rejected this massive theft of their lands.

This led to war and, predictably, a victory for the Zionists. The Palestinians had already been crushed by the British during the uprising of 1935-39, while the Arab armies that opposed the creation of Israel were poorly trained, poorly led, outnumbered – yes, they were outnumbered – and without a joint command. Israel won the war handily, acquiring 78 percent of historic Palestine, and drove out 800,000 Palestinians from the areas they controlled. In this first Israeli-Arab war, the Zionists had nearly achieved their goal. In June 1967, all of Palestine passed under Jewish control.

Almost immediately, the Zionist ideologues began inverting the truth about Israel. A racist, colonial settler-state that was established on the backs of imperial powers, and whose founding was premised on the dispossession of Palestinians, was now cast as a newly independent country, in the same class as India and Indonesia, which had won their independence from colonial subjugation. The Zionist struggle was even more heroic because, unlike India and Indonesia, they also had to fight off fanatical Arab neighbors unwilling to accept the existence of Israel.

The chief moral asset of the Zionists in their makeover of Israel was the Holocaust. This had created a vast fund of sympathy for the Jews, sympathy born of guilt. The Zionists conserved this sympathy capital through endless commemoration – in movies, media and museums. Better yet, they augmented the Holocaust capital by arguing that Jews had suffered horrors that were unique in history. Never before had a people been targeted for total extermination; never before had they faced death through incineration. Fortified with the shield of Holocaust capital, and armed with the sword of uniqueness, the Zionists have demanded that their actions should be exempt from the moral scrutiny of concerned world citizens. They should be given a free pass.

This Holocaust capital placed Israel beyond critique. First, Israel was equated with Jews. Second, Jews were equated with the survivors of the Holocaust.

Once these equations were established, Israel became the object of all the natural sympathy that belonged to the Holocaust survivors. As the haven, the last refuge for the world's super victims, Israel was now above reproach. It followed that anyone who dared to call Israel to account could only be an anti-Semite. This was a powerful tactic.

Among other things, this meant that there could be no Palestinian victims. It was logically impossible for a Palestinian to be a victim of Israelis. The Israelis, as survivors of the Holocaust, were super victims, perennial victims. Given this, how could the Israelis victimize anyone? All the talk of Palestinian suffering must be slander, the product of Arab anti-Semitism, which they had borrowed from the Nazis. In the court of Western opinion, the Palestinians did not have a prayer.

Worse, Israeli victimhood nullified Palestinians rights. The rights of the Palestinians – to their land, their freedom and dignity – counted for nothing if they collided with the infinitely superior claims of the Israeli super victims. Indeed, any Palestinian action in defense of their rights – if pressed against Israel – automatically earned the charge of immorality. Thus, Zionists charged that Palestinians, by opposing unrestricted immigration of Jews in the 1930s, had sent Jews to Nazi death camps. Under this logic, the very existence of the Palestinians was immoral.

Israel's victimhood could also justify violence against the Palestinians. The Israelis had earned the right to inflict any violence on the Palestinians that did not exceed their own suffering at the hands of the Nazis. As the world's super victims, there was no risk that their own violence could ever cross the limit where it would become unacceptable. The Israelis would remain blameless as long as they were not transporting Palestinians to gas chambers. Among others, Chaim Weizmann, the first president of Israel, employed this logic when protesting the West's muted concerns over the condition of Palestinian refugees. The problem of Palestinian refugees, he argued, was nothing compared to the murder of six million Jews.

It was easy stripping the Palestinians of their most basic rights – to their homes, lands, villages, towns, heritage and history. The Israelis demolished these rights with propaganda masquerading as history. The Palestinians had forfeited these rights because they had fled their homes voluntarily, following orders from Arab radio stations; they were not fleeing from Jewish terror. This concoction entered history books in Israel and the United States. No one asked for the evidence; no one asked if this made sense. No one asked if the Zionists had not planned this exodus all along. After all, how could a Jewish state *in* Palestine exist with all the Palestinians still in place?

The Zionist ideologues went about demonizing the Arabs too. They argued that the Arabs rejected the 1948 partition of Palestine because of a primeval Arab hatred for Jews, hatred that is akin to European anti-Semitism. The Arabs were excoriated for doing what any people faced with destruction would have done – fight against those who sought their destruction. Implicitly, the Zionists argued that the Arabs, or any race of inferior worth, did not possess a right to defend themselves against destruction by a superior people, such as the European Zionists. This was the logic of European racism.

In a similar vein, they have argued that Arab refusal to integrate Palestinian "refugees" demonstrated Arab intransigence and, not to forget, perversity. Wars have always created refugees, the Zionists maintained, but they do not linger in refugee camps; they are routinely absorbed by the host countries. If the Palestinians still live in refugee camps – in Jordan, Lebanon, Egypt and Syria – that is because these Arab countries have used them as pawns in their campaign against Israel. The Palestinians too have cooperated in this dastardly game – by refusing to leave the camps.

This is standard Israeli practice: denouncing their victims for not cooperating in their own demise. Israel engaged in large-scale ethnic cleansing of Palestinians because *it had to*; this was a *necessary* consequence of the Zionist plan for a Jewish state in Palestine. Why cannot the Arabs and Palestinians understand this? The Palestinians should have gone gently into the good night of national extinction prepared for them by the Zionists; they and their Arab compatriots display nothing but their inveterate anti-Semitism in demanding the right of return. Why should Israel alone have to endure such baseless, boundless hatred?

There was a deeper irony in the Zionist position. The Zionists demanded that the Arab countries should solve the problem of Palestinian refugees. Jordan, Lebanon and Syria hosted them: so they should absorb them. There would be no Zionism if the same logic were applied to the Jews who had lived in Europe for more than two thousand years. Instead, the Zionists argued that the Jewish communities in Italy, Britain, France, Russia and Spain were a distinct people. The Jews had resisted assimilation for some two thousand years, but now to safeguard Jewish identity and security they demanded a separate state for the Jews. Oddly, the homeland the Zionists sought for European Jews – a European people – was not to be founded in Europe, but in the heart of the Arab world, in Palestine.

A new lie was born when Arafat rejected the scraps offered to the Palestinians at Camp David in July 2000. The lie is that Arafat walked away from "an extremely generous offer," which gave the Palestinians 90 percent of the West Bank and Gaza. Indeed, the offer made at Camp David was very generous to Israel: it gave the Israelis control over the borders of the West Bank and Gaza, their water resources, their air space, and nearly all of old Jerusalem. Israel would keep most of the settlements, together with road links to Israel that Palestinians would need permits to cross. Camp David demanded that the Palestinians formalize a new system of apartheid sponsored and ratified by the United States.

Once the second Intifada started and the Palestinians were back in the streets, fighting Israeli armor with stones, the Israeli Occupation Army responded predictably. Within the first week, they had killed more than a hundred Palestinians, many of them children. However, this was no problem for the Israelis. When the world took notice, this was expertly blamed on Palestinian parents. "Look, how much they hate us. Now, they are sacrificing their children to gain some cheap publicity." In no time, the American media, always taking their cue from Israeli officials, were parroting these meretricious charges.

And so the lies, deceptions and sophistry employed to defeat the Palestinians have persisted. Indeed, they have multiplied and metamorphosed to suit the changing circumstances, the changing needs of an anachronistic colonizing project. As soon as Israeli officials announce these lies, they are taken up by a thousand American anchors, reporters and columnists, taken up and circulated verbatim. They rapidly enter into American public discourse, sanctified by op-ed writers, bandied at Congressional hearings, and trumpeted by Presidential hopefuls. Israeli lies become history in America.

Over the past eighty years, the myths created by the Zionist colonizers have killed Arabs, Jews and a few Americans too. They have become venerable like the biblical narratives – of Cain's murder, Ham's curse, Hagar's abandonment – that have supported generations of murderous ideologies. These mythologies, old and new-fangled, will continue to poison the world as long as they command our attention, as long as they substitute for history. If we do not oppose these lies here in the United States, they may well end up destroying our dearest hope – of a better world, a humane world, united, giving an equal place to every branch of the human family. We must oppose these myths before they destroy our humanity, child by child, house by house, camp by camp, city by city – as they do today, in Nablus, Tulkaram, Qalqiliya, Ramallah, Bethlehem and Jenin.

CHAPTER NINE

Academic Boycott of Israel

*"Allah forbiddeth you not those who warred not against you on account of
religion and drove you not out from your homes, that ye should show them
kindness and deal justly with them. Lo! Allah loveth the just dealers."*
—Qur'an: 60: 8

July 2002

In early April 2002, moved by the massacres in Jenin and the wanton
destruction of civilian infrastructure in the West Bank cities by the
Israeli Occupation forces, two British academics, Hilary Rose and
Steven Rose, circulated a call for an academic boycott of Israel.[1]

This campaign was directed primarily at European academics, and
so when it reached me nearly two months later, in the first week of
July 2002, there were only six American academics among the signatories. I carefully read the boycott statement, which entailed non-
cooperation with "official Israeli institutions, including universities,"
and decided to sign on to the list. I also forwarded the call to friends
on my e-mail list.

Most of my friends chose to ignore my email. I do not know if they were
opposed to the boycott in principle, or did not wish to incur the risk of
supporting it. Only two responded to my email, and both were more
than a bit troubled that I should be supporting such an initiative. One
described this campaign as "destructive;" another objected that this
was an "attack" on academic freedom. Once my name was on the list of
signatories, I also received two pieces of hate mail.

---

1   The call for this boycott is posted at www.pjpo.org.

Soon, Leonid Ryzhik, a mathematics lecturer at the University of Chicago, initiated a counter petition. In an interview published in *The Guardian*, May 27, 2002, he said that the boycott campaign was "immoral, dangerous and misguided, and indirectly encourages the terrorist murderers in their deadly deeds."[2] In addition, this week, in *The Nation*, August 5-12, Martha Nussbaum, an eminent ethical philosopher, who was in Israel to receive an honorary degree from the University of Haifa, wrote that she felt "relaxed" to be in Israel and she was "determined to affirm the worth of scholarly *cooperation* in the face of the ugly campaign (emphasis added)."

Having declared my support for the academic boycott of Israel, I believe I must now explain why I do not view this campaign as "destructive," "ugly" or supportive of "terrorist murderers." On the contrary, I see this as a moral gesture, part of a growing campaign by international civil society to use its moral force to nudge Israelis, to awaken them to the ugly and destructive reality of their Occupation, which has now lasted for more than thirty-five years and shows no sign of ending any time soon. At last, the cumulative weight of Palestinian suffering has begun to break through the crust of Israeli protestations of innocence. Although tardy, world conscience is now preparing to engage Israeli intransigence.

Increasingly, the world outside the United States understands that Israel is not a normal country. The Zionist movement sought to establish an exclusively Jewish state in Palestine, a land inhabited almost entirely by Palestinian Arabs in 1900 and for many centuries before that. Since no people yet have been known to commit collective suicide, or followed the Nazarene precept of turning the other cheek to its tormentor, the Zionists would have to achieve their objective through old-fashioned means: conquest *and* ethnic cleansing. This is how Israel emerged in 1948, through conquest and ethnic cleansing of 800,000 Palestinians.

Yet this was not enough. Although Israel now sat on 78 percent of historic Palestine, this was still short of Zionist goals. In 1967, during its pre-emptive war against Egypt, Syria and Jordan, Israel corrected this shortfall. It occupied the West Bank and Gaza. In addition, the Israelis pushed another 300,000 Palestinians across the Jordan River.

2 Leonid Ryzhik's campaign against the academic boycott of Israel call is posted at www.petitiononline.com/ noboyctt/petition.html.

Although the Security Council promptly called upon Israel to withdraw from the territories it had occupied in 1967, this resolution had no teeth. After routing three Arab armies, two from the leading nationalist Arab states, Israel had succeeded in deepening its special relationship with the United States; this promptly led to a doubling in US military and economic assistance to Israel. Seen from the Arab world, Israel and the United States now became two faces of the same reality. Jointly, and with increasing success, they sought to destroy Arab nationalist aspirations.

As a result, thirty-five years later, Israel still occupies the West Bank and Gaza. In reality, this 'Occupation' is merely a fiction, a farcical cover under which Israel buys time, which it uses to insert armed Israeli settlers, to increase Israeli control and ownership of Palestinian lands, to push the Palestinians into ever shrinking enclaves, to escalate the violence against Palestinian resistance, and to deepen the misery of Palestinian lives, all in pursuit of a policy of slow ethnic cleansing. At the same time, Israelis prepare for a final round of ethnic cleansing.

The logic of the Occupation is transparent to all but the purblind. If Palestinian demography prevents annexation, and ethnic cleansing is not feasible at present, the creation of Bantustans in the West Bank offers the next best solution. If 1.3 million Palestinians can be contained in Gaza, with an area of 360 square kilometers, the creation of similar enclaves in the West Bank could free up 90 percent of it for Jewish settlements. It is time to give up the fiction of the Occupation, and describe this oppressive regime by its proper name. This is a new Apartheid: one country with two unequal peoples, Jews and Palestinians, the colonizers and the colonized.

I have two objectives in rehearsing the narrative of Palestinian dispossession. First, the Zionists have repeatedly denied and massively falsified this narrative. Therefore, we must affirm it, simply and forcefully, again and again, in the expectation that world conscience will bear witness to the Zionist project of wiping out the Arab presence from Palestine to make room for Jewish settlers.

Once we affirm this narrative; once we recognize that the creation of Israel was based on the destruction of Palestinians; once we admit that the dispossession of Palestinians was implemented through wars, ethnic cleansing, massacres, villages destroyed, cities besieged, homes demolished, children maimed and killed, prisoners tortured, ambulances bombed, journalists targeted, municipal records destroyed and trees uprooted; once we recognize all this destructiveness – already accomplished, and more of it unfolding everyday – the accusations about the "destructiveness" or "ugliness" of an academic boycott of Israel will be seen for what they are – ludicrous and, indeed, unconscionable.

Mr. Leonid Ryzhik argues that the academic boycott "indirectly encourages the |Palestinian| terrorist murderers in their deadly deeds." Does he mean to say that this boycott "indirectly encourages" the Palestinian resistance? Is the boycott troubling because it seeks to question, delay and obstruct the extension of the Zionist project to the West Bank and Gaza? We must affirm in the face of such posturing that resistance is an inalienable right of the Palestinians, as it was of all colonized peoples who have faced dispossession. Of necessity, colonial dispossession is implemented by force, by massive force; it follows, that if the victim *so* chooses, resistance to dispossession can also employ violent means within the bounds of morality.

The question is not, why do the Palestinians resist, or why do they resist by violent means? There is a different question before world conscience. Why have we for fifty years abandoned the Palestinians to fight their battles alone, as they were being battered by a colonizer whom they could not fight alone? Why have we remained passive while the Palestinians were battered, exiled from their lands, herded into villages and towns that have been turned into concentration camps, exposed to the mercy of a colonizer who freely draws upon the finances, political support and military arsenal of the world's greatest power? In despair, marginalized, pauperized, and facing extinction as a people, if the Palestinians now use the only defense they have – to weaponize their death – who is to blame?

Finally, as Western conscience engages the Palestinian question, we can hope that this will mitigate the deep despair of Palestinians. When they learn that academic communities in Britain, France, Germany, Canada and the United States, hitherto indifferent to their tragic plight, are calling on Israel to end its Apartheid, the Palestinians may rethink their tactics. When they can see that Western audiences too are beginning to see the justice of their cause, the Palestinians may choose to renounce their acts of despera-tion. The academic boycott of Israel leverages moral suasion to reduce the violence of the colonizer as well as the colonized.

There are people who are shouting "Foul" at the academic boycott on the plea that this curtails the academic freedom of Israelis. I will readily admit that it does; this boycott can only work by shrinking some of the interna-tional avenues available to Israeli scientists for pursuing their work. Still, this curtailment is temporary; it will end the instant Israel ends the Occupation. It is also of limited scope. It only seeks to limit some of the advantages Israeli scientists derive from their interactions with the global scientific community. It does not threaten any fundamental academic freedoms.

In addition, we must look upon this curtailment of academic freedom in a larger context. Although academic freedom is an important value, one that all civilized societies should cherish, it is not an absolute value; there are other values that we cherish, other values that are more important, more fundamental than the right to academic freedom. I believe it is reasonable and moral to impose temporary and partial limits on the academic freedom of a *few* Israelis if this can help to restore the fundamental rights of millions of Palestinians – to life, to property, to ancestral lands, to sovereign control over their destiny, and to equal treatment under the law. We can deny this only if we confess to a disproportion in the value we accord to Israeli and Palestinian rights.

I refuse to be intimated by the cant about the 'sanctity' of academia, about mixing politics and science. More than ever before, universities help to reproduce the power structures of their societies; they are a potent source of ideologies of imperialism, race and class exploitation. Israeli universities are no exception. Through their links with the military, the political parties, the media and the economy, they have helped to construct, sustain and justify Israeli Apartheid. I might have hesitated in adding my name to the boycott if I knew that Israeli academics had taken the lead in organizing rallies, staging sit-ins, passing resolutions protesting the Occupation, refus-ing military service in the Occupied territories, or working on projects that reinforced the Occupation. On the contrary, nearly all of Israeli academia has shown that it is a party to the Occupation.

Of course, one might argue that this boycott is wasted effort; it can have no appreciable impact on Israeli society and policies. This is a question about the efficacy of the boycott. It is well known that Israeli scientists cherish the cooperation of the world's scientific community as well as access to international funding. We can expect, therefore, that if the boycott spreads, this can begin to reduce the effectiveness of Israeli scientists. Perhaps more important, Israelis will find it harder to ignore the message that the boycott sends to them: that Israeli violations of Palestinian rights are repugnant and will not be allowed to stand.

The academic boycott is one of the few handles that international civil society can use to bring pressure against Israeli Apartheid. Because of the power of the pro-Israeli lobbies in the United States, Israel continues to violate Palestinian rights with impunity. If any other country had been guilty of similar violations – nay, even half those violations – it would have invited economic sanctions, and even military intervention from the United Nations.

The capitulation of the United States to the pro-Israeli lobby has serious consequences for Palestinians and the future of world peace. It has meant that Israel can wage war against a civilian population – using jets, rockets, tanks, armored vehicles, explosives and bulldozers – with impunity. Abandoned, isolated, beleaguered and unarmed, a few Palestinian men and women have responded to this massive force by weaponizing their own death, provoking still greater violence from the Israeli military machine. Paradoxically, by the deaths they inflict and their own, the Palestinian 'suicide bombers' have forced world conscience to acknowledge that if they act beyond the pale of reason it is because the Israeli Occupation – so methodical, so streamlined, so overwhelming in its efficiency – leaves them with few tools with which to resist but the sacrifice of their own lives. The academic boycott is one small step that a slowly detribalizing world has now taken to stop the daily affront to our common humanity that is perpetrated on the West Bank and Gaza. This symbolic act should be endorsed, even applauded, by all men and women who have risen above the blind tribalism that hobbles mankind.

CHAPTER TEN

Crossing the Line

"This book sounds an alarm: Israel, through the deep and pervasive power of its lobby, threatens deeply-cherished American values—especially free speech, academic freedom and our commitment to human rights."
—Paul Findley (1985)[1]

September 2002

In 1982, when Paul Findley went down in his re-election bid after serving in the Congress for twenty-two years, the principal pro-Israeli lobby in Washington took credit for his defeat. What was the Congressman's crime? He had crossed a line drawn by the Israeli lobby for American officials and politicians: he had violated the Israeli ban on meeting Arafat.

This past week I too had a little taste of the same medicine. No, I am not a public figure, nor had I met with Arafat or any other Palestinian degraded to "terrorist" ranks by Israel's lexical offensive. I am only a professor, an obscure peddler of dissent, who, once tenure was secured, had been left reasonably well alone by school administrators, colleagues, and assorted self-appointed censors. How then did I get into trouble?

Over the past year, I began to cross that thin line, which I should have known one crosses only at some peril. I began to talk and write about Israel. This would not have been remarkable if I had been reading from the script; but I was not. Instead, I began to call a spade a spade. In other words, I was stepping over the line.

---

1 Paul Findley, *They Dare to Speak Out* (Westport, CT.: Lawrence Hill and Co., 1985): v.

Although invisible, this line is like a charged electrical cable. I first stepped on this cable when I spoke on the attacks of 9-11 at Northeastern University in October 2001. I had planned on providing a historical backdrop to the attacks on the Twin Towers, drawing attention to the record of French, British and American interventions in the region. My principal concern was that some Americans, so soon after September 11, might greet such an attempt with hostility. To my pleasant surprise, I was wrong. At the end of the seminar, several students and faculty stepped forward to thank me for speaking out in these difficult times.

However, there was unhappiness too over my remarks. A few hours after the talk, the Chair of Economics informed me that a professor had emailed to complain that I had "deviated" from the announced theme of the seminar. Later, the same day, as I was walking across the campus, a professor I had never met before accosted me. He told me that he was at my talk, and proceeded to accuse me of "hate speech." I could think of one passing reference to the peculiar history of Israel that might have nettled this irate professor.

Disoriented by the attacks on the Twin Towers, many Americans felt that the 9-11 had "changed everything." I shared in America's grief at the wanton loss of human lives, the first in their recent history. Although I had known this grief before, many times before, September 11 was changing me too. I was concerned over the curtailment of civil liberties in the United States, the growing attacks on Islam, and the triumph of lobbies who wanted the United States to wage endless wars against the rest of the world. Stepping out of my academic shell, I felt it was time to speak to some real issues.

Among other things, in early April I signed a petition that called for the academic boycott of Israel. In addition, I forwarded the petition to a few colleagues at Northeastern University. When one of them objected to this boycott, and declared that it was "destructive," I had to explain why I thought this campaign was morally justified. I wrote an essay, "An Academic Boycott of Israel," which was first published in *Counterpunch.Org* on July 31, 2002; it has since appeared on many more websites, newspapers and discussion groups. This produced both angry and supportive emails; only one threatened violence. Overall, I was pleased at the response.

There was worse to come. On September 3, 2002, the *Jerusalem Post* carried a report on my essay under the heading, "US Prof Justifies Palestinian Terror Attacks." The *Post* report did not mention the title of my essay or give any hint of its substance. The next morning I received several angry emails. Some of these were copied to the Chair of Economics and other administrators at Northeastern University. Over the next two days, I received calls from *The Jewish Advocate*, *Boston Herald*, *Bloomberg News* and *The O'Reilly Factor*. Although flattered by the attention, I declined the invitation to talk to the honorable Mr. Bill O'Reilly.

On September 5, taking the cue from the *Post*, the *Herald* published another malicious and sensational report on my essay. It was headlined, "Prof Shocks Northeastern with Defense of Suicide Bombers." It claimed that my article "sent shock-waves through the Fenway campus yesterday," but quoted only one Professor at Northeastern. The *Herald* report too did not refer to the title or substance of my essay, justifiably raising suspicions about the reporter's motive. Although I had sent a timely response to their email, the *Herald* reporter claimed that he could not contact me by phone or email.

It is curious how these reports had inverted the objective of my essay. My essay made a case for an academic boycott, a quintessentially non-violent act, as an alternative to the recent Palestinian acts of desperation. By showing greater solicitude for the Palestinians' desperate plight, I argued, international civil society could give hope to this beleaguered people, and persuade them to act with greater patience in the face of Israel's brutal military Occupation. The *Post* and *Herald* had twisted a moral case for non-violent action into justification for terror.

It would appear that I had crossed the 'line' in advocating an academic boycott of Israel, and I had to be punished. To quote Taha Abdul-Basser (*Boston Herald*, September 9), what the *Post* and *Herald* "actually find distasteful is the thought that intelligent, well-spoken people of conscience should call for a moral stand against the oppressive and unjust behavior of Israel." At least in the United States, the Israeli narrative has nearly monopolized public discourse on policies towards the Middle East. This narrative speaks only of Jewish claims to Palestine, and presents Israel as a victim of Arab hatred of all things Western, a beleaguered outpost of Western civilization in an ocean of Arab barbarism. My essay was unacceptable because it questions this narrative.

The attacks against me perhaps are not over yet. As I was finishing this essay on the night of September 8, I learned that I had been 'spoofed' – an addition to my lexicon. Someone had stolen my identity and sent out e-mails, containing malicious anti-Semitic diatribe, to administrators and colleagues at Northeastern. The spoof was quite crude, making it hard for anyone who knew me to believe that it could have originated from me. Or, perhaps, I am being naïve.

In the days following the September 11 attacks, President Bush had advanced a vision of the world framed in Manichean terms. Either you are with us, or you are against us. The Arabs are evildoers. We have always been good to them; they attack us only because they envy our freedom and our prosperity. Dissenting with President Bush was blasphemous; it gave comfort to terrorists. This is the new-fangled theology of America's war against terrorism, whose ramifications are being worked out feverishly every day by hawks of every stripe.

America's "war against terrorism" is legitimizing state terror the world over. Israel, Russia, China, India and many lesser powers have appropriated this new theology to suppress the legitimate resistance of various oppressed peoples as terrorist activities. In addition, America's hawkish lobbies are using the new theology to stifle discourse by smearing their opponents with the brush of terrorism. The *Post* and *Herald* have employed this tactic against me.

If we allow these attacks on free speech to stand, if we allow the corporate media, the right-wing zealots and pro-Israeli lobby to regulate our thoughts, we may soon witness the narrowing of all discourse to the parroting of official lies, we will be rallying behind illegal wars, and applauding the curtailment of our own liberties. We will only be free to mouth slogans. "Down with our enemies! Down with terrorism! Down with Arabs! Down with Islam!"

CHAPTER ELEVEN

Israelization of the United States

"And even so do We try some of them by others, that they say: Are these they whom Allah favoreth among us?"
—Qur'an: 6: 53

April 2003

The images of the American armada plowing through the deserts of Iraq, bombing military and civilian targets, laying siege to Iraqi cities, targeting Iraqi leaders, shooting civilians, blinded by sandstorms, stalled, ambushed, shocked by the Iraqi resistance, facing suicide attacks, suggests an eerie but inescapable comparison. Is this America's West Bank? Is this the Israelization of the United States – heading to its logical conclusion?

Most Americans have been taught by their captive media to interpret what happens *today* in the Middle East in terms of what happened *yesterday*. The clock of history in this region always starts with the most recent "suicide" attack mounted by Palestinians against "peaceful," "innocent" Israeli "civilians." If, somehow, these Americans could be persuaded to take the long view, they might begin to understand that the war against Iraq is perhaps the culmination of a process that had been long in the making: the Israelization of the United States.

The founding fathers of Zionism understood clearly that *their* colonial project had no chance of succeeding without the patronage of a great power. This is the first tenet of the Zionist doctrine. The Zionists tried but failed to persuade the Ottoman Caliph to open up Palestine to Jewish colonization; he declined their financial inducements. Later, the Zionists worked very hard to interest the Germans, French, and the

British in their plans, but without much success. Then came World War I and the British found themselves in a tight spot in the middle of this war. They sought Jewish help in accelerating US entry into the war. In return for their help, the Zionists got the vital support they had sought since 1897. In the infamous Balfour Declaration of November 1917, the British promised "to use their best endeavor" (what charming language) to facilitate the creation of a "national home for the Jewish people" in Palestine.

The British occupied Palestine in December 1917 and soon opened it up to Jewish immigration. At the end of the war, according to the terms of a secret agreement, the British and French vivisected the Arab territories of the Ottoman Empire to splinter Arab unity. Syria was carved up four ways: Lebanon, to create a Maronite-dominated state; Jordan, to reward one of the sons of the collaborating Sharif Hussein of Makkah; a French-controlled Syria; and the British mandate of Palestine, the future Israel. With little loss of time, the Jewish settlers began setting up a parallel Zionist administration, with its security arrangements, in British-occupied Palestine.

The die was cast for the Palestinians. They were no match for the combined Zionist and British forces; and there was no help from weak Arab 'states' hamstrung by imperialist control. Still the Palestinians fought to save their homeland. When the British halted Jewish immigration into Palestine in 1939, the Zionists mounted a terrorist campaign. The British lost nerve and passed the buck to the United Nations or, effectively, to the United States, which dominated that august body. Motivated in part by anti-Semitism and still strong Christian sentiments, but also swayed by a determined Jewish campaign, the United States pushed a partition plan that strongly favored the Jews. The Palestinians rejected the partition plan. They and other Arabs mounted a feeble resistance, but were routed by the Zionists. In 1948, the Israelis expelled 800,000 Palestinians from their homes (in what became Israel) and never allowed them to return.

It should be understood that the creation of Israel did not – at least in the early years – advance America's strategic interests. At the time, the United States and Britain exercised firm – and very profitable – control over the oil resources of the Gulf through a clutch of weak and pliant monarchies. The emergence of radical governments in Egypt in 1952, and, later, Syria, only deepened the dependence of the oil-rich Arab monarchies on Western powers. When the Iranian nationalists sought to nationalize their oil in 1952, the Americans and British organized a coup, and reinstated the deposed King. In other words, the British and Americans were firmly in control of the region – without any help from Israel. A "special relationship" with the Israeli interloper could only undermine this control by inflaming Arab nationalist sentiments.

The record of American assistance to Israel shows that the special relationship did not develop until the late 1960s. US aid flows to Israel remained well below $100 million annually until 1965, and, more importantly, very little of this was for military hardware. The aid flows doubled in 1966, increased six fold in 1971, and five fold again in 1974 when it rose to $2.6 billion, going up to $5 billion in more recent years.[1] Further, this aid was disbursed mostly in the form of grants, and nearly all of it was spent on military hardware. Indeed, these terms indicate a very "special relationship," not available to any other country.

Most commentators, especially those on the left, attribute the emergence of this special relationship to Israel's stunning 1967 victory over Egypt, Syria and Jordan. They argue that this victory convinced the US that Israel could serve as a vital ally and a counterpoise to Arab nationalism and Soviet ambitions in the region. But this explanation is both one-sided and simplistic. It completely ignores the part Israel played in initiating this relationship, deepening it and making it irreversible.

If the special relationship was the product of an Israeli victory over Arabs, the US should have embraced Israel as a vital ally after its first victory over Arab armies in 1948 or after 1956 when it seized the entire Sinai in a lightning strike. Why did US have to wait until 1967 *after* Israel had humiliated the leading nationalist states and Soviet allies in the region? Arguably, the downsizing of Arab nationalists should have reduced Israel's usefulness to the US. In addition, the doubling of American aid flows to Israel in 1966 as well as the cover-up of the 1967 Israeli attack on the USS Liberty – a reconnaissance ship – off the Sinai coast, indicate that a special relationship had been developing well before the 1967 war.

---

1 "U.S. Assistance to Israel," Jewish Virtual Library: http://www.us-israel. org/ jsource/US-Israel/U.S._Assistance_to_ Israel1.html (2003).

If America's special relationship with Israel was slow to develop, in large part, this was because Israel was doing quite well without it. At least in the 1950s, the British were still the paramount power in the Persian Gulf, a position it would yield only slowly to the United States. In addition, Israel entered into a very fruitful military relationship with France, who supplied not only heavy arms and combat aircraft but collaborated on its nuclear weapons program. Israel was quite confident of its military superiority over its Arab adversaries even in these early years. Apparently, the British and the French too knew about this, since they persuaded Israel to invade Sinai in 1956 as part of their campaign to regain control of the Suez Canal. This confidence was well-placed. Within a few days, Israel had taken the Sinai from the Egyptians.

If the war of 1967 produced stunning Israeli victories, it also drove Israel to look for a new partner. First, since it had started the war against French advice, President De Gaulle suspended all arms shipments to Israel. In order to make good the loss, Israel turned to the US, which had the added advantage of being the world leader in military technology. At the same time, Egypt and Syria would seek to rebuild their decimated military by pursuing an even closer relationship with Soviet Union. Given the logic of the Cold War, this persuaded the US to develop Israel as a counterweight against the growing Soviet influence in the region. The conditions were now ripe for the growth of a special relationship between Israel and the US.

The Israeli decision to realign itself with the US was pregnant with conse-quences. Israel would have to persuade Americans that their vital interests in the region – protecting their oil supplies, rolling back Arab nationalism, and containing Soviet influence – could be best served by building up Israel, militarily and economically, as the regional hegemon. This would not be an easy task since American support for Israel was certain to alienate the Arab world. And Americans knew this.

The Israelis undertook this task with seriousness. In casting itself as the regional hegemon, Israel was playing a high-risk, high-stakes game that could succeed only if it was supported and financed by the United States. Moreover, caution demanded that Israel could not build its new strategy on a special relationship that Americans would be free to reverse. In order to make this an enduring relationship, Israel would bolster it at two levels.

At the grass-roots level, the Israeli lobbies worked to build an emotion-ally intense American identification with Israel. This was pursued in a variety of ways. Most importantly, American consciousness was saturated with guilt over Jewish suffering. In his book, *The Holocaust Industry*, Norman Finkelstein has shown that the sacralization of the holocaust began only *after* 1967, and how the guilt this produced has been used to silence Israel's critics. Americans now feared that criticism of Israel would be seen as anti-Semitism. As a result, few dared to criticize Israel in public.

Israel was also portrayed as a democracy, constantly under attack from Palestinians and Arabs. Two explanations of Arab hatred of Israel were offered. It was a species of anti-Semitism. Like its older European cousin, Arab anti-Semitism was unprovoked; it had no causes. Alternatively, unable to modernize, the Arabs hated Israel because it was the only country in the region that was both free and prosperous.

At the political level, organized American Jewry amplified its efforts to increase the pro-Israeli bias of American politics. While individual Jews continued to play a distinguished role in liberal and left causes, nearly all the major Jewish organizations now worked feverishly to put pressure on the media, the Congress and the Presidency to offer unconditional support to Israel. In several states, Jewish money, votes and media tilted elections towards the most pro-Israeli candidates. In addition, Jewish organizations worked more effectively to *defeat* candidates who took positions even mildly critical of Israel. This is documented in Paul Findley's book, *They Dare to Speak Out*.

Once Israel's special relationship with the US was in place, it would acquire its own logic of success. This logic worked through several channels. First, as Jewish organizations worked to shape US policies towards Israel, they would improve their tactics, and their initial victories would bring more Jewish support and, in time, more success. This logic even worked to turn temporary reverses to Israel's advantage. People who argue that the US special relationship with Israel was prompted by its victory in 1967 should also note that its near-defeat in 1973 led, the following year, to a more than five-fold increase in the US aid package to Israel to $2.6 billion. Egypt took this message to heart, deciding that it would be futile to challenge this spe-cial relationship any longer. In 1978, it signed a separate peace with Israel, after US promised to sweeten the deal with an annual aid package of $2 billion. Its chief rival eliminated, Israeli hegemony over the Middle East was now more secure.

Iran's Islamist revolution in 1979 added new strength to Israel's special relationship with the US. The overthrow of the Iranian monarchy, the second pillar of American hegemony in the Middle East, increased Israel's leverage over US policies. In addition, the accession to power of Islamists raised the bogey of the Islamic threat to the West. The Israeli lobby, especially its Middle East experts, had been making the case for some time that the Islamist movements in the Middle East opposed the US *per se*, and not merely its policies towards Israel. The alarm caused by the Iranian Revolution gave strength to this interpretation.

The end of the Cold War in 1990 stripped the special relationship of its old rationale. Israel would now have to invent a new one to continue to sell itself as a strategic asset. It would now market itself as the barrier, the breakwater, against the rising tide of Islamic fundamentalism. For many years, the chief opposition to the corrupt and repressive regimes in the Arab world, whether dictatorships or monarchies, had taken Islamist forms. Pro-Israeli apologists in the media and academia – mostly Jewish neoconservatives and Middle East experts – argued that the West now faced a new Islamic enemy, global in its reach, who hated the freedoms, secular values and prosperity of the West. Bernard Lewis, the "doyen" of Middle East experts and a passionate Zionist, solemnly intoned in September 1990 that this was nothing less than a "clash of civilizations."[2] This was a clever move, but also a necessary one, to convert Israel's conflict with the Arabs into a new Crusade, the war of the West (read the United States) against Islamdom. It was a clever move also because it had support from Christian fundamentalists, who were now a strong force in the Republican Party.

The new Crusaders worked in tandem with Islamicate extremists in the Al-Qaida camp who also wanted to provoke a war between Islamdom and the US. Every time Osama's men struck at American targets, it was exploited by the pro-Israeli lobby to promote the Clash thesis. When the nineteen hijackers struck on September 11, 2001, they could not have chosen a better time.

---

2   Bernard Lewis, "The roots of Muslim rage," *The Atlantic Monthly* (September 1990): 60.

The man at America's helm was a born-again Christian, backed by right-wing Christians, and with a cabinet that took its advice on foreign policy mostly from neoconservatives with strong Israeli ties. The neoconservative's plan for a new Crusade had been ready long before 9-11. They had the President's ear after 9-11, and the President bought into their plan.

In no time, President Bush had been converted into a new Crusader. He described Ariel Sharon as a "man of peace," after embracing every one of his extremist positions on the Palestinians: reoccupation of the West Bank, repudiation of Oslo, removal of Arafat and dismantling of the Palestinian authority. He laid out his binary doctrine – you are with us or against-us – and prepared for pre-emptive wars against the "axis of evil."

The new Crusade is now underway. The world's only superpower, commanding one-fifth of the world's output, and nearly one-half its military expenditure, has entered Iraq to effect regime-change, to bring 'democracy' to a people it has emasculated with bombs and sanctions for twelve years. In this new Crusade, the United States stands at the head of a numerous "coalition of the coerced," now including forty-five countries. However, America's "strategic asset in the Middle East" – Israel – is curiously missing from the long list of coalition partners. Israel stayed out because the United States was afraid that its entry would alienate its Islamic allies. This serves Israel quite well: why should it waste Israeli troops when Americans are eager to do the job. Israel can eat its cake and have it too. That is a trick no magician could replicate. The Israelization of the United States is complete.

CHAPTER TWELVE

Illuminating Thomas Friedman

"Among the People of the Scripture there is he who, if thou trust him with a weight of treasure, will return it to thee. And among them there is he who, if thou trust him with a piece of gold, will not return it to thee unless thou keep standing over him. That is because they say: We have no duty to the Gentiles."
—Qur'an: 3: 75

June 2003

The publishers, Farrar, Straux & Giroux, maintain a webpage on Thomas Friedman, the foreign affairs columnist for the *New York Times*. The webpage proudly proclaims that Friedman is in a "unique position to interpret the world for American readers. Twice a week, Friedman's commentary provides the most trenchant, pithy, and illuminating perspective in journalism."[1]

I will not contest the claim that Mr. Friedman is in "a *unique position* to interpret the world for American readers (emphases added)." That is plain enough: he writes for the NYT, arguably America's most influential newspaper. However, do his commentaries provide "the most trenchant, pithy, and illuminating perspective in journalism"? What do his commentaries "illuminate" – his Middle Eastern subjects or his own biases?

Consider his column, "The Reality Principle," from the NYT of June 15, 2003.[2] Quoting an Israeli political theorist, Yaron Ezrahi, he argues that only the United States, "an external force," can rescue the Israelis and Palestinians from their self-destructive war against each other. The United States of America is the "only reality principle." The United

---

1   "Thomas L. Friedman," Farrar, Straus & Giroux (2002-2003): http://www. thomaslfriedman.com/index.htm.
2   Thomas Friedman, "The Reality Principle," *New York Times*, June 15, 2003, Section 4 , Page 13 , Column 1.

States alone can save the day "with its influence, its wisdom and, if necessary, its troops."

How illuminating is this?

Is the United States altogether "an external force" in its dealings with Israel? No American politician or media commentator can candidly examine this question without serious damage to his career. It is much safer to take the position that Israel is a client state of the United States, a strategic asset that polices America's friends and foes alike in the oil-rich Middle East. This is also the premise behind Friedman's description of the United States as the "only reality principle" in the conflict between Israel and the Palestinians.

The notion that Israel serves American interests in the Middle East is insupportable. At the least, it ignores three refractory facts. If indeed the United States acted in its own best interests *vis-à-vis* Israel, why would the American Israel Public Affairs Committee (AIPAC) exert itself so mightily to ensure that the US Presidency, Congress and media remain firmly committed to Israeli hegemony over its neighbors? In other words, why would American Jewry engage in such a monumentally wasteful exercise? Then, there is the curious fact that the United States was deeply concerned, during the two Gulf Wars, to keep Israel *out* of these conflicts. If Israeli were a strategic asset, would it not be helping the United States in these two wars? Third, on the rare occasions when a US President has opposed an official Israeli position, even when this was a mild rebuke, he has been forced to backtrack after running into massive opposition from both parties in the Congress. Who controls the Congress: the President or the Israeli lobby?

There are a few more glittering gems embedded in Mr. Friedman's column. Although Israel has the right to "pursue its mortal enemies, just as America does," he explains, it cannot "do it with reckless abandon." "America will never have to live with Mr. bin Laden's children. They are far away and always will be. Israel will have to live with the Palestinians, after the war. They are right next door and always will be." Now that should be illuminating to an America that was "changed for ever" by the events of 9-11, an America whose daily nightmare now is the looming threat of a chemical, biological or dirty-bomb attack on its home ground.

Next, consider Friedman's fears that the Palestinians are "capable only of self-destructive revenge, rather than constructive restraint and reconcilia- tion." Again, how illuminating that Friedman should exclude Israelis from this anxious train of thought. There is amnesia here too. It is odd (or is it illuminating?) that NYT's foreign affairs columnist forgets some perti- nent history. The Palestinians demonstrated seven years of "constructive restraint and reconciliation" between 1993 and 2000, even as the Israelis – in clear violation of the Oslo Accord – continued their colonization of the West Bank, confiscating Palestinian lands, and building and expanding settlements that laid siege to Palestinian communities. In the end, what did the Palestinians get for relinquishing their historical right to 78 percent of historical Palestine? The Israelis made the now-notorious "generous offer" of Palestinian Bantustans. That is when the Palestinians, threatened with extinction, mounted their second Intifada.

Friedman asserts that on the Israeli side, only the "extremist Jewish set- tlers" oppose the two-state solution. In other words, all the other Israelis – the 'moderate' Jewish settlers and the Israelis settled inside the green line – support the two-state solution. Could it be that a small band of "extrem- ist Jewish settlers" – these settlements did not crop up in one day – has imposed its extremist vision on the overwhelming majority of Israelis? How does that happen in the only democracy in the Middle East? Now, isn't that illuminating?

Is there a subliminal message in Friedman's discourse on "The Reality Principle?" I think there is one. It is contained in a single word – "troops." Only the United States, he claims, can save the day "with its influence, its wisdom and, if necessary, its *troops* (emphasis added)." Friedman is suggest- ing – of course, he is only suggesting – that "if necessary" the United States should take its war on "terrorism" to Gaza and the West Bank.

In 1993, the United States-cum-Israel chose Yasser Arafat and his "security services" to "discipline their own people." When Arafat "proved unwilling to do that consistently," Bush/Sharon replaced him with Mahmoud Abbas. It now appears that Abbas too may refuse to take his marching orders from Jerusalem or Washington. Of course, the Israelis could finish the job on their own, but it would be too dangerous. As Friedman puts it, "If Israelis try to do it, it [the cancer] will only metastasize." Friedman has a solution: give the job to American troops.

Twice a week Friedman delivers his perorations on the Arabs, Iran, Israel, Turkey, the Middle East and the Islamicate world more generally. In addition, over the years, as the NYT's regular commentator on the Middle East, he has built a reputation as America's chief opinion-maker on the region. Does he deserve that reputation? Does he offer a balanced, objective, or *American* perspective on the region? Out of political correctness, most Americans will answer in the affirmative, but I have some nagging doubts.

In a recent television interview with Charlie Rose, Mr. Friedman said, "Israel was central to my life as it was to all my friends." He was reminiscing about his years in high school. "Today," he laments, "I'm probably the only one of my friends who is still emotionally involved in Israel."[3] Now, I would not have mentioned this if Friedman were not America's journalistic sage on Arabs and Muslims. However, since he is, I may be excused for thinking that this confession is pertinent to his sermons on the Middle East.

Isn't that illuminating?

---

3   "Friedman: Will Jews Still Care?" *Forward*, June 6, 2003: www.forward. com/ issues/2003/03.06.06/news3b.html.

CHAPTER THIRTEEN

Lerner, Said and the Palestinians

"Every indigenous people will resist alien settlers as long as they see any hope of ridding themselves of the danger of foreign settlement. This is how the Arabs will behave and will go on behaving so long as they possess a gleam of hope that they can prevent 'Palestine' from becoming the land of Israel."
—Ze'ev Jabotinsky (1923)[1]

June 2003

Very few intellectuals in our times would measure up to Edward Said in the eulogies he received upon his death last year. Indirectly, every obituary, tribute, essay, reminiscence honoring his memory was a rebuke to the mercenaries who populate our media, academia and that execrable category, think tanks. But would they notice?

Yet, I chanced upon one obituary notice that I found troubling. I was troubled because it was from Rabbi Michael Lerner who has risked the opprobrium of America's Jewish establishment by his opposition to the Israeli Occupation of the West Bank and Gaza.[2] At one time, he had to seek police protection in the face of death threats from pro-Israeli Americans.

It is not that the Rabbi does not praise Edward Said. He pays "tribute to a great thinker and writer whose contribution to contemporary intellectual life deserves our respect and appreciation." Said was a "powerful and passionate advocate for his *own* people, the Palestinians (emphasis added)." Is that all?

1 Ze'ev Jabotinsky, "The iron wall," *Rassvyet*, 4 November 1923: www. Marxists.de/ middleast/ironwall/ironwall.htm
2 Michael Lerner, "Edward Said," *Tikkun*, November/December 2003.

The Rabbi reserves his deepest respect, however, for the way in which Edward Said "publicly challenged Arafat and his *thuggish* ways (emphasis added)." Actually, challenging Arafat became a commonplace amongst Palestinians after he traded the rights *of* Palestinians for policing rights *over* them. The pointed reference to Arafat's "thuggish ways" is gratuitous. This phrase belongs to the lexicon of Zionist demonization of Palestinians.

Then come the accusations against Said. He did not "sympathize with the plight of European Jews and the way that their returning to the place they perceived to be their ancient homeland was not an act of Western colonialism." It is a circuitous sentence, a bit jumbled and problematic too.

Here is how I make sense of the Rabbi's syntax. First, he posits that the creation of Israel was not an "act of Western colonialism," something Edward Said knew or should have known. From this, the Rabbi infers that Said's opposition to Zionism was due to his lack of sympathy for (a) the "plight of European Jews" and (b) their right to return to "the place they perceived to be their ancient homeland."

The first charge is scandalous. Only someone seized with anti-Semitic loathing could lack "sympathy" for the centuries of suffering endured by European Jews. Unwittingly, therefore, the Rabbi accuses Said of anti-Semitism, which I am sure the Rabbi will promptly disavow. Or, is the Rabbi saying that European Jews had earned the right – because of their long suffering – to a Jewish state in Palestine, even if this would lead to the destruction of Palestinian society. Said's sin, then, is that he does not recognize *this* Jewish 'right.' On this account, we have to acquit Edward Said. The Rabbi will agree that self-destructive sympathy does not come naturally to most people.

The second charge stems from the premise of a Jewish right of return. In this case, we are asked to concede that the "perception" that Palestine is "their ancient homeland" gives European Jews the right to return. And this right is comprehensive. It empowers European Jews to 'repossess' Palestine – take it away from the Palestinians – in order to establish a state *of* the Jewish people.

The Jewish right of return claims legitimacy by appeals to its ancient nationalist mythology. No system of law elevates a perceived claim, by an individual or group, into a legally enforceable right. Nor does any system of law confer on any people a perpetual right to a country they once inhabited (or may have inhabited), much less one they left (or claim to have left) some eighteen hundred years ago. In effect, then, the Rabbi faults Said for not accepting Jewish mythology as law for the Palestinians.

Rabbi Lerner also accuses the Palestinians – and Said, by association – of immorality. "He never took the step of acknowledging that Palestinian resistance to Jewish immigration in the years when Jews were trying to escape the gas chambers of Europe or the displaced persons camps of 1945-48 was immoral." At best, the argument is tendentious.

Is the Rabbi conceding – perhaps unwittingly – that Palestinian resistance to Jewish immigration was moral *before* Hitler opened the gas chambers? Was it moral then because Jews were entering Palestine under a Zionist plan – first conceived in 1897 and ratified by Britain in 1917 – whose goal was to create a Jewish state that would dispossess the Palestinians. This organized Jewish immigration amounted to a Jewish invasion that would necessarily lead to the displacement and dispossession of Palestinians.

Should the Palestinians have ceased their resistance because Nazi persecution of Jews in Europe – by accelerating Jewish immigration into Palestine – was bringing their own demise nearer, and making it more certain? Did the Zionists at this time start a dialogue with the Palestinians, explaining to them that the Jews escaping Nazi persecution would enter only as refugees, seeking temporary shelter in Palestine before they could be relocated to countries where they would be welcome? Indeed, Nazi persecution became the perverse – if unintended – engine for completing the Zionist project. Should it then have mattered to the Palestinians that the Jewish immigrants who would accelerate their dispossession were fleeing persecution?

There is another flaw in the Rabbi's train of thought. He assumes that Palestine was the only destination for Jewish refugees escaping Nazi persecution. On the face of it, it sounds implausible that none of the Allied countries (or their vast colonies), whose war effort could have been greatly aided by the influx of Jewish skills, expertise and capital, would have offered refuge, permanent or temporary, to the Jews fleeing Nazi Europe.

In support of this assumption, the Zionists point to the resistance to Jewish immigration in the United States. But this will not wash. One has to ask if the world Jewish hierarchy, by now fully committed to the creation of Israel, had a real interest in exerting its power to overcome American opposition to Jewish immigration. If the Jewish lobbies in the United States could offset the State Department's opposition to the creation of Israel, were they not capable of overcoming the Administration's resistance to Jewish immigration. Moreover, the United States was not the only feasible destination for Jewish refugees.

Rabbi Lerner's difficulties have their source in the deep contradictions of Zionism. This was a nationalist project unlike any other because the people – European Jews – it defined as a nation did not possess the territorial attributes of a nation; they did not constitute a majority in any of the territories that they inhabited. In fact, they were everywhere a small minority. It was imperative for this nationalist project, therefore, to acquire a territory where it could exercise the collective rights of nationhood, viz. sovereignty and statehood.

The founders of the Zionist project knew instinctively that it would be impractical – indeed suicidal – to try to acquire territory for a Jewish state within Europe. Instead, they decided that they would harness the support of European powers to create the territorial basis of their state *outside* of Europe. Britain was the first great power to sponsor the Zionist project.

Palestine offered the ideal location. Its historical value – as the site of the ancient Jewish state and the land promised by Yahweh to the Hebrews – would be useful in mobilizing Jewish support for the Zionist project. Since it was not yet a European colony, it would be easier to persuade a European power to help create a Jewish state in Palestine, serving as a "rampart of Europe against Asia, an outpost of civilization against barbarism."[3] Palestine contained Christian holy lands too, and this was another incentive for Europeans to take it away from the Muslims and give it to the Jews, a Biblical people. Finally, the project would realize the anti-Semite's dream of cleansing Christian Europe of its Jewish population.

Inevitably, since its inception, the Zionist project had two defining features. It was an imperialist project – a form of surrogate imperialism – since Britain, the leading imperialist power, would acquire Palestine in fulfillment

---

3 Theodore Herzl, *The Jewish state* (1896): www.geocities.com/Vienna/6640 /zion/ judenstaadt.html.

of a deal with an influential segment of the Jewish bourgeoisie. Necessarily, it was also a colonial-settler project, since it sought to create a state *of* European Jews *on* Palestinian land. This would entail, in some combination, the displacement and marginalization of the Palestinians.

These are the "wrongs" that the Zionists regard as right, as legitimate, as moral, as necessary for Jewish survival, for Jewish power. Rabbi Lerner is a committed Zionist. He makes no bones about that. Though an American himself, he informs us – without comment – that his son had served with the Israeli Occupation Army in the West Bank.[4] As a Zionist, the Rabbi accuses the Palestinians – and Edward Said – for not acknowledging the wrongs done to them as right, as moral, as necessary.

Of course, Rabbi Lerner has more heart than most Zionists. He concedes that the Palestinians too have "rights" to Palestine, the same as the Jews. He concedes this *because* you cannot be a pro-Israeli without conceding these rights: because there can be no prospect of Jewish security without mollifying the Palestinians. The "equal" rights he grants the Palestinians, however, only allows them a "state" on 22 percent of historic Palestine. He does not contemplate any Palestinian right of return. No "equality" there.

The creation of Israel was a power play. It was born out of the contradictions of the history of European Jews, a contradiction that would be resolved by the confluence of Jewish influence and Western imperial power, combining to serve the interests of both. The cost of this project to Palestinians, to Arabs, to Muslims, was not even an issue in an era dominated by Western racism and bigotry – of the Christian, Jewish and secular variety.

As the contradictions of the Zionist project deepen, forcing it to draw the United States directly into the conflict, that same racism and bigotry are being mobilized in the West, and especially the United States, to support another assault on the rights of the Palestinians, Arabs and Muslims. Slowly, reflexively, a segment of the Muslim population, a small segment still I believe, is being energized to take back their lands, their dignity and rights, their place under the sun. Some of them are even imitating the bloody-mindedness of their foes.

---

4   Rabbi Michael Lerner, "It's time to atone when we see only our own pain," *Los Angeles Times*, October 13, 2000.

Is this the clash of civilizations between the West and the Islamicate world predicted by Samuel Huntington? Was this conflict inevitable given the confluence of four factors: the dependency of US economy on Middle Eastern oil; the insertion of Israel in the Arab heartland; the advanced Israelization of the United States, a consequence of the Zionist project; and an Islamicate world, a large segment of the Periphery, beaten in the nineteenth century, divided, humiliated, expropriated, now reaching a quarter of the world's population, and struggling to regain its rights, its autonomy, its dignity, its splintered wholeness?

Are Islamicate societies seeking to reconstitute their life on the primordial foundations – lost in the stress of modernization – of a perennial encounter "between God as such and man as such," between the transcendent, creative principle of the universe and a theomorphic man endowed with intellect, free will and speech?[5] Alternatively, are these societies today what their adversaries say they are – raging over their loss of power, over being left behind by the West? Did they 'fail' to modernize because of flaws in the 'deep structure' of their culture; and are they now seeking, out of spite, to destroy the leader of the modern, democratic and powerful West?

We cannot tell where this contest – at bottom, an economic contest – will take us. It may end quickly, producing a 'thousand years' of US-Israeli hegemony over the Islamicate world; or it may lead to the decline of American power in that region. If it is the latter, it may restore a balance between the West and Islamdom, an equilibrium shattered in the nineteenth century. However, these options are simplistic. History may hold surprises, as it often does, especially for those who think they have the power to make things happen according to well-laid plans. The unintended consequences have a habit of making *things* a bit messier. The two American victories – over Nazis and the Soviets – do not translate into an ineluctable law of invincibility. The Islamicate peoples are not defending outmoded systems or some unnatural tyranny. They are defending something more basic: their lives, their livelihood and the way they want to live.

---

5 Frithjof Schuon, *Understanding Islam* (Bloomington, IN: World Wisdom Books, 1994): 1.

CHAPTER FOURTEEN

On Being Good Victims

"Captain Gordon Pim stated in his speech that it was a philanthropic principle to kill natives; there was, he said, "mercy in a massacre."
—Sven Lindqvist, Exterminate the Brutes (1996)

August 2005

At last Mr. Elie Wiesel has spoken of the 'dispossessed' in Palestine. It is appropriate that he should do so; that is what the world has long come to expect of him. A Holocaust survivor and Peace Laureate, Mr. Wiesel has dedicated his life to preventing another holocaust, acting on the conviction that "...to remain silent and indifferent is the greatest sin of all..."[1]

And so Mr. Wiesel speaks of the grief of dispossession in words that convey his deep empathy for the victims. In a NYT column of August 21, 2005, he writes about the "heart-rending" images of dispossession. "Some of them are unbearable. Angry men, crying women. Children led away on foot ...." The victims are "obliged to uproot themselves, to take their holy and precious belongings, their memories and their prayers, their dreams and their dead, to go off in search of a bed to sleep in, a table to eat on, a new home, a future among strangers."

Some of you may be surprised at Mr. Wiesel's grief for the victims *in* Palestine. It appears uncharacteristic. Now, no one would accuse Mr. Wiesel of reserving his humanitarian work only for Jews. Indeed, according to his own testimony, he is not only a "devoted supporter of Israel," he has "also defended the cause of Soviet Jews, Nicaragua's Miskito

---

1   Marie Arana, "Elie Wiesel: A Debt to Memory," *Washington Post* (August 14, 2005): BW10.

Indians, Argentina's Desaparecidos, Cambodian refugees, the Kurds, victims of famine and genocide in Africa, of apartheid in South Africa, and victims of war in the former Yugoslavia."[2] In Mr. Wiesel's world, however, the Palestinians do not qualify as victims.

Rightly, Mr. Wiesel accuses the world of indifference – and silence – as the Nazis worked to exterminate the Jews. Yet, he too has chosen – and as a matter of principle – to maintain a deafening silence about the suffering of Palestinians. This is how he enunciated this principle many years ago: "I support Israel – period. I identify with Israel – period. I never attack, I never criticize Israel when I am not in Israel."[3] Those words suggest that the commitment to Israel is visceral; he believes in a strictly monogamous relationship.

It is not only that Mr. Wiesel will not criticize Israel when he is not in Israel. Israel can never do anything that could merit his criticism. "Israel didn't do anything except it reacted…. Whatever Israel has done is the only thing that Israel could have done … I don't think Israel is violating the human rights charter…. War has its own rules."[4] Israel is not only above criticism: it has always been the victim of Arab and Palestinian wars. Israel is utterly innocent.

Sadly, there is no surprise in Mr. Wiesel's column; nothing to celebrate here. Mr. Wiesel has not renounced his high principle. The 'dispossessed' people in his column are not Palestinians: they are the illegal Jewish settlers in Gaza. Instead of commiserating with the Palestinians, Mr. Wiesel is engaging in a new game of blaming the victims – and calling attention to a new form of Jewish victimization. Implicitly, this is his message: 'There never was any ethnic cleansing of Palestinians – in 1948, 1967 or later. All this is a lie, an anti-Semitic slur. But look at what is real. It's happening right before your eyes: the ethnic cleansing of Jews in Palestine. You can see it everywhere, on *Fox*, CNN, CBS, the *Washington Post* and the NYT.'

This is merely the latest, most ingenious move in the splendid Zionist strategy to paint Israel and Israelis as victims. Israelis never dispossessed anyone. But Israelis are being 'dispossessed' today in their promised land, in

---

2   *Elie Wiesel* (Elie Wiesel Foundation for Humanity). <www.elieweselfoundation.org/ElieWiesel/index.html>
3   Noam Chomsky, *The Fateful Triangle: The United States, Israel & The Palestinians* (Boston, MA: South End Press, 1983): 16.
4   Norman G. Finkelstein, *An introduction to the Israel-Palestine conflict.* <www.normanfinkelstein.com/article.php?pg-4& ar-10>

their own country. How tragic: they are the only Jews to be ever dispossessed by their own army. If there were ever any misgivings about Israeli intentions towards Palestinians: the expulsion of Jews from Gaza should dispel them. Look, the Israeli government will even dispossess Israeli Jews to accommodate Palestinians.

In this new role as the 'dispossessed,' the Israelis have new opportunities too for blaming the real victims – the Palestinians. What is the Palestinian crime now? Faced with "the tears and suffering of the [Israeli] evacuees," the Palestinians have chosen *not* to "silence their joy and pride ..." Instead, they have organized "military parades with masked fighters, machine guns in hand, shooting in the air as though celebrating a great battlefield victory." Mr. Wiesel is telling the Palestinians that they cannot enjoy even their hard-won little victories – for which they have paid over the last eighty years in blood and tears.

The logic by which the Zionists have blamed the Palestinians is quite extraordinary. They demand that the victim must empathize with his tormentor; he must understand his tormentor's grief, the grief that drives him to torment his victims, and the terrible grief he feels even as he torments his victims. In other words, the victims of Israel must show saintliness that is even beyond saints. If the Palestinian hates his tormentors, he is anti-Semitic. If he resists his tormentor, he is a terrorist. If he celebrates his little victories, he is insensitive.

This is the language of racial superiority – the doctrine that believes in a hierarchy of races, where the higher races have rights and inferior races are destined for extinction or a marginal existence under the tutelage of higher races. Under the Zionist doctrine, the Jews are a higher race. According to some versions this superiority is divinely ordained: God made his covenant with Israelites not with the Ishmaelites. This superiority is also empirically established: the Zionists wanted to take Palestine from the Palestinians – and they made it a fact.

The Israelis are not only superior in their strength. They are superior in their magnanimity. The Palestinians still live: don't they? Isn't this proof of Israeli magnanimity. The Israelis merely pushed the Palestinians out of their lands; they did not incinerate them in ovens. They blow up their houses, but generally give them time to get out of the way. Aren't the Israelis incomparably kinder than the Nazis?

Let the Palestinians celebrate their extraordinary luck: they were *not* expropriated by the Germans or Anglo-Saxons. The Herero in Southwest Africa, the natives in the United States, or the Tasmanians were not half as lucky. 'Give up your futile terrorism,' the Zionists tell the Palestinians. 'Take the Bantustans we have created for you: and be grateful. We have both power and money: we can reward your gratitude. If you behave we might even give you a few passes for day jobs in Israel. You could make a good living scrubbing floors and washing toilets.'

The Zionists are incensed when the Palestinians reject this 'generous offer.' 'This is not in our script,' they scream. The outrage is understandable. They don't expect such insolence from inferiors. The Zionists find it hard to understand *how* any people could reject their claim to Palestine. But that is what the Palestinians have chosen to do – what any other people in their condition would have done. It is this humanity of the Palestinians, ordinary yet incontrovertible, that is so galling to those raised in the logic of Zionism.

As the Zionist project has unfolded through wars, through ethnic cleansing, through expropriation, through an occupation that has involved one society – in its entirety – in the relentless destruction of another people, how many Zionists can assert in sincerity – despite the military successes of their project – that their humanity is still intact, that Israelis today are better exemplars of the highest values of Jewish traditions than the generations of Jews who preceded them?

Israel has fashioned itself into a society whose primary vocation is to devise new stratagems, produce new lies, invent new traps, and build new walls to imprison another people who by their will to resist continue to challenge and frustrate their plans to expropriate them. The Palestinians have stretched thin the ability of Israelis to retain their humanity in their role as occupiers. Those who have made it their life-long vocation to defend *all* Israeli atrocities suffer a similar loss in their humanity. I suppose Mr. Elie Wiesel knows this all too well in the inner sanctums of his conscience. Or is he so far advanced in this malady that he has become blinded to his own affliction?

CHAPTER FIFTEEN

Voiding the Palestinians: An Allegory

"Palestine belongs to the Arabs in the same sense that England belongs to the English or France to the French."
—Gandhi[1]

"Palestine will be as Jewish as England is English."
—Chaim Weizman[2]

July 2004

On October 29, 2003, a leading Israeli daily, *Ha'aretz*, reported a rape-murder that occurred more than fifty years ago at Nirim, an Israeli military outpost in the Negev. The victim was a Palestinian girl, in her early or mid-teens, or younger; the perpetrators of this crime were members of the 'Israeli Defense Force.'[3] Six days later, *The Guardian* also reported this crime, but US papers did not think this was news that is fit for print.[4] In the United States, the media prefers to shield Israel from adverse notice.

What is the significance of a single rape-murder in the long and tortuous history of the dispossession of one people by another? No dispossession ever makes a pretty picture. Moreover, the dispossession of Palestinians is no ordinary dispossession. It is not ordinary because it involved the complete *voiding* of one people by another: Palestine had

1 Mohandas K. Gandhi, *Harijan*, 74, November 20, 1938: 239-242.
2 Chaim Weizmann, *Trial and Error* (Greenwood: 1921/1972).
3 Aviv Lavie and Moshe Gorali, "I saw fit to remove her from the world," *Ha'aretz*, October 29, 2003: http://www.haaretz.com/hasen/spages/ 355227.html
4 Chris McGreal, "Israel learns of a hidden shame in its early years," *The Guardian*, November 4, 2003: http://www.guardian.co.uk/israel/Story/ 0,2763,1077148,00.html

to be emptied of its ancient Palestinian population to make room for Jews. It is not ordinary because much of this emptying was telescoped within a few short months (in 1948) rather than over centuries or decades. It was not ordinary because the people doing the voiding had themselves been voided from their spaces in Europe, a people with brilliant accomplishments, voided from the spaces they had helped to enrich. It is not ordinary because the voiding, the violence it demanded, had been carefully planned, orchestrated, justified, explained, excused, and, after it's success, celebrated and glorified in Israeli and Western media.

What is the significance of a single rape-murder – I ask again – in the voiding of Palestine implemented through the deceit of declarations and the mockery of mandates; through repeated wars and grinding repressions; through the backing of great powers and support of the world's organized Jewry; through ethnic cleansings, orchestrated massacres and obliterated villages; through bombings of cinder block apartments, hospitals, schools and workshops; through armed settlements built on hilltops; through house demolitions, curfews, sieges, trenches, and bypass roads dividing communities; through countless daily humiliations at a hundred checkpoints; and now through a gargantuan wall, coiling, advancing, ominous, that dreams of squeezing the last drop of blood from beleaguered Palestinian communities in the West Bank?

Perhaps this single rape-murder *is* significant. The voiding of a people necessarily involves suffering on a monumental scale. The Zionists built their Jewish state by destroying the lives of millions of Palestinians over three generations. The scale of this suffering has been documented in reports of human rights organizations, in statistics of villages destroyed, houses demolished, and men, women and children evicted from their homes, robbed, incarcerated, bombed, shot at, tortured, killed. However, statistics do not tell stories; they will not grip the reader with the pain of the victims. As the Holocaust reveals its hellish intent in images and artifacts, so the narrative of Palestinian voiding must be conveyed in images, metaphors and allegories, each of which contains in miniature, in essence, the great pain that the Palestinians have endured for more than eighty years.

We must read the Ha'aretz disclosure of the rape-murder in the Negev as an allegory of the fate decreed by the god-like Zionists for an inferior Arab population. Read with understanding, the report reveals the darkness at the heart of the Zionist project, its racism, its moral obtuseness, its blindness to the irony of the grave injustice the Zionists intended to do to the Palestinians. The rape-murder of a nameless Palestinian girl – most likely a minor – by IDF soldiers graphically conveys the unequal contest between the Zionists and Palestinians, as the Zionists sought to void the Palestinians so that they could resurrect a Jewish state that had been dead for some eighteen hundred years.

The only written record of the rape-murder, before the Ha'aretz report, is to be found in the diary of David Ben-Gurion, the first prime minister of Israel. He made a terse but telling entry about this episode. "It was decided and carried out: they washed her, cut her hair, raped her and killed her."[5] Ben-Gurion could be describing a military operation, efficiently completed, according to plan, without hesitation, and without any loss of time. His verbs are active verbs: they speak of strong men, determined men, confident of their power to decide, to execute, to wash, to cut, rape and kill. The decisiveness, the finality of their actions is awe-inspiring.

On the morning of August 12, 1949, the Platoon Commander at the Nirim outpost in the Negev, Second Lieutenant Moshe, organized a patrol with six soldiers. During their patrol, they shot and killed a Palestinian *after* he threw down his rifle and was running away. Later, they captured two unarmed Arab men with a girl. The men were driven away with shots fired over their heads, but the girl was taken back to the outpost at Nirim. The patrol had *decided* that she was "fuckable." On their way back to the outpost, the patrol shot and killed six camels, leaving them to rot.

At the outpost, while Moshe was away on another patrol, the Platoon Sergeant, Michael prepared the girl for rape. He removed her traditional garments, forced her to stand under a water pipe, and washed her with his own hands, while everyone watched. The washing done, he dressed her in a jersey and shorts, and took her back to a hut where he raped her. When the girl complained to Moshe about the rape, he ordered his men to wash her – again – "so that she would be clean for fucking." The soldiers cut the girl's hair, washed her head with kerosene, placed her under the water pipe, and sent her back to the hut in jersey and shorts. She was now clean.

---

5   Lavie and Gorali, "I saw fit to remove her from the world."

Later the same day, the soldiers at the Nirim outpost gathered in a large tent for the festivities of Sabbath eve. The Platoon Commander, Moshe, inaugurated the Sabbath by blessing the wine, a soldier read from the Bible, after which there was singing, eating, drinking, jokes and fun. Before the party ended, Moshe asked his men to decide the Palestinian captive's fate with a vote. They had two options: the captive could work in the kitchen; or they could have her. In the Middle East's only democracy, the girl's fate had to be decided *democratically*. The soldiers chanted, "We want a fuck." Commander Moshe *carried* out the will of the majority. He and his sergeant went in first, leaving the girl unconscious.

The next morning, when the Palestinian girl protested, the Platoon Commander threatened to kill her. And, indeed, later, he ordered Sergeant Michael to execute the girl. They stripped her before execution; a soldier wanted his shorts back. The Sergeant, accompanied by a medic and two soldiers, took the girl out in the desert and shot her in the head as she ran. Overcome by pity, just in case she was alive and in pain, a soldier pumped a few more bullets into the girl's body. Washed clean, her hair cut, raped repeatedly, the Palestinian captive now lay dead in a shallow grave.

Second Lieutenant Moshe drove down to Be'er Sheva later that same evening to watch a movie. At the theatre, he met his Battalion Commander, Major Yehuda Drexler, who had ordered that the Palestinian captive be taken back to where she had been found. When the Major asked his subordinate if he had done so, Moshe replied: "They killed her, it was a shame to waste the gas." A Palestinian's life is not worth a gallon or half of gas.

When Captain Uri, the Company Commander, asked Second Lieutenant Moshe to explain what had happened to the Palestinian girl, this is what he wrote in his report:

> "In my patrol on 12.8.49 I encountered Arabs in the territory under my command, one of them armed. I killed the armed Arab on the spot and took his weapon. I took the Arab female captive. On the first night the soldiers abused her and the next day I *saw fit to remove her from the world* (emphasis added)."

That was all. It was dismissive in its terseness, as if to say it would be a waste of our time discussing the rape-murder of a Palestinian. However, if you insist on a report, here it is: We found an Arab girl, raped her, and "I saw fit to remove her from the world."

It is that last phrase that is so haunting, imperial, Biblical, even divine. It sums up the ethos of a whole age, an imperial age that took pride in its superior race and its civilizing mission. An age in which various Europeans nations "saw fit" to conquer, colonize, enslave, exterminate, displace, 'liberate' or 'educate' the rest of humanity, anyone different from them in color or religion. No matter what injury the Europeans inflicted on the natives, it had to be good for them. Nothing but goodness could flow from such superior beings. Zionism and its fruit, Israel, are but late flowerings of that Imperial age.

At the trial for this rape-murder, which was held in secret the same year, Second Lieutenant Moshe denied raping the girl. "Morally speaking," he argued, "it was impossible to sleep with such a dirty girl." Most likely, he knew that this was an argument that would carry weight. It is a basic premise of the civilizing mission. "The native is always dirty, his clothes filthy, his manners crude." There is an added twist here. "It isn't raping an Arab girl that would have been immoral, but that she was dirty." The Court acquitted Moshe of rape, though he received a sentence of 15 years for murder.

Moshe offered a second defense. He told the Court repeatedly that Captain Uri, one of the Company Commanders in the battalion, had told him in private that when it came to the Arabs, he should engage in "killing, slaughter." The Court rejected this charge with its own psychoanalysis. The Judges wrote: "The court believes that the words "killing, slaughter" originate in a psychosis that seems to have taken root in the officer's blood, to the effect that Arabs were to be massacred indiscriminately." The Court chose not to cross-examine Captain Uri on this point.

Sergeant Michael pleaded that he was merely following orders when he executed the girl. The judges rejected his plea, but passed a "very light" sentence of five years in prison because of extenuating circumstances. "At the time there was a *general feeling of contempt for the life of Arabs in general* and infiltrators in particular, and sometimes wanton events occurred in this sphere. All this helped to create an atmosphere of 'anything goes.' We are *convinced* that this atmosphere existed at the Nirim outpost too (emphases added)." The judges at the Nuremberg trial too could have urged the same extenuating circumstance when passing sentences on Nazi criminals. After all, the Nazis too operated in a general climate of deep hatred against Jews, a hatred that had been bred for close to two thousand years. Thankfully, the judges at Nuremberg did not use this argument.

In addition, when Moshe accused Captain Uri of urging "killing, slaughter" against Arabs, the judges dismissed this is as the invention of a psychotic mind. Yet, in arguing for a reduced sentence, they use the argument that there existed at the time "a general feeling of contempt for the life of Arabs in general." Were the judges at the murder-rape trial of the Palestinian girl schizophrenic? Or, were they only protecting their own kind?

Those who are familiar with the tragedy of Palestinian dispossession will have read – as I have – in the events of August 12 and 13, 1949, at the Nirim military outpost in the Negev, an allegory of that dispossession. In two days, this nameless girl, a minor, was made to suffer the degradation, shame, abuse, rape and, eventually, death, which has been the fate – figuratively, and, in many cases, literally – of the Palestinians and their homeland for more than eighty years. We observe several striking parallels between the two gory narratives. We see it in the girl's capture by a platoon of soldiers; in the Commander's decision to decide her fate by a vote; in the question about the girl's fate that is put to vote (use her as a slave worker or sex slave); in stripping the girl of her traditional garments, washing her, cutting her hair; raping her, the officers going in first; in the order for her execution when she protests; in the secret trial held; in the officer's language ("I saw fit …"); in the acquittal from rape charges; in the light sentences; and in the judges' use of extenuating circumstances.

And now the parallels are being pushed towards a final convergence – in the final obliteration of the national existence of Palestinians – with the building of the strangulating wall; with levels of unemployment among Palestinians reaching 70 percent; with malnutrition among Palestinian children reaching famine levels; with the acceleration in the pace of ethnic cleansing; the unashamed American backing for the war-criminal, Ariel Sharon's extreme right-wing policies; and growing demands for a final round of ethnic cleansing to rid historical Palestine of all Palestinians. At least, that is the intent of the Neoconservatives, Christian Zionists and Israel's right-wing Likudniks. It is an intent that all right-thinking people – including right-thinking Americans and Israelis – must oppose before the American-Israeli warmongers, with their fingers on nuclear buttons, push the world over the precipice.

CHAPTER SIXTEEN

Israel Builds A Wall

Before I built a wall I'd like to know
What I was walling in or walling out.
—Robert Frost

July 2004

On July 9, 2004, fourteen of the fifteen Justices on the International Court of Justice delivered an 'advisory opinion' on Israel's apartheid barrier that accurately reflects the world's growing moral outrage over Israel's determination to push the Palestinians to the wall and beyond. Aptly – and yet, to our shame – the only contrary opinion was rendered by Justice Thomas Buergenthal, an American.

The Justices declared that the wall being built by Israel, "the occupying Power, in the Occupied Palestinian Territory, including in and around Jerusalem, and its associated régime, are contrary to international law." There is no ambiguity in the judgment of the International Court: no prevarication over the legality of the wall. The case is closed. The Israeli Wall violates international law.

The Justices told Israel that it is "under an obligation" to stop work on the wall, dismantle those portions of the wall that have been built, annul the legislative régime erected to support its construction, and render compensation for the damage it has already inflicted on the Palestinians in the Occupied Territories.

Finally, the Justices called upon the United Nations – especially the General Assembly and the Security Council – to "consider what further action is required to bring to an end the illegal situation resulting from the construction of the wall and the associated régime, taking due account of the present Advisory Opinion."

In these dark times, when American power has tied itself irrevocably – for the foreseeable future – to every Zionist aim against the Palestinians, be it ever so indefensible, the moral clarity of these judicial opinions will bring hope and encouragement to ordinary humans who do not always find it easy to sustain their struggle in the face of new oligarchies that practice their dark craft in the name of the men and women they trample upon methodically. Countering concerted pressure from the United States and its allies, the fourteen Justices, five from the European Union, have decided to apply the universal principles of justice to the actions of an Occupation that in its malicious intent, its devastating effects, its lengthening history, and its potential for fueling wars has no parallels in recent times.

Yet, as predictably as it is tragic, the Zionists in Israel and their allies in the United States – both Christians and Jews – have responded to International Court's 'advisory opinion' with tired clichés about Palestinian terrorism and Arab anti-Semitism. Once again, they are enunciating from the media perches they command that the Palestinians are terrorists and anti-Semites to boot; and the Israelis, always under threat and in peril, are their innocent victims.

In editorials and speeches ringing across Israel and America, a thousand apologists are protesting that beleaguered Israel is building a 'security fence' – not a wall – whose only purpose is to safeguard innocent Israeli civilians against the primordial violence of Palestinians. In the columns of the New York Times, of July 13 2004, a former Israeli Prime Minister, explains that this "security barrier" is "temporary," it extends into "less than 12 percent of the West Bank," and it does not kill Palestinians, it merely harms their "quality of life" while saving Israeli lives. The unsophisticate that he is, the Israeli Prime Minister of course cannot appreciate that a 'reduced' quality of life easily feeds into higher mortality. There are smarter ways of killing than in death camps with poison gases.

If the League of Nations, in the early stages of the Nazi campaign of ethnic cleansing, had had the moral courage to ask the Permanent Court of International Justice – the predecessor to the ICJ – to pass judgment on the legality of this campaign that, at this stage, included the herding of Jews into concentration camps, how might the Nazis have responded to an 'advisory opinion' that declared the herding of Jews to be in violation of international law and called the Nazis to immediately cease such actions?

The Nazis might have chosen one of several arguments in their defense. Given the overt racism of the times, they could have appealed to their historical right – as communicated by the World Spirit – to exclusive ownership of the German Deutschland; the Jewish interlopers in Germany had to be removed to make room for the original and rightful owners. Had they taken a defensive line, they might argue that the 'relocation' of Jews was a temporary measure, undertaken in the face of clear intelligence of British plans to use Jews as a fifth column in their war against Germany. Alternatively, they might claim that this was a humanitarian move, gathering Jews into districts set apart for them and where they would be free to observe the *halacha*, which they had been unable to do in the past. They were only making amends for past lapses. And, of course, they might have claimed that the Justices were ganging up against them, singling them out, driven by a new wave of anti-Germanism fomented by the British and Americans.

There is a terrible irony in the chorus of loud Zionist condemnations that have greeted the ICJ's ruling. To the eternal shame of the times, when the Jews were being herded into the concentration camps – where most of them would die – they had very little help from the Allied powers, the self-designated keepers of world conscience. The United States and Britain closed their doors to Jewish immigration. Certainly, there were no rulings from the Permanent Court on the barbarity of German plans of genocide. Bitterly, and justifiably, the Jews have accused the world of letting them die in the Nazi terror. No Courts, no governments offered effective support, material or moral.

No one came to the support of the Palestinians either, as the British awarded their country to the Zionists, as the British after occupying Palestine allowed European Jews to settle the country, form militias, and prepare to drive out the Palestinians. No Western publics raised a voice when 800,000 Palestinians were terrorized into fleeing their homes in 1948 and stripped of their right to return. No Western publics supported the Palestinians when they began to resist the Israeli occupation of West Bank and Gaza. Instead, taking the cue from Israel, the Western powers branded the Palestinians as terrorists, and refused to recognize their existence as a people. The moral indignation of the Western publics has only been aroused in the past decade, starting with the First Intifada, which revealed the brutal face of the Israeli Occupation, crushing, pulverizing, expropriating a mostly unarmed people.

Yet the Zionists today relentlessly accuse these Western publics of anti-Semitism, of singling them out because they are Jews. For too long, the Zionists have acted with impunity against the Palestinians, because they have succeeded in using the Holocaust to shield themselves against the censure of Western publics. That makes the Occupation a perfect crime, without any perpetrators. Better yet: the perpetrators became the primary victims of those they victimize.

However, lately, world conscience has been stirring, waking up to the insufferable conditions imposed upon Palestinians by the Israeli Occupation. World conscience is affirming itself in a hundred ways: in the Internationals who risk death to stop the demolition of Palestinian homes; in the willingness of the Belgian Court to try Ariel Sharon for war crimes; in the reminders by South Africans that this Occupation is worse than the Apartheid they had endured; in the academics who initiated a movement to boycott Israeli academics; in the students protesting investments in the Israeli economy; in the world-wide marches, protests and activism against the Israeli Occupation. And now the International Court of Justice has spoken, loudly and clearly, against Israel's apartheid wall.

Indeed, increasing numbers of Israelis are speaking out – even members of their armed forces, those who have seen the ugliness of the Occupation at first hand because they were its direct enforcers. Hundreds of Israeli soldiers have refused to 'serve' in the West Bank and Gaza, risking jail sentences. Other Jewish voices are being raised, warning that Israel is losing its soul, that the Occupation is brutalizing young Israeli men and women, who then brutalize their families, their spouses, their children. Increasingly, Israeli soldiers are taking their own lives. This is not a distant colonial Occupation, thousands of miles away from the European home base, that could be held down by a handful of soldiers and hired natives. Every Israeli – indeed a large segment of world Jewry – participates in this Occupation.

Is there a danger that the world may begin to look upon Israel as the moral equivalent in our own times of Nazi Germany? This 'moral equivalence in our times' does not require that Israel duplicate *all* the crimes of Nazi Germany. Instead, the world will be asking if, relative to the morality and the constraints of *our* times, Israel has gone as far as Nazi Germany did in more barbarous times, when the extermination of 'inferior races' was regarded as the right of White Europeans.

It would appear that as Israel builds the apartheid barrier whose intent is to wall the Palestinians in, sealing them inside a few miserable Bantustans, it is simultaneously building another wall, invisible but no less solid in construction, that is walling Israel out, disconnecting it from the human community, its laws, its hopes and its sympathies. Increasingly, in the years ahead, the world will be asking this question unless the Israelis demonstrate conclusively that they are ending the long night of their occupation over the West Bank and Gaza.

SECTION THREE

THE WAR AGAINST

Global

Terrorism

CHAPTER SEVENTEEN

A History of September 11

"Lo! The noblest of you in the sight of Allah, is the best in conduct."
—Qur'an: 49:13

November 2001[1]

Occasionally, a student at Northeastern University, troubled by my analysis of US foreign policy, will challenge me with the question, 'Why are you here if you don't like the United States?'

I answer that this is the most rational thing to do. I came to the United States only after I had tried living in several countries on four different continents. I was born in Palestine, but the Zionists took over that country in 1948, and the Haganah expelled my family from our ancestral village in Galilee. We moved to Korea, but the Americans soon followed us there with a devastating war to defend their 'freedom.' My next destination was democratic Iran, but a CIA-inspired military coup overthrew its government in 1953. I left the medieval city of Isfahan when the coup plotters restored the Shah to the Peacock Throne. One after another, I tried living in Congo, Chile, Nicaragua and Guatemala, but each time the CIA destabilized these countries. In 1988, after many misadventures, I finally understood that there is only one country the CIA was not very likely to destabilize: the United States. That is when I moved to Massachusetts.

I wish to present for your consideration two verses from the Qur'an; they will explain my *locus standi* as a social scientist. (I am assuming that this is still permissible; the President has told us repeatedly that the US is not at war against Islam, only against Islamic terrorists.)

---

1   This essay started as a talk delivered at a symposium on September 11 at Northeastern University.

> *O Mankind! Be careful of your duty to your Lord Who created you from a single soul and from it created its mate and from them twain spread abroad a multitude of men and women.* (4:1)
>
> *O mankind! Lo! We have created you male and female, and have made you nations and tribes that you may know one another.* (49:13)

Mark the words. God speaks to humankind: not to the Israelites, not to the Arabs, not to whites or blacks, but to all of humanity. Mark the words. God speaks to men *and* women. Mark the words. God reminds us that we carry the same genes *because* we have the same parents. Mark again the words. God says: Your differences are a blessing: they provide you with opportunities for getting to know each other, to learn from each other, and to compete with each other in doing good works.

Twelve hundred years later, we come across a human document, *The Declaration of Independence*, which proclaims the "self-evident" truth that "all Men are created equal, that they are endowed by their Creator with certain inalienable Rights, that among these are Life, Liberty and the Pursuit of Happiness." It is time to ask again, before the anger of September 11 consumes us, if we have upheld this "self-evident truth" in this great country, especially in our dealings with Africa, Latin America and Asia.

I will avoid the temptation to explore the meaning of September 11 in the language of tribalism, in terms of *them* and *us*. In these critical times, we should try harder than ever not to privilege any country, race or people. It is also vital that we locate these attacks in time, in the matrix of historical time, and not view them through the prism of selected images that are being played up *ad nauseum* on our television screens. Only by acquiring a historical understanding of September 11, we can hope to avoid the fatuous reasoning that says, "We were attacked because *we* are so good; and they hate us because *they* are so evil."

Our world was created in two great waves of European expansion that had the effect of producing a global capitalist system centered in Western Europe and the United States. Starting in 1492, the first wave of expansion broke against the shores of the Americas, and very quickly led to the extermination of much of its indigenous population. In order to create an export economy in the Americas, soon Africa was integrated into this emerging

Atlantic economy as a source of cheap labor: this labor entered the Americas as slaves. Around 1800, the Industrial Revolution spurred the second wave of expansion, which was directed against all peoples of color and, before the end of the nineteenth century, it had led to the colonization of nearly all of Africa and Asia. Core capital penetrated these two continents in order to degrade and restructure their economies to produce cheap primary goods for export to the Core countries.

This global capitalist system followed a powerful logic. It deepened the economic and social inequalities between rich and poor societies, between the Core and the Periphery. The Core capitalists, based in the most advanced capitalist countries, used their economic power, financial leverage and military might to extend and dominate their foreign markets. Often, this persuaded the Core countries to gain political control over these markets. This system of domination ensured that capital, technology, and manufactures would be concentrated in the Core countries, while the Periphery combined its cheap labor with land to produce primary exports.

This global system of inequalities is not stable. Karl Marx thought that it is unstable because of a conflict at the heart of capitalism, between the capitalists – the propertied classes – and the dispossessed workers. He maintained that the workers in the Core countries are a revolutionary force, and they would eventually overthrow the system, expropriate the capitalists, and create a socialist society. This did not happen. At its core, the capitalist system turned out to be more dynamic and flexible than Marx had predicted. The Core countries used the rapid growth in their productivity to co-opt the workers: they raised their wages and elevated them into the ranks of the middle classes. With the gradual acquisition of political rights, the workers chose to use political means to improve their bargaining power and living conditions *within* the capitalist system. Thus capitalism managed to contain the class conflict in the Core countries.

However, the global system produced two additional contradictions not foreseen by Karl Marx that would prove to be more destabilizing. The Core countries – and occasionally would-be Core countries – competed with each other to acquire *exclusive* control over markets and resources in the Periphery. In addition, the marginalized capitalist and professional classes in the Periphery were gradually mobilizing under nationalist and socialist ideologies to end foreign control over their lives. The first contradiction pre-cipitated two World Wars, in the first half of the twentieth century, between two sets of countries at the Core. In turn, the first World War precipitated the Russian Revolution, the first massive challenge from the Periphery to the dominance of the global capitalist system. The two World Wars, cumu-latively, also weakened all the core countries in Western Europe, several of whom had colonial possessions in Africa and Asia. Taken together, the two World Wars and the Russian Revolution, prepared the conditions for the lib-eration movements in the colonies to press harder against their now weak colonial rulers. This produced a rapid dismantling of the colonial empires starting in the late 1940s.

The weakening of Europe and Japan, the emergence of the Soviet Union as a great power, the dismantling of empires, and the Cold War: these events converged in the late 1940s to create a window of opportunity for the coun-tries at the Periphery. The centralization of political power in the Core coun-tries – a process that had been going on for the previous two centuries – would now be reversed for a change. Much of the Periphery would gain various degrees of power to make important decisions regarding the struc-ture of their economies. China and India, for different reasons, were among the leading beneficiaries of this tendency; they emerged as unified coun-tries under nationalist governments that were committed to autonomous development. The Arabs and Africans were not so lucky. Their lands had been vivisected by the imperialist powers; they gained independence as fragmented entities, still dominated by Britain, France and, increasingly, the United States. In addition, the great powers inserted a new contradiction – Israel, a Jewish colonial-settler state – in the heart of the Arab world.

This window of opportunity did not last very long. With help from the United States, the core economies of Japan and Europe quickly recovered from the devastation of World War II to enter into a period of unprecedented growth. Slowly capital from the leading core countries began to re-establish their positions of dominance in much of the Periphery. More ominously, the planned economies in the Soviet Union and Eastern Europe failed to sustain their earlier promise of rapid growth. As they kept falling behind the core capitalist countries, their communist leadership lost faith in their own system. As a result, the collapse of communism in the early 1990s was sudden and catastrophic. The path was now clear for the Core countries to regain their unchallenged dominance in the global economy. And that is what they did with a vengeance.

Instead of their old rivalries, the Core countries now presented a united front to the Periphery, with the United States in the driver's seat. During the Cold War, the Core countries had sought to manage their interests in the Periphery jointly through two key multilateral institutions, The World Bank and the IMF. In the 1990s, they strengthened the role of these two institutions and added a third, the World Trade Organization (WTO), to impose their neoliberal rules on global trade and property rights. Quickly, these three institutions assumed the functions of a quasi-world government – an international bureaucracy backed by the Core countries – defining and policing the new global economic regime. Increasingly, during the 1990s, this global triad opened up the markets of the former East Bloc and Third World countries for domination by multinational corporations from the Core countries. Core capital now occupied an eminence in the global economy it had never experienced before. Once again, power had been centralized.

The reversal in the fortunes of much of the Periphery was dramatic. Their ruling classes were fully co-opted: they now joined the World Bank and IMF in advocating and implementing neoliberal policies in their economies. In Latin America and the Arab/Islamicate countries, they waged open warfare against their own peoples. These contradictions are deepest in the Arab world, which labors under a four-fold burden. It is subjugated because it is a part of the Periphery; it is subjugated for its oil; it is subjugated in order to facilitate Israeli expansionism; and it is subjugated because of the West's atavistic fear of Islam. Western triumphalists declared that this was a perfect world. Their leading representative, Francis Fukuyama, concluded that history had ended: it had arrived at its final destination. The West had finally created a world that "is completely satisfying to human beings in their most essential characteristics." This triumphalism would be short-lived since it was based on a rather naïve reading of history. Shortly, the triumph of Core capital produced successive waves of economic dislocations in Latin America, Africa, and East and Southeast Asia. But it would face more serious challenges from the disenfranchised populations in the Middle East.

The attacks of September 11 are a reminder that history has no terminus. In the 1990s, the contradictions of history have deepened, forcing long-simmering conflicts to the surface. The tectonic plates of the global system are rubbing harder against each other. We are witnessing the first eruptions of conflicts – between the Core and the Periphery and within these two segments of the global economy – that have so far been papered over by a media and academia servile to the interests of corporate capital. Once again, we live in a world whose rules have been restructured to the advantage of the richest, both globally and within each country. However, globalization and global poverty do not mix well. A growing cabal of billionaires, more visible and more united that before, now confronts growing masses of starving, desperate and angry people in every quadrant of the globe.

In concluding, I wish to invite all Americans – with one of the highest proportions of college graduates anywhere in the world – to reflect on the conditions that forced them, more than two hundred years ago, to rebel against the legal and established authority of Britain, the 'mother country' of the American colonies. This is how *The Declaration of Independence* justified this rebellion:

> "… when a long Train of Abuses and Usurpation, pursuing invariably the same Object, evinces a Design to reduce them under absolute Despotism, it is their Right, it is their Duty, to throw off such Government, and to provide new Guards for their future Security. Such has been the patient Sufferance of these Colonies; and such is now the Necessity which constrains them to alter their former Systems of Government."

In all fairness, can the honorable citizens of the United States, 'the greatest country in the world,' deny the oppressed peoples of the world today the same Right, the same Duty, to follow the same line of Reasoning, and carry it to the same Conclusion – restore their Inalienable Rights? Can we grant that the Wretched of the Earth have the Right, as Americans did, to seize their own Freedom?

CHAPTER EIGHTEEN

Race and Visibility

"Surely We created man of the best stature. Then We reduced him to the lowest of the low, save those who believe and do good works, and theirs is a reward unfailing."
—Qur'an: 95: 4-6

December 2001

When I crossed the border into United States in 1988, after living in Canada for two years, I had the curious feeling that my wife, my son and I, still brown-skinned and dark-haired, had somehow become invisible.

We walked the streets of Hamilton – a small university town in Central New York – or nearby Utica and Syracuse, each of them overwhelmingly white, without attracting any unwanted attention. The motorists did not gawk at us while we waited at the curb for the walk signal. At restaurants, there were no heads turning in our direction. The shoppers and cashiers did not greet our entry into the stores with a quizzical, perplexed look, following our very steps. Even our neighbors left us alone.

I was relieved at this loss of visibility. It was a signal change from my experience in Canada recently as a professor, and several years before when I was attending graduate school in London, Ontario. The only time I felt comfortable stepping outside the campus was in the cold winter months, when bundled in jacket, hood, scarf and gloves, I became nearly indistinguishable from every one else. In summer, when I had to shed these sartorial covers, I ventured out only at night, under the cover of darkness. I had no wish to invite racial slurs from teenagers, sober or drunk, driving by in their convertibles, pickups and jeeps.

I enjoyed this invisibility even at my teaching job at Northeastern University. Yes, there was a little edginess when I first entered a class, a mild dismay, anticipating the strange accents and manners of 'another Indian professor.' For the most part, I managed to lay these fears to rest, and week after week, my students would concentrate on *what* I had to say, undistracted by *who* said it. However, this invisibility proved to be fragile.

When I began to depart from the scripted texts, drawing attention to the ideological intent of economics, its Eurocentric biases, and its disregard for facts, not a few of my students began to take a harder look at *me*. Over time, as I elaborated my critique, it made me more visible. My ethnicity and origins, my brown skin and dark hair, their texture and opaqueness, began to obstruct their view. I became proof of the absurdity of my critique. I felt like the black carpenter whose comments on the uxorial problems of white clergy invited a sharp rebuke from the philosophic Kant. He declared, "This fellow was quite black from head to foot … a clear proof that he was stupid."[1]

Then, all of a sudden, September 11 introduced a new dynamic. The nineteen hijackers of Arab and Muslim background, their planes crashing into the Twin Towers, had unleashed a fury that would overthrow many governments, abridge many liberties, and rearrange many lives, here at home and abroad. This first massive attack on Americans on their own soil had shaken America. They were now united – in grief, anger and indignation – against *anyone* ethnically connected to the perpetrators of this undeserved and 'unprovoked' act of violence. Almost instantly, I could sense from my little corner of the world, that this anger, volcanic and intense, would reorder the world in a hurry. Soon, this foreboding came true.

Almost as soon as I walked into the Attleboro station to catch the 6:30 AM train, I noticed a change. One by one, the heads, the eyes, the glances turned to me, as they would towards a suspect, towards a face one recognizes from a poster for the most wanted. The commuters, many of whom had taken this train with me for years, now felt uncomfortable at my presence. In their newborn sense of insecurity, they began to perceive a connection between the hijackers and me. My Pakistani ethnicity was indistinguishable from the Arab background of the nineteen hijackers. A crust of visibility began to thicken around me. I was back in Canada.

---

1 Emmanuel Eze, *Race and Enlightenment: A Reader* (Blackwell: 2000): 38.

The trajectory of America's reaction to September 11 has been unfortunate but predictable. The US administration quickly painted the world in two unmistakable colors, white and black; no shades of gray to confuse the already shaken citizenry. President George Bush had enunciated a new doctrine. "You are either with *us* or you are against us." Ergo, if you are not with us, you are black – and that makes for great visibility. This would be a global war, a Manichaean contest, between the United States, symbolizing "infinite justice" and "enduring freedom," and Osama bin Laden, with his global terrorist network, commanding the evil hordes of Islamic totalitarianism.

Instantly, the United States gave Pakistan "a second chance" to prove itself. Without losing a moment, Pakistan's military junta took up the challenge. The attack on Afghanistan was soon unfurled; the mightiest concentration of military power in human history was deployed against a war-ravaged, famine-stricken country. The smart bombs, the cluster bombs, the daisy-cutters, the bunker-busters began to descend on Afghanistan. Not a few fell on villages, hospitals, mosques and Red Cross warehouses.

The Americans opened two additional fronts. The Al-Qaida network would have to be starved of funds. They issued two lists of political parties, financial institutions, charities and individuals suspected of links to Al-Qaida, their assets frozen. More ominously, America began a descent into a Hobbesian state, where the liberties of *some* Americans and *all* aliens would be traded against the security of *other* Americans, 'real' Americans.

The attacks of September 11 led to an instant boom in racially motivated attacks against persons of Arab, Pakistani and other Islamicate ethnicities. This has produced a growing number of arrests and detentions; but when their numbers crossed 1000, the count became a state secret, unavailable to the public. The United States passed new laws and edicts allowing the FBI to tap phones and to enter into homes without notice. The government could now hold aliens, both legal and illegal, without trial for as long as a year. Military courts could try terrorist suspects in secrecy and hang them in the absence of a unanimous verdict.

I am thankful in these dangerous times to be on sabbatical, away from my students, who would be spared, at least for a while, my talk about the toy economies that falsify reality, abstract from history, and elevate the interests of particular classes and particular nations (USA, among others) to the category of the Universal Good. My sabbatical had freed me at the right time from the unpleasant task of curtailing my own speech. Cloistered in my academic cell, I could become invisible.

I did, however, in the first weeks after September 11, put up a red, white and blue flag on my office door. The inspiration for this came from my wife when she began plastering our front door, mailbox and her car with small paper flags. When a colleague commended me for my patriotism, I answered that I was only exercising my right of free speech – or what was left of it. It was a comic gesture, an ironic attempt to regain the invisibility that I had lost in the aftermath of September 11.

CHAPTER NINETEEN

A Day that Changed America?

"The best Jihad is to speak the truth before a tyrannical ruler."
—Muhammad[1]

December 2002

In the aftermath of September 11, 2001, the fear, foreboding and out-rage of many Americans was crystallized in a single phrase: it was "a day that changed America forever."

These words conveyed a tragic sense of loss, a sudden passage from innocence to grieving, a descent from security to peril, an exit from exhilaration to angst. Suddenly, Americans, given to cruising at heav-enly heights, had crash landed on terra firma; they faced terror in the heart of America. Momentarily, America had collided with the reality of a world mired in wars, poverty and disease; it had been struck by the shards of economies devastated, polities derailed, environments degraded by a rapacious globalization. In short, for one brief hour, America had glimpsed the agony endured for centuries by more than four-fifths of humanity, or what still goes by that name. It was as if, Americans had been expelled from their Eden, banished from the land of perpetual bliss.

These wounds carried a revolutionary potential. Now that September 11 had rudely shattered Americans out of their cocooned bliss, ended their disconnection from the real world, they would avidly seek to expand their knowledge about its geography, history, politics and, most importantly, its peoples. They would ask not only about *who* had

---

1 Abū Dawūd, *Sunan Abū Dawūd*, II, 438, in: Mohammad Hashim Kamali, *Freedom of Expression in Islam* (Cambridge: Islamic Text Society, 1997): 11.

183

perpetrated the horrors of September 11, but *why*? They would not rest until they had answers to two troubling questions that delve into the origins, the logic and the genesis of September 11.

The first question concerns good and evil. Why had the 'goodness' of America been repaid by the evil of September 11? Many if not most Americans believe that they are a nation of do-gooders; that their country stands at the pinnacle of human evolution; it embodies better than any nation ever has the values of freedom and justice; it is a beacon of light to all mankind, fighting foreign tyrannies, propagating democracy, and sharing its own prosperity, ideas and technology with the world's less fortunate nations. If all this is indeed true, why did September 11 happen to us? Or, could it be that *we* have been duped, that the image of American munificence was just that, an image that concealed the reality of an ugly, imperialistic power like all others before?

The second question concerns the efficacy of America's vaunted military power. Americans know that their country is the only superpower, a distinction solidly built upon unrivalled economic strength, leadership in cutting-edge technologies, and a vastly superior work force – advantages that allow the US government to gather intelligence worldwide, deploy troops worldwide, hit targets worldwide, and destroy incoming missiles before they can reach American shores. In short, they are convinced that they have the capacity to annihilate any country that dares to challenge them. However, none of this helped on September 11 when a handful of men, armed with nothing more lethal than box-cutters, attacked two venerable icons of American power, and within an hour killed some three thousand Americans, caused property damage worth tens of billions of dollars and still greater damage to the economy. Why was our government, they might well ask, spending 350 billion dollars a year on military hardware, troops, surveillance, intelligence and training if it could not stop nineteen men from "changing America forever?"

These are the questions that America's mass media might have asked after September 11 had they been free from corporate control. If the mass media had raised these questions, they would also be debated on college campuses, in churches, town halls and in the halls of the Congress. If this discourse could occur, it would slowly but surely effect a sea change in

American perceptions about how their country projects its power overseas; about the ideals abandoned in our dealings with weaker nations; about our readiness to trample freedoms abroad, sacrifice non-American lives, and devastate entire economies in order to advance the corporate interests of a few Americans. If this discourse had occurred, Americans would finally wake up to the ugly realities of America abroad and mobilize – as they had mobilized against slavery and racial discrimination before – to force their government to pursue the same ideals abroad that it honors at home. If all this had indeed come to pass, then truly we could say that America had decisively defeated the perpetrators of September 11 – by changing America and the world for the better.

However, this is not how America changed after September 11. Americans could not be allowed to ask the 'right' questions because this might lead them to the 'wrong' answers – wrong, that is, for corporate America, for America's powerful oil interests, for the military establishment, for the Zionist lobby, for racists and for religious bigots. America's outrage over September 11 would not be answered by debate, discussion and dull inquiry. It would be placated by righteous indignation, by talk of evil antagonists, by promises of vengeance, by wars without end. America's grief would be hijacked by groups whose interests, security, power and profits batten on paranoia, bigotry, racism, wars and conflicts. Almost instantly, these forces responded to September 11 by orchestrating the deafening drumbeat of war. On September 11, Osama bin Laden had dared America. America obliged – with wars against Afghans and Palestinians, to be followed in time by wars against Iraqis, Iranians, Syrians, Saudis, Egyptians, Pakistanis and others.

President George Bush and his neoconservative warmongers took the lead in all this. They had found in the tragedy of September 11 the trigger for the war plans they had been hatching since the end of the Cold War in the early 1990s. Within days, George Bush *et al* had laid out their plans for global war before the American public. Even before the hijackers had been identi-fied, they were linked to Al-Qaida, a "collection of loosely affiliated terrorist organizations." Their attacks were declared to be "an act of war against our country." This was no ordinary war, however. The Al-Qaida had launched a civilizational war; "they hate us," they are "enemies of freedom," they "hate our freedoms," they want to "disrupt and end a way of life." Al-Qaida's goal "is remaking the world—and imposing its radical beliefs on people everywhere." In other words, Al-Qaida wanted to impose their fundamentalist Islam on the United States and Europe.[2]

Wars spawn wars. So if Al-Qaida had started a war, the United States would have to respond in kind. The President declared that "the *only way* to defeat terrorism as a threat to our way of life is to stop it, eliminate it, and destroy it where it grows (emphasis added)." This global war "on terror begins with Al-Qaida, but it does not end there. It will not end until every terrorist group of global reach has been found, stopped and defeated." In time, this war will be extended to "nations that provide aid or safe haven to terrorism." In addition, this would not be a short war: it will be a "lengthy campaign, *unlike any we have ever seen* (emphasis added)." It will also be a total war, including "dramatic strikes, visible on TV, and covert operations, secret even in success." The Bush strategy was clear. Magnify the terrorist threat, fuel it, and prepare the nation for a war that would be global, total and unending.

Roma locuta est, causa finite est. President Bush had spoken, and the case was closed. All the organs of mainstream media concurred with Bush. The country was in the midst of a war, and it would tolerate nothing which carried a hint of dissent. Dissent was unpatriotic; some said it was treasonous. The Bush doctrine – you are against us if you are not with us – applied to individuals as well as states. The United States was now a country with one party, the party of Bush-Cheney-Rumsfeld-Ashcroft. Nevertheless, the survivors of the victims of September 11 stuck to their demand for an independent investigation into September 11. When their persistence became embarrassing, the President reluctantly agreed, more than a year after September 11, to appoint an Independent Commission. Yet, in choosing Henry Kissinger to chair this Commission, the President ensured that it would be ineffectual. As one commentator quipped, he had put Dracula in charge of the blood bank.

Even without Kissinger to chair it, the Independent Commission on September 11 is unlikely to deliver any surprises. Its mandate only demands that it identify the factors that *allowed* the attacks on WTC and Pentagon to

---

2   All the quotes in this and the next paragraph are from President George Bush's speech of September 21, 2001, given to a joint session of Congress: www.guardian.co.uk/ Print/0,3858,4261868,00.html

occur. The Commission will not hold any hearings in Grozny or Gaza, in Baghdad or Basra, in Kashmir or Kabul, in Cairo or Karachi, in Jakarta or Jeddah, in Caracas or Kolkata, in Nairobi or Nouakchott. The Commission will not enter into the world of the hijackers; it will not probe into their lives, their grievances; it will not ask why the hijackers took their own lives to take American lives; it will not ask why the hijackers did not deliver their message by less violent means.

Presumably, all these questions had been answered definitively by Bush *et al.* The perpetrators of September 11 were evil, who acted from ineradicable spite, from a nihilistic rage against the modern world, against all that America represents, her freedom, democracy, progress and prosperity. After these incontestable answers, there was only one thing that remained to be done. Send the stealth bombers, cruise missiles, daisy-cutters and bunker-busting nukes to exorcise these demons.

Now, more than a year after that tragic morning on September 11 when nearly three thousand Americans were consumed in an inferno that descended from the skies, after all the rubble from the Ground Zero and the Pentagon has been cleared, can we say that America has changed forever? Did America embrace the potential for change contained in that terrible moment, the potential to connect with the inverse of our own world, a world whose sufferings, whose tyrannies, whose pathologies are deeply connected to ours in ways unknown to us? Were we overwhelmed by the slow dawning of the burden we bear, as the vanguard of the human enterprise, as the champions of Christian charity, to do something – even a little bit – to enrich, empower, enlighten and embrace those left behind? If Americans had taken up this challenge, if we *could* take up this challenge, then we would have turned a corner – and *that* would be a departure from old ways of doing things.

Instead, the captains of capital, the marshals of mass media, the priests of prejudice, the zealots of Zion, have laid out plans for wars, total, global and unending to stop Americans from demanding change and to stop the rest of the world from getting the changes they deserve. As the wounds of global capitalism deepen, as the dark satanic mills of capitalist greed grind more than half of mankind deeper into poverty, as entire continents are devastated, as agro-corporations seek to chain millions of farmers to terminator seeds, as the middle classes in the rich countries slowly sink into poverty, as the consciousness of these depredations finally threatens to become global, the concentrated power of capital seized upon September 11 to divert Americans with gladiatorial combats on a global scale.

Let the drums of the news networks roll, let the combats begin, let blood be spilled daily, let entire countries be depopulated, let us convert mass extermination into a spectator sport. Let us sit back in our living rooms with Coke and Budweiser, and watch the greatest country in the world notch miraculous military victories over dictatorships that we in years past had commissioned to murder their own people. Let us take deep draughts of sweet revenge. Only death will bring life, the death of all our enemies. Only devastation will bring peace. Only by these paradoxes will America be redeemed.

CHAPTER TWENTY

Why 9-11 and Why Now?

"... no other conquering nation has ever treated savage owners of the soil with such generosity as has the United States."
—Theodore Roosevelt (1889)[1]

"All told, the North American Indian population ... which had probably numbered in excess of twelve million in the year 1500, was reduced by official estimates to barely more than 237,000 four centuries later. This vast genocide historically paralleled in its magnitude and degree only by that which occurred in the Caribbean Basin is the most sustained on record."
—Ward Churchill (1994)[2]

December 2002

If the attacks of September 11, 2001 are indeed 'unique,' without precedent in the long history of Western contacts with the 'lesser breeds', it is important that we make an effort to understand why they happened now, and what they say about our world?

The uniqueness of September 11 is not hard to establish. If we accept the officially sanctioned definition of terrorism, which restricts the term to violence directed against civilians by non-state actors, the attacks of September 11 gain a unique place in history because of their deadly human toll, some three thousand lives. On the other hand, these attacks pale into insignificance when compared to the civilian carnage perpetrated by states, not excluding the United States, over the past five hundred years.

---

1 Theodore Roosevelt, *The Winning of the West, Vol. 4* (New York: Putnam, 1889): 54.
2 Ward Churchill, *Indians Are Us* (Common Courage Press, 1994): http:// web.mit.edu/ thistle/www/v9/9.11/ 1columbus.html

A second claim to 'uniqueness' concerns the methods employed by the attackers. They had not employed guns, explosives, bombs or missiles. Instead, so we have been told, their weapons consisted of box-cutters and plastic knives. Armed with these, and their determination to die *with* their victims, the hijackers had flown civilian jets into the Twin Towers and the Pentagon. The German composer, Karlheinz Stockhausen, carried away by the power of the moment, described the self-immolation of these terrorists as "the greatest work of art ever." Later, retracting under pressure, he described the destruction as "Lucifer's greatest work of art."[3]

President Bush presented the third claim to 'uniqueness.' In his first address after September 11 to members of the Congress, he pointed out that "Americans have known wars – but for the past 136 years, they have been wars on foreign soil, except for one Sunday in 1941. Americans have known the casualties of war – but not at the center of a great city on a peaceful morning."[4] In other words, the attacks of September 11 were the first foreign assault against an American city in 136 years.

Noam Chomsky offered a different take on the uniqueness of September 11. This was a "terrible terrorist atrocity," he wrote, but it was "not unique in scale, by any means." "What's unique about it, is the victims. This is the first time in hundreds of years that what we call the West – Europe and its off-shoots – have been subjected to the kinds of atrocities that they carry out all the time in other countries and that is unique. The guns are pointed in the other direction for the first time."[5] The Indian writer and activist, Arundhati Roy, sums this up in a striking metaphor. The attacks of September 11, she wrote, "were a monstrous calling card from a world gone horribly wrong."[6]

Since 1492 the West has been on the offensive. For five hundred years now, the steel of their sword, lance, gun and bomb has been planted in the bones and flesh of Africans, Australians, Asians and Native Americans. For five hundred years, the Western powers divided the world into two unequal moieties, one planted on top of the other, one rising as the other sank,

---

3 "Attacks Called Great Art," *The New York Times*, September 19, 2001, p. E3; and Kirsty Scott, "September 11 Apology by Hirst," *The Guardian*, September 20, 2002: www. guardian.co.uk/arts/news/story/0,11711,795385,00.html.

4 "Text of George Bush's Speech," *Guardian*, September 21, 2001: www.guardian.co.uk/ Print/0,3858,4261868,00.html.

5 "Noam Chomsky: Interview by Chris Spannos," www.vcn.bc.ca/ redeye/interviews/ chomsky. html.

6 Arundhati Roy, "The Algebra of Infinite Justice," *The* Guardian, September 21, 2001: www.guardian.co.uk/ Print/0,3858,4266289,00.html.

one battening as the other sickened. For five hundred years, entire continents were devastated, societies overthrown, their civilizations denigrated,
and their peoples subjugated, herded into slavery and stranded without
dignity. All this was the product of a new dynamic that welded power and
capital, states and markets, in a cumulative process that divided the world
into a dominant Core and a dependent Periphery, giving birth to unequal
development, the inequalities growing cumulatively. Once it had been set
in motion, this process could not be overthrown.

For five hundred years, the non-Western societies retreated, vacating their
political, economic and cultural space before the surge of Western power.
It must be asserted, however, that they never retreated without a fight; they
fought against constantly increasing odds; they hid in ambush after every
defeat; they stole the weapons of their enemies; after every defeat, they plotted and mobilized for the next battle. On many occasions, they stalled the
advance of Western arms; they even won a few stunning victories. Finally,
the tide began to turn with the Russian Revolution of 1917 and the Turkish
success in repelling European invaders from the Anatolian peninsula in
1923. Slowly, the liberation movements began to gather momentum. Then,
starting in the 1940s, with the colonial empires in retreat, the Periphery
began to win back some breathing space.

Yet never in all these years could the victims attack their tormentors on their
home turf, in their fortified playgrounds, inside the lavish retreats where they
enjoyed the spoils of their conquests. Not once in all these years could the
victims carry their resistance into the citadel of their oppressors. Though
many peoples were crushed over these dim centuries, though many were
driven into extinction, though many more were sold into slavery, though
proud empires were laid waste, though ancient cultures were cast aside, not
once could the victims breach the bastions, scale the citadels of Western
power. Not once could the millions of Americans, Africans and Asians, whose
lives were trapped in fear for centuries, bring fear to the homes of their tormentors. Inside their homelands, the captains of plunder were safe, beyond
the reach of the wrath and the retribution of their countless victims.

September 11, 2001, changed that. On this fateful day, the victims had scaled
the citadel of Western power, they had breached the impenetrable defense
shield of the world's greatest power, they had cut through its security perime-

ter, and visited destruction inside its inner sanctum. On September 11, it would appear that the victims had desecrated the holy of holies. They had attacked two of the most visible icons of American financial and military power.

Do these attacks mark a turning of the tide? Do they mark the beginning of a new form of guerilla warfare, one that will be fought on the home turf of the United States? Did these attacks result from some new vulnerability created by changing technologies, the new connectivity between continents, or the new globalization? Were these attacks allowed to happen? Are they a new 'Operation Northwoods' executed surreptitiously by some cabal in the centers of power? Or are they flukes, a one-time disaster, the result of a momentary lapse in the defenses of the world's greatest power?

There are questions too about the attackers, their identity and their motives. Did they represent America's victims in Cuba, Haiti, Congo, Vietnam, Cambodia, Nicaragua, El Salvador, the Philippines, Afghanistan and Iraq? Had they acted out of sympathy for the victims of the United States and Israel in Palestine? Were they announcing their revulsion against the immorality of a world which allows tens of millions of children to die before they reach their fifth birthday, a world which now supports a growing trade in body parts? Are they Jehadists acting out of an atavistic faith which seeks to revive its glory by the force of arms? Or are they nihilists, rebels, madmen, deranged by the advance of modernity, by genetic engineering, terminator seeds, surrogate motherhood, designer children, stem-cell research and human cloning?

The answers to these questions – and many more like these – could have filled the pages of America's storied newspapers and magazines for many months. But theirs editors and columnists serve corporate masters; they cheer America's overseas wars; they think no sacrifice of foreign lives too great for advancing the profits of corporate America; they sanctify the crimes of a racist, expansionist, colonial-settler state; they can discover few virtues, little worth preserving outside the borders of their own great country. America's mass media works to ensure that no idea that can compromise the interests of corporate America ever enters the mind of Americans.

Was September 11 then a fluke, a contrived event, a shard from the past, history catching up with the amorality of power, the result of a new dynamic created by globalization and a new connectivity? Alternatively, should we accept the official answer, and see the hijackers of September 11 only as evil men, cold-blooded murderers, acting out of malicious spite, products of a failing civilization? Do we have the right to think, to evaluate, to empathize, to imagine, to choose? Do we dare to resist the machinery that manufactures consent?

In the world of social dynamics, few events are so simple that they can be traced back definitively to a single cause, as if we were examining not a social phenomenon but a disease that is carried by a single vector, a single malevolent life form that can then be destroyed with antibiotics. Should we ignore the complexity of the real world, the layers of causation, the interconnections amongst humans – even between tormentors and their victims – and reach for convenient answers, answers that exonerate us, answers that invert reality, even transforming villains into heroes, tormentors into victims? Sadly, that is what our media and academia do, because they are beholden to money and power.

We might assert, and quite accurately, that September 11 happened because of skyscrapers: the attacks would never have occurred if the 'monstrous' Twin Towers did not exist. If our media were dominated by interests inimical to tall buildings – for reasons of aesthetics, economics or politics – this is the explanation that would have prevailed. The solution too would have been simple: level America's skyline. We would have created a wrecker's paradise, a boom for demolition companies.

Alternatively, we might argue that the culprits were the passenger jets. Who can deny that these jets were the instruments of destruction chosen by the hijackers? The hijackers had used no cluster bombs, no cruise missiles, no daisy-cutters; they had simply turned these flying behemoths into massive weapons. "Ban commercial air travel," the cry could have gone up. In fact, this solution did make sense in the immediate aftermath of the attacks, when the United States grounded all commercial flights for a few days. It was a sensible thing to do. However, if the anti-airline lobbies had been powerful we would have grounded them permanently and gone back to traveling the old-fashioned way – by ships and trains.

It is appropriate, however, that the search into the causes of September 11 began with the perpetrators of these attacks. Very quickly the nineteen dead hijackers were identified; we learned that they were male, young, Arab and Islamic. Once this identification had been made, a great deal of the surmise, analysis, investigation and response turned on the Arab-Islamic ethnicity of the hijackers. For many commentators, especially those with Zionist proclivities or evangelical vocations, this singular fact contained all the answers. The hijackers were messengers of death from the Arab-Islamic hell. For years, these fiends had brought death to innocent Israelis. And now they have directed their terror against the free, democratic and Christian West itself. Their hatred of the West has no political causes, no political grievances and no history: it springs from their race, their ethos, and their devilish, war-mongering creed.

This line of thinking led to some quick solutions. Ann Coulter, contributing editor of *National Review Online*, proposed, "We should invade their countries, kill their leaders and convert them to Christianity."[7] The solution appeared eminently logical. Since the Islamicate world is the source of terrorism, the United States should exorcise Islam, exterminate the Muslims or convert them to Christianity. That done, we can have peace and goodwill on earth. Although this may sound outlandish, the United States has been moving in this general direction since September 11. Already, we have invaded Afghanistan and are getting ready to invade Iraq in what promises to be the first leg of a plan of Middle Eastern conquests that will take us to Iran, Syria, Saudi Arabia and Egypt. After that, the sky is the limit.

There was another solution that the United States began implementing right after September 11, 2001. It is a solution in which it has long experience: racial profiling. Once again, the solution appeared logical. All nineteen hijackers were young Arab men. If the United States could get tough on Arabs, keep tabs on them, track them, screen them at the border, arrest them on suspicion, abridge their civil rights, all Americans could sleep in peace. This might just work if the terrorists are only capable of *repeating* September 11. What if the team Al-Qaida is recruiting even now includes Italian, Greek, Hispanic or Chinese Muslims? Should the United States extend racial profiling to these new groups? How will this affect the corporate project of globalization?

---

7   Ann Coulter, "This Is War," *National Review Online*, September 13, 03: www.nationalreview.com/coulter/coulter091301. shtml

Why did corporate and official America – the America projected by our mass media – respond to September 11 by reverting to old stereotypes? Americans are the knights in shining armor, once again slaying the dragons that had dared to breathe fire over their cities. Once again, they are battling the slovenly Arabs, the violent Muslims, the fanatic Orientals. At the dawn of the twenty-first century, the world's most advanced country is mobilizing for the modern world's first civilizational war. If this war unfolds according to plans – and when the plans begin to unravel – the memory of the Crusades might pale in comparison. That was a local war fought in one sector of the Islamicate world. Already this new war is being fought on a broader front that includes Afghanistan, Palestine, Iraq and Philippines. And it threatens to be a great deal more deadly.

In the 1990s, following the collapse of Soviet Union, two visions competed to shape America's dominance in the world. The first was the project of globalization. It strove to open up world markets to American capital, every corner of the world, including the Third World and the former communist countries. In the past, Europe had achieved this through force of arms, but even so it was incomplete. Now the United States could do a great deal more, without waging too many wars, without creating a formal empire. Instead, it would use its dominating presence in the global economy – backed no doubt by its unchallenged military might – to define the rules of the global economy, rules that would open up the world, as never before, to the free entry of American capital. This was the vision that dominated throughout the 1990s.

However, the hawks would have their day. The contradictions of globalization would bring this about. As globalization advanced, it deepened poverty in large sections of the Periphery, transferred jobs out of the Core countries, augmented the power of Corporations, and threatened the environment. Together, these developments produced a new countervailing force – an anti-globalization movement that was itself global. Driven by the same connectivity that was driving globalization, anti-globalization became global. By the late 1990s, anti-globalization posed a serious challenge to the corporate elites and their globalization project. At its edges the movement contained radical tendencies. Anti-globalization had to be contained.

Another imperial project was running into trouble. In May 2000, the Israelis beat a hasty retreat from South Lebanon, changing the mood of the

Palestinian resistance, and forcing Arafat to reject the Bantustans offered by Israelis in July 2000. Three months later, the second Intifada was born, forcing the Likudniks and their American allies – the neoconservative hawks – to turn to their second option that was aimed at the ethnic cleansing of Palestinians from the West Bank. This plan called for the entry of the United States itself into a war against the Arabs. At some point in the course of this war, it would be safe to drive the Palestinians out of the West Bank. In May 2002, Dick Armey, the House Republican Majority Leader, proposed to "transfer" the Palestinians to the deserts of Western Iraq.[8]

A third force was also brewing in the United States. It was the force of the religious right, the Christian Coalition: they hark back to the letter of the Bible, they read the old prophecies into modern history, and their worldview is Manichean. They are mostly Southerners and racists, who want America to launch a new Crusade against the Islamicate world. More importantly, they have been plotting to take over the Republican Party. And in 2000, they were already a major force in the Presidential election.

In the meanwhile, the neoconservative hawks also plotted. In a "Statement of Principles," announced in June 1997, they laid out plans for 'The New American Century,' an imperial century that would "increase defense spending signifi-cantly," "shape circumstances before crises emerge," "meet threats before they become dire," and "challenge regimes hostile to our interests and val-ues."[9] In another document, published in September 2000, these neocon-servatives complain that the "process of transformation" they wanted to effect "is likely to be a long one, absent some catastrophic and catalyzing event – like a new Pearl Harbor."[10]

Was September 11 the "catastrophic and catalyzing event" without which the neoconservatives could scarcely launch their 'New American Century?' Was it the inevitable escalation in a clash of civilizations, another twist in the unfolding inner logic of the Zionist project, or a symptom of a deepen-

---

8   "Rep. Dick Armey Calls for Ethnic Cleansing of Palestinians," *Counterpunch. Org*, May 2, 2002: http://www.counterpunch. org/armey0502.html.

9   The words in quotes are from the "The Statement of Principles," showcased on the website of *The Project For The New American Century*, signed by the major neoconservatives, including Dick Cheney, Donald Rumsfeld, Elliot Abrams, Paul Wolf-owitz, Norman Podhoretz, I. Lewis Libby and Eliot Cohen. See www.newamericancentury.org/statementofprinciples.htm

10 Tom Barry and Jim Lobe, "The Men Who Stole the Show," *Foreign Policy In Focus*, October 2002: www.fpif.org/papers/ 02men/box1_body.html.

ing crisis in the relations between the Core and Periphery? Was it serendip-ity, conspiracy or kismet that produced these fateful attacks? Perhaps, it was all of the above.

Whatever the forces that engineered September 11, this much is clear. It was seized precipitately by the quartet just described – the American Likudniks, Corporate America, the Zionists and the Christian Coalition – to launch their 'Project for a New American Century,' to proclaim endless wars, to seize the profits from the Arab oil fields, to shrink and downsize Islamdom, to make the world safe for American interests, and to create a hegemony that would last forever. Do we indeed stand at the dawn of a new American Century, whose birth threatens the world with wars, blood, grime, but also promises to deliver profits never dreamed of before?

A hundred years from now, standing in front of the majestic monuments raised to commemorate this grand American century, what will Americans think of Osama bin Laden? Will they remember this malevolent genius as the midwife who facilitated the birth of 'The New American Century?' On the other hand, if this project runs into trouble, if it produces blood and grime but no profits, who shall we blame for the human toll of this terrible catastrophe? We can of course blame bin Laden, the nineteen hijackers, the Jihadists, or the Muslims who hate our freedoms. Or, with some hon-esty and introspection, we can blame the cold hearts, minds cowed by fear, grasping cupidity and a terrible tribalism that delivered humankind, gagged and bound, into the power of the neoconservative Juggernaut.

CHAPTER TWENTY-ONE

Iraq is Free

"It is most hateful in the sight of Allah that ye say that which ye do not."
—Qur'an: 61: 3

March 2003

Iqra, recite, proclaim, affirm, avow, declare: *Iraq is free.*

Iraq has been freed from ten thousand years of tyranny; freed from darkest infamy; freed from cold villainy; freed from centuries of stasis; freed from nights of searing pain; freed from terrible torture; freed from sanctioned starvation; freed from laser-guided precision; freed from bombs that explode with shock and awe.

The whole world was witness to this historical moment. They saw the dark head of the tyrant, the granite head of Ozymandias draped in the fabric of freedom, effaced, his sneer blotted out, his terror nullified, brought down by the force of an armor-clad Bradley. Iraqis, many dozens of them, cheered lustily. A few even kissed the liberators on both cheeks, in authentic Arab style.

The naysayers, skeptics, doubting Thomases, pacifists, prophets of doom, and the patriotically challenged were wrong about America's war *in* Iraq. The millions who marched in the streets, protesting the war, are now gnashing their teeth. In deep shame, penitent, they have announced that they will march again in the millions, to curse, flog and flagellate themselves for marching *against* the war that freed Iraqis.

This was not a war *on* Iraq, much less a war *against* Iraq. It was a war *in* Iraq: a war *for* the Iraqis. It was not the first time that a great civilizing nation has fought a war *in* a barbarous land *against* its home-grown tyrants. Civilized nations have carried this burden uncomplainingly, showing equal dedication in freeing lands *of* their peoples and, when the occasion demanded, freeing peoples *of* their lands. The United States now carries the torch of freedom, bravely torching anyone who shows the gall to oppose the forward march of the brave and free.

Consider the freedoms this war has bestowed on Iraq.

First, this war has freed Iraq of its WMDs. It is not surprising if the Americans have not yet found any caches of WMDs inside Iraq: the experts knew this all along. In the days leading up to the war, the WMDs were smuggled into Syria for safekeeping. However, this only means that Americans will have to go the extra mile, into Syria. In time, Syria will smuggle the WMDs into Egypt, Egypt into Libya, Libya into Iran, and Iran into Sudan. Is this an Arab conspiracy – or what – to hitch a freedom ride on Bradleys and Abrams tanks?

Instantly, the American liberators have turned the Iraqis free to pillage their museums, strip their hospitals, plunder their universities, and loot their homes. The acutely funny Donald Rumsfeld explained: "It's untidy. And freedom's untidy. And free people are free to make mistakes and commit crimes and do bad things." Quickly, the Iraqis are learning that the gift of freedom comes at a price. They are eager to prove that their freedom is worth the price they are being asked to pay for it. If Madeline Albright could sacrifice the lives of half a million Iraqi children for *American* 'security,' surely the Iraqis can give up their national treasures for a fleeting taste of freedom.

The war has freed Iraq to spread the welcome mat to American Corporations. For thirteen long years, since Gulf War I, American capital was not free to outbid Russian, French and German capital in developing Iraq; this was an unconscionable abridgement of freedom. Now, the playing fields have been leveled. The Bechtels, Halliburtons, Northrops, Exxons and Triremes are free at last to claim their pound of Iraqi flesh.

There is good news too for the pastoral faction of American capital, for outfits like Franklin Graham's Good Samaritans. After years of softening with sanctions and bombings, their would-be-victims are free to receive the good word of the Lord. Even as I write, the Samaritan convoys are converging on Iraq, ready to trade American food and water for Iraqi souls. The Iraqis never knew a better bargain, getting something for nothing.

Iraq is now free, as Egyptians freed themselves after suffering their fourth defeat at the hands of Israel in 1973, to derive the inestimable benefits of 'normal' relations with Israel. After 55 years, Iraqi oil is now free again to flow to Haifa. In addition, Iraqi water too is free to flood the parched swimming pools in Israel and the West Bank settlements.

Freed from the threat of Iraq's WMDs, Israelis can now attack the Palestinian problem – the Palestinian menace in Judea and Samaria – with impunity. The pace of ethnic cleansing, too slow for an early final solution, can now be accelerated. Now that Iraq is free, with Americans in charge of its land and resources, it should be relatively easy teleporting the Palestinians to the deserts of Western Iraq.

The war has freed another Arab capital from the threat of Israel's Samson option. Once the unimpeded looting of their hospitals, universities and museums stops, the five million citizens of Baghdad can sleep in peace. Never again will they be troubled by nightmares of being incinerated in a nuclear inferno. Sanctions, wars and occupation are but a small price to pay for the inestimable gift of an Iraq free from Israeli threats of a nuclear holocaust.

If one counts all the advantages of America's war *in* Iraq – and I have barely started – history will record this war as the greatest opening in Iraqi history, a greater moment than the first founding of civilization on the banks of Tigris and Euphrates. Once the Iraqis awake to this shattering truth, they will also acknowledge their deep debt to Saddam Hussein. Without his anti-Zionism, his methodical recklessness, his development of WMDs, his support for terrorism, and his financing of Al-Qaida, the United States would never have waged a war to liberate Iraq. Without Saddam Hussein, the Iraqis would still be toiling under some vapid dictator, allied to Israel and receiving bribes from the United States. I can imagine a day, once the fog of America's war *in* Iraq clears, when repentant Iraqis may restore Saddam Hussein's statue to the high pedestal it had long occupied in Baghdad's

Central Square. In shock and awe, these are the words that American visitors will read inscribed on its base:

Saddam Hussein
A Brave Iraqi
Serendipitous Architect of Our Freedoms

CHAPTER TWENTY-TWO

Dialectics of Terror

"If you kill one person, it is murder. If you kill a hundred thousand, it is foreign policy."
—Anonymous

August 7, 2003

States are founded on a monopoly over violence; this is their very essence. They enforce this monopoly by amassing instruments of violence; but that is scarcely enough. They also use religion, ideology and laws to de-legitimize and exorcise violence by non-state agents.

This monopoly over violence creates its own problems. Unchallenged, the state can direct violence against its own population. This leads to state tyranny. The state can also wage wars to enrich one or more sectional interests. This defines the dual challenge before all organized societies: restraining state tyranny and limiting its war-making powers.

Often, a trade off exists between state tyranny and wars. Arguably, such a tradeoff was at work during the period of European expansion – since the sixteenth century – when Europeans slowly secured political rights even as they engaged in growing, even genocidal, violence, especially against non-Europeans. As Western states gradually conceded rights to their own populations, they intensified the murder and enslavement of Amerindians and Africans, founding white colonies on lands stolen from them. This inverse connection troubled few Westerners: it was the essence of racism.

The United States is only the most successful of the colonial creations; and this has left an indelible mark on American thinking. It was founded on violence against its native inhabitants, who were pushed to near-extinc-tion to accommodate the growing tide of European immigrants. Its history also includes the violence – on a nearly equal scale – perpetrated against the Africans who were torn from their continent to create wealth for the new Republic. Such a genesis, steeped in violence against other races, con-vinced most Americans that they had the divine right – like the ancient Israelites – to build their prosperity on the ruin of other, inferior races.

This racism goes a long way to explain why so many Americans give blind support to their government's interventions abroad. It is unnecessary – they might be saying – to look too closely into these interventions; after all, they *are* undertaken to secure 'our' interests. Even if these interventions result in deaths – for instance, the deaths of more than three-quarters of a mil-lion children in Iraq – most Americans keep a clear conscience about these deaths. In the felicitous phrase of Madeline Albright, the US Secretary of State, they know that "the price is worth it."

Few Americans understand that their country has long stood at the apex – and, therefore, is the chief beneficiary – of a global system that produces poverty for the greater part of humanity; that this system subordinates all social, cultural, environmental and human values to the imperatives of corporate capital; a system that now kills millions merely by setting trade, investment and property regimes that devastate their economies, deprive them of their livelihood, their dignity and eventually their lives. The cor-porate media, the school curricula, and the Congress ensure that most Americans never see past the web of deceit – about a free, just, tolerant and caring United States – that covers up the human carnage and environmen-tal wreckage this system produces.

The wretched of the earth are not so easily duped. They can see – and quite clearly, through the lens of their dark days – how corporate capital, with the United States in the lead, produces their home-based tyrannies; how their economies have been devastated to enrich transnational corporations and their local collaborators; how the duo stifle indigenous movements for human rights, women's rights and worker's rights; how they devalue indige-nous traditions and languages; how their countries are used as markets, as sources of cheap labor, as fields for testing new, deadlier weapons, and as sites for dumping toxic wastes; how their men and women sell body parts because the markets place little value on their labor.

The world – outside the dominant West – has watched how the Zionists, with the support of Britain and the United States, imposed a historical anachronism, a colonial-settler state in Palestine, a throw-back to a racist past, when indigenous populations in the Americas could be cleansed with impunity to make room for Europe's superior races. In horror, the world watches daily how a racist Israel destroys the lives of millions of Palestinians through US-financed weaponry and fresh-contrived acts of malice; how it attacks its neighbors at will; how it has destabilized, distorted and derailed the historical process in an entire region; and how, in a final but foreordained twist, American men and women have now been drawn into this conflict, to make the Middle East safe for Israeli hegemony.

In Iraq, over the past thirteen years, the world has watched the United States showcase the methods it will use to crush challenges to the new imperialism – the New World Order – that was launched after the end of the Cold War. This new imperialism commands more capital and more lethal weapons than the old imperialisms of Britain, France or Germany. It is imperialism without rivals and, therefore, it dares to pursue its schemes, its wars, and its genocidal campaigns, under the cover of international legitimacy, through the United Nations, the World Bank, IMF and World Trade Organization. In brief, it is a deadlier, more pernicious imperialism.

Under the cover of the Security Council, the United States has waged a total war against Iraq, a war that went well beyond the means that were necessary to reverse the invasion of Kuwait. The aerial bombing of Iraq, in the months preceding the ground action in January 1991, sought to destroy the country's civilian infrastructure, a genocidal act under international law; it destroyed power plants, water-purification plants, sewage facilities, bridges and bomb shelters. It was the official (though unstated) aim of these bombings to sting the Iraqis into overthrowing their rulers. Worse, the war was followed by a never-relenting campaign of aerial bombings and the most rigorous sanctions in recorded history. According to a UNICEF study, the sanctions had killed half a million Iraqi children between 1991 and 1998, the result of a five-fold increase in child mortality rates.[1] It would have taken five Hiroshima bombs to produce this grisly toll.

Then came September 11, 2001, a riposte from the black holes of global capitalism to the New World Order. Nineteen hijackers took control of passenger airplanes in Boston, Newark and Virginia, and rammed them, one after another, into the twin towers of the Word Trade Center and the Pentagon; the fourth missed its target, possibly the White House. Following a carefully rehearsed script, the nineteen hijackers enacted a macabre ritual, taking their own lives even as they took the lives of nearly three thousand Americans. The hijackers did not wear uniforms; they were not flying stealth bombers; they carried nothing more lethal (so we are told) than box cutters and plastic knives; they had not been dispatched or financed by any government. Nevertheless, using the principles of jujitsu, they had turned the civilian technology of the world's greatest power against its own civilians. As Arundhati Roy put it, the hijackers had delivered "a monstrous calling card from a world gone horribly wrong."[2]

The terrorist attacks of 9-11 shocked, perhaps traumatized, a whole nation. Yet the same Americans expressed little concern – in fact, most could profess total ignorance – about the hundreds of thousands of dead Iraqis, a horrendous toll exacted by daily bombings and crippling sanctions over a period of thirteen years. Of course, the dollar and the dinar are not the same. American deaths cannot be placed side by side with Iraqi deaths. The Iraqis were after all evil; they harbored ill will towards the United States. And evil people should never be given a chance to repent or change their evil-doing propensities. Senator John McCain said it succinctly: "We're coming after you. God may have mercy on you, but we won't."[3]

The simultaneous attacks of 9-11 required a high level of planning, training and skill. On this ground, some argued that it could not have been the work of "incompetent" Arabs. However, it would appear that there is greater political cunning at work in the conception of these attacks. Al-Qaida delivered what the Bush hawks wanted, a terrorist attack that would inflame

---

1   UNICEF, *Iraq Surveys Show Humanitarian Emergency.* (1999). <www.unicef.org/newsline/99pr29.htm>

2   Arundhati Roy, "The Algebra of Infinite Justice," *The Guardian*, September 21, 2001: www.guardian.co.uk/ Print/0,3858,4266289,00.html.

3   John Diamond and Bob Kemper, "Bush Lining Up Allies for Retaliation," *Chicago Tribune, September 13, 2001*: http://www. chicagotribune.com/ news/specials/911/showcase/ chi-warinafghanistan,0,1468693.story.

Americans into supporting a war against the Arabs. In turn, the Bush hawks gave Al-Qaida what it wanted, a war that would plant tens of thousands of Americans in the cities and towns of the Islamicate world.

The attacks of September 11, 2001, were products of a massive failure of intelligence and security in a country that spends tens of billions of dollars annually on intelligence gathering and hundreds of billions more on its military. It should have led to an immediate Congressional inquiry; in fact, this would not start for another year. Instead, President Bush declared that 9-11 was an act of war (making it the first act of war perpetrated by nineteen civilians), and proceeded to declare unlimited war against terrorists (also the first time that war had been declared against elusive non-state actors). In the name of a bogus war against terrorism, the United States appropriated the right to wage preemptive wars against any country suspected of harboring terrorists or possessing weapons of mass destruction (what are weapons for if not mass destruction?) with an intent (US would be the judge of that) to use them against the United States.

Osama bin Laden had the victory that he wanted: the world's only superpower was running mad after him and his cohorts. Al-Qaida now occupied the place vacated by the Soviet Union. No terrorist organization could have asked for greater recognition, and this was almost certain to help in Al-Qaida's recruitment drive. Secondly, by declaring war against Al-Qaida, the United States had tied its own prestige to the daily casualties of this war. Every terrorist strike – the softer the target the better – would be counted by Americans and the rest of the world as a battle lost in the war against terrorism. It should come as no surprise that the frequency of large-scale terrorist strikes has increased markedly since 9-11 – from Baghdad to Bali and Bombay. Thirdly, President Bush's war against terrorism has already placed 160,000 American troops in Iraq and Afghanistan, not counting additional thousands in other Islamicate countries. Already, it would appear that Al-Qaida is capitalizing upon this opportunity to open a broad front against the United States on its home turf.

Although the Crusader presence in the Levant, starting in the 1090s, lasted for nearly two centuries, this did not provoke a pan-Islamic Jihad against the 'Infidels.' On occasion, some Muslim states formed alliances with the Crusaders to contain the ambitions of rival Muslim states. It was only in

1187, after Salahuddin had united Syria and Egypt, that the Muslims took back Jerusalem. However, the Arabs did not carry their counter-attack to a decisive end; the Crusaders retained control of parts of coastal Syria for another hundred years. Indeed, several years later, Salahuddin's successors returned Jerusalem to the Crusaders on the condition that they would not fortify it. The Muslims did not look upon the Crusades, which loom so large in European imagination, as a civilizational war.

Of course, that was then, when Islamicate societies were prosperous, refined, tolerant, self-confident and strong. As a result, although the Crusades threw the combined might of Western Europe – that region's first united enterprise – to regain Christian holy lands, the Muslims took the invasions in their stride. Eventually, the resources of a relatively small part of the Muslim world were sufficient to end this European adventure, which left few lasting effects on the region. In the more recent past, Islamicate societies have been divided, fragmented, outstripped by their European adversaries, their states embedded in the periphery of the global economy, and their rulers allied with Western powers against their own people. This fragmentation of Islamdom is not a natural condition in the historical consciousness of Muslims.

More ominously, since 1917 the Arabs have faced settler-colonialism in their very heartland, an open-ended imperialist project successively supported by Britain and the United States. This Zionist insertion in the Middle East, self-consciously promoted as the outpost of the West in the Islamicate world, produced its own twisted dialectics. An exclusive Jewish state founded on fundamentalist claims (and nothing gets more fundamentalist than a twentieth-century imperialism founded on 'divine' promises about real estate made three thousand years back) was bound to evoke its counterpart in the Islamicate world. In 1967 when Israel inflicted a humiliating defeat on Egypt and Syria – the leading proponents of Arab nationalism – this created an opening for the insertion of Islamists into the region's political landscape. One fundamentalism would now be pitted against another.

This contest may now be reaching its climax – with the United States entering the war directly. In part at least, it is the unfolding of the logic of the Zionist insertion in the Arab world. On the one hand, this has provoked the growth of Islamist movements, some of which were forced by US-supported repression in their home countries to target the United States. On the other hand, the Zionist occupation of lands rich in Biblical lore has encouraged the growth of Christian Zionism, predicated on the conviction that all the Jews of the world must assemble in Israel before the Second Coming of Christ. At the same time, Zionist propagandists – based in America's think tanks, media and academia – have worked tirelessly to arouse old Western fears about Islam and Muslims. They paint Islam as a violent religion, perennially at war against infidels, opposed to democracy, fearful of women's rights, unable to modernize, and raging at the West for its freedoms and prosperity. They never tire of repeating that the Arabs hate Israel because it is the only 'democracy' in the Middle East.

Arguably, the US occupation of Iraq is in some trouble. Already, there has been a retreat from plans to bring about regime change in Iran, Syria, Saudi Arabia and Egypt. There is still talk of bringing democracy to Iraq and the Arab world, but it carries little conviction even with American audiences. There is new-fangled talk now of fighting the "terrorists" in Baghdad and Basra rather than in Boulder and Buffalo. Further, after two years of bristling unilateralism, the United States is back at the Security Council, imploring the world to share the financial and human costs of their occupation of Iraq. It is unlikely that Indians, Pakistanis or Egyptians will play human shield for American troops in Iraq. In any case, it is unlikely that any rechristening of the Occupation will fool the Iraqi resistance.

What can be the outcome of all this? During their long rampage through history, begun in 1492, the Western powers have shown little respect for the peoples they encountered in the Americas, Africa, Asia and Australia. Many of them are not around to recount the gory history of their extermination through imported diseases, warfare, and forced labor in mines and plantations. Those who survived were forced into peonage, or consigned to mutilated lives on reservations. Many tens of millions were bought and sold into slavery. Proud empires were dismembered. Great civilizations were denigrated. All this had happened before, but never on this scale. In part, perhaps, the extraordinary scale of these depredations may be attributed to what William McNeill calls the "deep-rooted pugnacity" of Europeans.[4] Much of this, however, is due to historical accidents which elevated West Europeans

---

4   William H. McNeill, *The Rise of the West* (Chicago: University of Chicago Press, 1991).

– rather than the Chinese, Turks, or Indians – to great power status based on their exploitation of inorganic sources of energy. If we are to apportion blame, we might as well award the prize to Britain's rich coal deposits.

In the period since the Second World War, some of the massive historical disequilibria created by Western powers have been corrected. China and India are on their feet; so are Taiwan, South Korea, Singapore, Hong Kong and Malaysia. These countries are on their feet and advancing. However, the wounds of imperialism in Africa run deeper. The colonial legacies of fragmented societies, deskilled populations, arbitrary boundaries, and economies tied to failing primary production continue to produce wars, civil wars, corruption, massacres and diseases. Yet, the West can ignore Africa; the deaths of a million Africans in the Congo do not merit the attention given to one suicide bombing in Tel Aviv. Africa can be ignored because its troubles do not affect vital Western interests; at least not yet.

Then there is the failure of the Islamicate world to reconstitute itself. As recently as 1700, three major Muslim empires – the Mughal, Ottoman and Safavid – together controlled the greater part of the Islamicate world. By 1800, after a period of rivalry among indigenous successor states and European interlopers, the Mughals had given way to the British in much of India. The Ottoman Empire disintegrated more slowly, losing Egypt and its European territories in the nineteenth century, and then during the First World War the remaining Arab territories were divvied up amongst the British, French, Zionists, Maronites and a clutch of oil-rich protectorates. The Iranians alone held on to most of the territories acquired by the Safavids. In short, the colonial onslaught had fragmented Islamdom, divided it into some forty states, none with the potential to serve as a core state; and this fragmentation was most striking in Islamdom's Arab heartland. In addition, significant Muslim populations now lived in states with non-Muslim majorities.

Why did the Muslims fail to reconstitute their power? Most importantly, this was because Muslim power lacked a demographic base. The Mughal Empire ruled over a non-Muslim majority; the Ottomans faced a similar situation in their European territories. More recently, the Muslims have been the victims of geological 'luck,' containing the world's richest deposits of oil, the fuel that drives the global economy. The great powers could not let the Muslims control *their* lifeblood. The Muslims suffered a third setback from a historical accident: the impetus that Hitler gave to the Zionist movement. Now there had emerged a powerful new interest – a specifically Jewish interest – in keeping the Arabs divided and dispossessed.

It appears, however, that Muslims have not acquiesced in their fragmentation or the capitulation of their governments to Anglo-Zionist power. We have watched the resilience of the Muslims, their determination to fight for their dignity in Afghanistan, Bosnia, Palestine, Chechnya, Kashmir and Mindanao – among other places. In the meanwhile, they have overcome their demographic weakness. At the beginning of the twentieth century, the Muslims constituted barely a tenth of the world population; today that share already exceeds 23 percent, and continues to rise. Moreover, unlike the Chinese or Hindus, the Muslims inhabit a broad swathe of territory from Nigeria, Senegal and Morocco in the west to Sinjiang and the Indonesian Archipelago in the east. It would be hard to corral a population of this size that spans half the globe. More likely, the US-British-Israeli siege of the Islamicate world, now underway in the name of the war against terrorism, will lead to a broadening conflict with unforeseen consequences that could easily turn very costly for either or both parties.

Can the situation yet be saved? In the weeks before the launch of the illegal war against Iraq, when tens of millions of Europeans and Americans marched against the war, it appeared that the war-mongering 'democracies' could be stopped from executing their belligerent designs; that the marchers would defeat the ideologies of hatred and the tactics of fear-mongering; it appeared that if the demands for diplomacy were denied, the marchers would resort to civil disobedience to stop the carnage. However, once the war began, the protesters melted away like picnicking crowds when a sunny day is marred by rains. In retrospect, the protests lacked the depth, organization and grit to graduate into political movements. America does not easily stomach anti-war protestors once it *starts* a war. Wars are serious business. Once the killing begins, America's wars must have the undivided support of the whole country. Support for wars becomes support for *our* troops.

The anti-war protesters may yet regroup, but not before many more body bags arrive in the continental United States, before many more young Americans are maimed for life, before many tens of thousands of Iraqis are dispatched to early deaths. Attempts are already underway to invent new lies to keep Americans deluded about the war; to tighten the noose around Iran; to hide the growing casualties of war; to lure poverty-stricken Mexicans and Guatemalans to die for America; to substitute Indian and Pakistani body bags for American ones. America's war mongering cannot be stopped unless *more* Americans can be taught to separate their government from their country, their leaders from their national interests, and their tribal affiliation from their humanity.

This can be done. We now posses a new medium – the internet – to create a new consciousness, to get past the mercenary media, the pusillanimous politicians, the spineless social scientists, the serenading schools, and putrid prejudices. If some of us had done a better job getting past these hurdles in time, the nineteen hijackers may never have delivered their monstrous calling card, and they and their three thousand victims might still be alive today. Still, the hijackers chose the wrong means to deliver their message; by targeting civilians, they played right into the game plan of the Bush hawks. The result has been more profits for favored US corporations, greater freedom of action for Israel, and more lives and liberties lost everywhere. At least, this is what the ledger of history shows for now.

CHAPTER TWENTY-THREE

Semantics of Empire

"Saddam Hussein is a man who is willing to gas his own people ..."
—George Bush, March 22, 2002

"As he (George Bush) said, any person that would gas his own people is a threat to the world."
—Scott McClellan, White House spokesperson, March 31, 2002

"Saddam Hussein is a tyrant who has tortured and killed his own people."
—Hillary Clinton, October 10, 2002

"He poison-gassed his own people."
—Al Gore, December 16, 1998

December 2003

We might glean a few insights about the semantics of the global order – and the reality it tries to mask – from the way in which the United States has framed the moral case against Saddam.

Saddam's unspeakable crime is that he has "tortured his *own* people." He has "killed his *own* people." He has "gassed his *own* people." He has "poison-gassed his *own* people." In all the accusations, Saddam stands inseparable from his *own* people.

Rarely do his accusers charge that Saddam "tortured people," "gassed people," "gassed Iraqis," or "killed Iraqis." A google search for "gassed his *own* people" and "Saddam" produced 5980 hits. Another search for "gassed people" and "Saddam" produced only 276 hits.

It would appear that the indictment of Saddam gathers power, conviction, irrefutability, by adding the possessive, proprietary, emphatic 'own' to the people tortured, gassed or killed. What does the grammar of accusations say about the metrics of American values?

It is revealing. For a country that claims to speak in the name of man, abstract man, universal man, the charge is not that Saddam has killed people, that he has committed murders, mass murders. Instead, the prosecution indicts him for killing a people who stand in a specific relation to the killer: they are his *own* people.

This betrays tribalism. It springs from a perception that fractures the indivisibility of mankind. It divides men into tribes. It divides people into "us" and "them:" "ours" and "theirs." It elevates "us" above "them:" "our" kind above "their" kind. It reveals a sensibility that can feel horror only over the killing of one's *own* kind.

Life is sacred at the Core. In the United States, *we* have an inalienable right to life. It is protected by law; it cannot be taken away without due process. Americans are proud, sedate, in the illusion that *their* President never kills his *own* people; their history is proof of this. An American President would never think of killing his *own* people.

Saddam's crimes are most foul because he has tortured his *own* people; he has killed his *own* people; he has gassed his *own* people. He has violated the edict of nature. His actions are so terribly *un*-American.

Saddam's unnatural crimes trouble us, however, not because we feel empathy for his victims. His crimes *predict* trouble for us. If he can kill his *own* kind how much more willingly would he kill *us*? In Scot McClellan's version: "any person that would gas his own people is a threat to the world (read the United States)."

Of course, Saddam might plead innocence to this charge. "You've got it all wrong about the people I kill. The Kurds I killed are not my *own* people. They are not even Arabs and, worse, they wanted to break up Iraq and create their own independent Kurdistan. What would you do to your Blacks, Amerindians, Hispanics or Asians, if they took up arms to carve out independent states of their own? Were not the Southern whites your own people? But you killed a half million Southerners when they took up arms against you in the 1860s. More recently, you killed your own kind at Waco."

Now, as the United States prepares to try Saddam for torturing, gassing and killing his *own* people, does this absolve *us* of killing the same people because *they* are not our *own*? Is the killing of Iraqis a crime only when the perpetrators are local thugs – once in our pay – and not when *we* take up the killing and execute it more efficiently, on *our* account?

In the colonial era, racism inoculated people against feeling empathy towards those *other* people in the Periphery. Those *other* people were children, barbarians, savages, if not worse. We had to kill them if they could not be useful to us, or if they stood in the way of *our* progress. There wasn't much squeamishness about that. It was good policy.

In the era of the Cold War, we went easy on the language of racism, though not always on its substance. When we sent our men and women to kill hundreds of thousands of Vietnamese and Koreans, we justified this by claiming that we were doing it to protect *our* freedoms. Of course, it was all right to kill others for *our* freedoms.

However, in the new era, the US contracted the killing to thugs in the Periphery. This was a win-win for us. We kept our hands free from bloodstains, so we could smell like roses. At the same time, we could point to colored killers (in our pay), and say, "Look, they are still incapable of civilization." What is more, we could use their savagery as justification for killing colored peoples on our own account.

More recently, the US has gone back to killing on its own account. Starting in the 1980s, taking advantage of their costly foreign debts – which we helped create – we began a general economic warfare against the Periphery, stripping down their economies for takeover by Core capital. In this new war, the colonial governors and viceroys have been replaced by two banks – the World Bank and the IMF – and a trade enforcer, the WTO. Like the famines in British India, this war has produced tens of millions of hidden victims, dead from hunger and disease.

In 1990, the US introduced a new, deadlier form of economic warfare: it placed Iraq under a total siege. This instrument was chosen because we knew that Iraq was vulnerable: it imported much of its food, medicines, medical equipment, machinery and spare parts, nearly all paid for by oil exports. Imposed to end the Iraqi occupation of Kuwait in 1990, the siege was lifted in 2003, some thirteen years later and only *after* the US had occupied Iraq. Altogether, this US-imposed siege had killed more than a million and a half Iraqis, half of them children.

Once again, the US is the world's nerve center of reactionary ideologies. The post-War restraints on the use of deadly force now gone, the United States revels in the use of deadly force. Not that alone, it wants to be *seen* using deadly force. It wants to be feared, even loathed for its magnificent power, raining death from the skies as never before, like no other power before. At manufacturing death, we brook no competition.

Imperialism, militarism and wars create their own rationale. In time, Islamist enemies were created and magnified, with help from the Zionists. Rogue states stepped out of the shadows. The swamps began to spawn terrorists. Weapons of mass destruction proliferated. Sagely Orientalists suddenly awoke to an Arab "democracy deficit." Islam, they declared, is misogynist, anti-modernist and anti-democratic. The civilizing mission was Arabized. Once again, the musty odors of jingoism, militarism, racism and religious bigotry infested the air. Like a godsend, the attacks of September 11, 2001, galvanized America. Imperialism and racism rode into town, cheek by jowl, hand in hand.

The new colonization project has now snagged its chief prize. An Arab Ozymandias brought low. The man who tortured, killed and gassed his *own* people is in American hands. Our civilizing mission displays its trophy. We are repeatedly invited to peep into the oral orifice of this bedraggled Saddam. "Ladies and gentlemen, we got him."

The images of Saddam the captive, haggard, resigned, defanged, are images of our raw power. Our power to appoint, anoint, finance and arm surrogates in the Periphery; and when they go wrong, our power to wage war against their people; destroy their civilian infrastructure, poison their air, water and soil with uranium; lay siege to their economy; and, finally, to invade and occupy their country. We will go to any lengths to save the people of the Periphery from *our* tyrants.

Come, then, wretched denizens of the Periphery, there is cause to rejoice. Lift your Cokes and offer a toast to the Boy Emperor even as he launches wars to establish a thousand years of Pax America. He will bring down all outmoded tyrannies, and root out rogue states, dictatorships and monarchies. He will extirpate all fundamentalists, hunt down all terrorists, track down all drug lords, and scrap all unfriendly WMDs. This will be the great cleansing of all self-created challenges to the Empire. In the end nothing will stand between the Empire and the Periphery, between Capital and Labor, between Thesis and Anti-Thesis.

Rejoice: the Empire is hastening its day of reckoning with history, its tryst with destiny, its long descent to memory.

CHAPTER TWENTY-FOUR

America, Imagine This!

"To know is nothing at all; to imagine is everything."
—Anatole France

December 2004

Over the past three years, I have followed the mainstream public discourse on the abhorrent attacks of 9-11 with the eerie feeling that I was watching a new version of Hamlet where the King of Denmark – the Prince Hamlet's father – dies a natural death. The Prince of Denmark's enigmatic, feverish, even murderous, behavior stems from some strange sickness of his mind. He just hates his noble uncle, Claudius, who succeeds to the throne of Denmark upon his father's death.

Once the perpetrator of a crime has been identified, it is natural for the family of the victim to ask: why? After 9-11, Americans too were asking such questions. 'Why did the 19 Arabs attack us?' 'What was their motive?' 'Why did they take their own lives to inflict death upon us?' 'What did they want from us?' 'What had we done to make them so angry, so suicidal?' These questions could easily take a dangerous turn. They had to be preempted.

Losing no time, on the evening of September 11, President Bush sought to restrict the questioning. "Today," he opened his speech, "our fellow citizens, our way of life, our very freedom came under attack in a series of deliberate and deadly terrorist acts." But that was not enough. A few days later, in his speech to the joint session of the Congress, the President fixed the question for Americans. Americans are asking, he told us, 'Why do they hate us?'

This canonical question became the steel frame which has bounded the official, establishment discourse on the etiology of September 11. In this clever formulation, 'they' refers not only to the nineteen hijackers, or the few radical Islamists who target the US with their violence, but it encompasses all Arabs, all Middle Easterners, indeed all Muslims. Likewise, 'us' does not refer to America's war-mongering elite, the neoconservatives, the Zionists, or the Crusader Christians, but to all of America – the greatest country in the world, the beacon on the hill, the last great hope of mankind, the fortress of democracy, the defender of all civilized values.

The answer to this question – now narrowed – also had to be fixed, determined for ever. President Bush's speech-writers provided the answer. It was categorical. "They hate our freedoms: our freedom of religion, our freedom of speech, our freedom to vote and assemble and disagree with each other." This singular indictment summarized, captured and explained the temperament, the values, the nature and the perverse proclivities of nearly a billion and a half Muslims, with more than fourteen hundred years of history behind them.

On the lofty banner of American hubris, unfurled after the attacks of 9-11, are inscribed in black letters the words, 'The Muslims hate our freedoms.' This is now the accepted, formulaic substitute for all discourse, all questioning and probing into the history of America's relations with the peoples of the Islamicate world over the past six decades. Three words now have the power to terminate all discourse on 9-11 in mainstream America. 'They hate us.'

The 9-11 Commission website informs us that it was "chartered to prepare a *full and complete account of the circumstances surrounding* the September 11, 2001 terrorist attacks, including preparedness for and the immediate response to the attacks. (emphases added)." Yet, the 500 page report of the Commission contains not a single mention of any possible connection between 9-11 and US policies towards the Middle East. Presumably, American policies, even when they wreak havoc, are like acts of God. There can be no blowback.

There is a deep irony in all this too. The US administration, led by neo-conservative ideologues, has convinced a majority of Americans that the Muslims attacked their country because they hate our freedoms. What then is the remedy the US proposes to combat the 'terrorism' that emanates from the Islamicate world? It proposes to invade and occupy their countries so that US marines can inject the serum of freedom into their moribund bodies. It appears that the Muslims do not hate freedoms per se; they only hate *our* freedoms because *they* don't have it. We must conquer them in order to bring this gift to them.

The speed and ease with which President Bush's lies sink into the psyche of so many Americans is truly astounding. To his flock, he is like a Moses bringing divinely inscribed tablets from Mount Sinai. His words, however inarticulate, however disjointed in their logic, however divergent from facts, are the word of God. It appears that 9-11 has turned President Bush into the leader of an American cult.

Is there a cure for this delusion? I will propose a therapy that involves a modest exercise of the imagination. Modest, I emphasize. Not the layered imagination of mystics, not a poet's flight of fancy, or the hallucination of madmen. Just a little pedantic imagination, well within the reach of most ordinary humans willing to exit momentarily from the present into an imagined and imaginary world.

Let America now imagine this. Imagine waking up tomorrow in an upside-down world, one in which the history of America's relations with the Arabs is inverted. Iraq is now the global hegemon, the world's richest democracy, a beacon of freedom; Iraq and the Arab democracies dominate the world and what was once the USA. Imagine that the Arabs have used their power to replace a United States of America with fifty nominally independent states – with states for native Americans, Latinos, Blacks, Indian Americans, Vietnamese Americans, Iranian Americans, Italian Americans, German Americans, French-Americans, Anglo-Americans, Jews, Mormons, Sikhs, Jehovah's Witnesses, the Amish, Hutterites, etc – with most of these states run by despotic Iraqi surrogates.

Iraq, after colonizing New England and ethnically cleansing its native inhabitants, has converted it into an exclusive, racist, colonial-settler state for Arabs brought in from Sudan who were dying from a severe drought, the worst in a thousand years. This state, *Arabistan*, is by far the most powerful of the states on the American continent. It is Iraq's strategic asset in the Americas, periodically mounting incursions against the neighboring states from where the New Englander refugees mount occasional guerilla attacks on Arabistan.

Starting in March 2003, the Iraqi marines, supported by two divisions from Palestine, had invaded and occupied Texas. The Iraqi administration argued that this was a preemptive invasion to *prevent* the fanatical Texans from developing biological weapons. However, some Arab publications on the Left have argued that the Texan oilfields were Iraq's real target. It is well known that production from the Iraqi oil fields has been declining for several years.

What would the Americans, now split, divided, corralled into fifty racial, ethnic and sectarian states do if they found themselves in such a world? Would they resent the surrogate despotisms that ruled over them with Iraqi arms and money? Would some of their young men, faced with overwhelming Iraqi power, resort to suicide attacks within Iraq itself? Would they too hate the Iraqis and Arabs and attack them because they are free, prosperous and democratic?

What would the New Englanders do, now scattered in refugee encampments in New York, Michigan, Pennsylvania and Ohio? Would they dream of returning to their country? Would they demand the right to return to their homes in New England? Would they demand compensation for the homes they had lost? Would they hate the Sudanese settlers who now lived in their homes, their towns and cities?

What would all the other Americans do if the New Englanders began to wage a campaign of terror against Iraqi interests in the former USA? What would they do if Arabistan – the Iraqi surrogate – then *retaliated* by bombing New York, Detroit, Washington and Albany? What would they do if the Iraqi media accused them *ad nauseum* of hating Iraq's free, open, democratic society?

If only Americans could imagine all this – imagine all this for even a few seconds – how would this change the way they *think* about what their country, the United States, together with its democratic ally, Israel, have been doing to the Arabs? Can Americans imagine this? What would it do if they could imagine this – even for a few seconds? Would they recognize in their imagined pain, in their imagined humiliation, in the imagined wars and destruction imposed upon them, the *real* wars, occupations, massacres, ethnic cleansings, tortures, bombings, sanctions and assassinations endured by Palestinians and Iraqis for more than eight decades?

Would they?

CHAPTER TWENTY-FIVE

Thomas Friedman's Muslim Problem

The Mulla sent a small boy to get water from the well. 'Make sure you don't break the pot!' he shouted, and gave the child a clout. 'Mulla,' asked a spectator, 'why do you strike someone who hasn't done anything?' 'Because you fool,' said the Mulla, 'it would be too late to punish him after he broke the pot, wouldn't it?[1]

July 2005

It appears that Mr. Thomas Friedman has a Muslim problem. He has a great deal of trouble thinking straight when writing about Muslims; and, as the *New York Times*' resident expert on Islam, he displays this malaise frequently, often twice a week.

In the wake of the recent bombings in London – as atrocious as bombings get anywhere – Mr. Friedman sums up his thoughts on this terrible tragedy in the title of his column of July 8, 2005, "If it's a Muslim Problem, It Needs a Muslim Solution." The conditional 'If' is merely a distraction. I could say that it is a deceptive ploy, but I will be more charitable. It is perhaps the last gasp of Mr. Friedman's conscience, mortified by his own mendacity.

Always the faithful acolyte of Bernard Lewis, Mr. Friedman interprets every Muslim act of violence against the West (and that includes Israel) as the herald of a clash of civilizations. In his own words, when "Al-Qaeda-like bombings come to the London underground, that becomes a civilizational problem. Every Muslim living in a Western society suddenly becomes a suspect, a potential walking bomb."

---

1   Idries Shah, "Learn how to learn," in: *The pleasantries of the incredible Mulla Nasrudin* (New York: Penguin Books, 1968): 54.

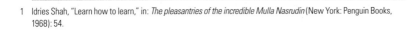

First, consider the inflammatory assertion about *every* Muslim in the West suddenly becoming "a potential walking bomb." If this were true, imagine the horror of Westerners at the thought of some 60 million potential walking bombs threatening their neighborhoods. Thankfully, the overwhelming majority of Westerners did not start looking upon their Muslim neighbors as "walking bombs" after the terrorist attacks in New York, Madrid or London. Despite the high-pitched alarms raised in very high places, the overwhelming majority of Europeans and Americans knew better than Mr. Friedman.

It appears that Mr. Friedman is propounding a new thesis on civilizational wars. 'The Muslim extremists,' he charges, 'are starting a civilizational war. It all begins when they bomb our cities, forcing us to treat all Muslims here as potential terrorists. This is going to pit us against them. And that is a civilizational problem.'

The terrorist acts of a few Muslims are terrible tragedies: but do they have a history behind them? Is there a history of Western provocations in the Muslim world? Does the Western world at any point enter the historical chain of causation that now drives a few angry Muslims to acts of terrorism? The only history that Friedman will acknowledge is one of Western innocence. There is no blowback: hence, no Western responsibility, no Western guilt.

Mr. Friedman speaks on this authoritatively and with clarity. The Muslims world has produced a "jihadist death cult in its midst." "If it does not fight that death cult, that cancer, within its own body politic, it is going to infect Muslim-Western relations everywhere." His two-fold verdict is clear. Inexplicably, the Muslims have produced a death cult, a religious frenzy, that is driving those infected by it to kill innocent Westerners without provocation. Equally bad, the Muslims have done nothing to condemn, to root out this death cult they have spawned.

There is not even a hint of history in these words. The historical amnesia is truly astounding. Does Mr. Friedman know any history? Of course, he does; but the history he knows is better forgotten if he is to succeed in demonizing the Muslim world. The oppressors choose to forget the history of their depredations, or substitute a civilizing mission for their history of brutalities, bombings, massacres, ethnic cleansings and expropriations. It is the oppressed peoples who know the history of their oppression: they know it because they have endured it. Its history is seared into their memory, their individual and collective memory. Indeed, they can liberate themselves only by memorializing this history.

Which part of the history of the Muslim world should I recall for the benefit of Mr. Friedman? I will not begin with the Crusades or the forced conversion of the Spanish Muslims and their eventual expulsion from Spain. That is not the history behind the "jihadist death cult." I could begin with the creation of a Jewish state in 1948 in lands inhabited by Palestinians; the 1956 invasion of Egypt by Britain, France and Israel; Israel's pre-emptive war of 1967 against three Arab states; the meticulously planned destruction of Palestinian society in the West Bank and Gaza since 1967; the Israeli occupation of Lebanon, stretching from 1982 to 2000; the massacre of 200,000 Bosnian Muslims in the 1990s; the devastation of Chechnya in 1996 and since 1999; the brutalities against Kashmiris since the 1990s; the deadly sanctions against Iraq from 1990 to 2003 which killed one and a half million Iraqis; the pogrom against Gujarati Muslims in 2002; the US invasion of Iraq in April 2003 which has already killed more than 200,000 Iraqis. Clearly, there is a lot that Mr. Friedman has to forget, to erase from his history books.

Mr. Friedman's memory only goes back to the latest terrorist attacks of Muslims against Western targets. That is not say by any stretch that these terrorist attacks are defensible. Clearly, they are not. But they will not be stopped by willfully and perversely erasing the layered history behind these acts. They will not be stopped by more wars and more occupations. If Mr. Friedman would unplug his ears, that is the clear message flowing everyday from the American or American-supported occupations of Palestine, Iraq and Afghanistan.

Frustrated by what he sees as the unwillingness of the Muslim world to smash the "jihadist (read: Islamic) death cult," Mr. Friedman issues a dire warning: 'Smash your cultists or we will do it for you. We will do it in a "rough and crude way," by denying visas to Muslims and making every Muslim in our midst "guilty until proven innocent."' This clinches my point that Mr. Friedman cannot think straight when he talks about Muslims. Apparently, he does not realize that his proposal to deny visas to nearly a quarter of the world's population would seriously jeopardize globalization – his own pet project. Incidentally, this also raises another question. Why wasn't Mr.

Friedman pushing his visa proposal after 9-11? But, in those heady days he was too busy peddling the war against Iraq as the panacea for the troubles of America and Israel.

What is Mr. Friedman's agenda in all this? No doubt, he will claim he is a man of peace: no less than George Bush or Ariel Sharon. We know that Mr. Friedman is no naïf; neither are we gullible fools. Mr. Friedman can sense that the history he tries so hard to camouflage – the history of Western domination over the Muslim world – may change before his eyes. He has been hoping that the United States can forestall this by wars, by occupying and re-making the Arab world, creating a second, deeper Balkanization of the Middle East that his neoconservative allies have been pushing under the rubric of democratization.

Already that project is in tatters. Despite all their inane rhetoric about fighting the terrorists in Baghdad, the policy makers in Washington know that their wars in Iraq and Afghanistan are spawning more terrorists than they can handle, and not just in Iraq and Afghanistan. The terrorists have struck Western targets in Bali, Riyadh, Istanbul, Karachi, Madrid, and now London. The United States could have leveraged these terrorist acts to strike Iran or Syria or both. But these plans are now on hold. Even Mr. Friedman admits that "there is no obvious target to retaliate against." One has to add, the targets are obvious enough, but they look much harder after Iraq.

In desperation, Mr. Friedman has now issued two new threats. He is warning Muslims living in the West, 'If your coreligionists do not stop their terrorist attacks against us, we will hold you hostages here.' To the Muslims living outside the Western world his message is equally sanguine, "Smash the terrorists or forget about ever setting foot in the United States."

Perhaps, judging from the endless rush of visa applicants at US consulates in Muslim countries, Mr. Friedman thinks this will bring the Muslim masses to their senses. In every street, every neighborhood, Arabs, Pakistanis and Indonesians will form anti-terrorist vigilante groups, and hunt down the terrorists. If this works out, it could be the cleverest coup since the marketing of Coke and Pepsi to the hungry masses in the Third World.

Regrettably, the visa proposal will not work. The United States has already mobilized nearly every Muslim government – with their armies, police and secret services – to catch the Muslim terrorists. Not that the Musharrafs and Mubaraks have failed. Indeed, they have caught 'terrorists' by the truck loads, and dispatched many of them *ex post haste* to Washington.

In this enterprise, it is the United States that has failed. It has been producing terrorists much faster than the 'good Muslims' can catch them. Perhaps, after Madrid and London the rhetoric about fighting the terrorists in Baghdad is beginning to strain even the ears of the faithful in the red states. Perhaps, the faithful are now ready for a new tune. Perhaps, in time the Muslim world will take Mr. Friedman's advice, suppress terrorism, and deny business visas to Americans unless the United States pulls out its troops from every Muslim country. After that Mr. Friedman might wish he had thought a little harder about the law of unintended consequences!

CHAPTER TWENTY-SIX

Real Men Go To Tehran

"Anyone can go to Baghdad. Real men go to Tehran."
—Senior Bush Official, May 2003

January 2006

The United States and Israel have been itching to go to Tehran since the Islamic Revolution of 1979. That Revolution was a strategic setback for both powers. It overthrew the Iranian monarchy, a great friend of the US and Israel, and brought to power the Shi'ite Mullahs, who saw themselves as the legitimate heirs of the Prophet's legacy, and, therefore, the true defenders of Islam.

As a result, the Iranian Revolution was certain to clash with both the US and Israel, as well as their client states in the Arab world. Israel was unacceptable because it was an alien intrusion that had displaced a Muslim people: it was a foreign implant in the Islamic heartland. But the US was the greater antagonist. On its own account, through Israel, and on the behalf of Israel, it sought to keep the Middle East firmly bound in the chains of American hegemony.

The US-Israeli hegemony over the Middle East had won a great victory in 1978. At Camp David, the leading Arab country, Egypt, chose to surrender its leadership of the Arab world, and signed a separate 'peace' with Israel. This freed Israel to pursue its plans to annex the West Bank, Gaza and Golan Heights, and to project unchecked power over the entire region. The Arab world could now be squeezed between Israel in the West and Iran to the East, the twin pillars of US hegemony over the region's peoples and resources.

The Iranian Revolution of 1979 ended this partnership. At that point, real men in Washington would have loved to take back Tehran from the Mullahs but for the inconvenience of Soviet opposition. But great powers are rarely stymied by any single development however adverse. It took little encouragement from Washington to get Iraq to mount an unprovoked invasion of Iran. In the twentieth century, since Sharif Hussein of Makkah first took the bait, few Arab leaders have seen the difference between entrapment and opportunity.

The war between Iran and Iraq served the United States and Israel quite well. It blunted the energies of Iran, diverting it from any serious attempts to export the revolution, or challenging American influence in the region. The Israeli gains were more substantial. With Egypt neutered at Camp David, and Iraq and Iran locked in a bloody war, Israel was free during the 1980s to do what it pleased. It expanded its settlements in the West Bank and Gaza, destroyed Iraq's nuclear reactor at Osirak, expelled the Palestinian fighters from Lebanon, and established a long-term occupation over much of Southern Lebanon. Israel was drawing closer to its goal of commanding unchallenged power over the Middle East.

The end of the Cold War in 1990 offered a bigger opening to the United States and Israel. Freed from the Soviet check on their ambitions, and with Iran weakened by its war with Iraq, the United States began working on plans to establish direct military control over the region, in the style of earlier colonial empires. This happened quickly when, with American assurance of non-intervention in intra-Arab conflicts, Iraq invaded Kuwaiti in August 1990.

The US response was massive and swift. In January 1990, after assembling 600,000 allied troops in Saudi Arabia – about half of them American – it pushed Iraq out of Kuwait, and mounted massive air strikes against Iraq itself, destroying much of its industry, power-generating capacity and infrastructure. The US had now established a massive military beachhead in the oil-rich Persian Gulf. It established permanent military bases in Saudi Arabia, continued its economic sanctions against Iraq, created a Kurdish autonomous zone in the north of Iraq, and, together with Britain, continued to bomb Iraq on a nearly daily basis for the next thirteen years.

With the US beachhead in place, where did the real men in the US and Israel want to go next? There was no secrecy about their plans. At a minimum, the Neoconservatives in the US and their Likud allies in Israel wanted 'regime change' in Iraq, Syria and Iran. This would be delivered by covert action, air strikes, or invasion – whatever it took – to be mounted by the US military. Israel would stay out of these wars, ready to reap the benefits of their aftermath.

The Likud plans were more ambitious. They wanted to redraw the map of the Middle East, using ethnic, sectarian, and religious differences to carve up the existing states in the region into weak micro-states that could be easily bullied by Israel. This was the *Kivunim* plan first made public in 1982.[1] It would give Israel a thousand years of dominance over the Middle East.

The attacks of September 11, 2001 were the 'galvanizing event' that put these plans into motion. The US wasted no time in seizing the moment. Instantly, President George Bush declared a global war against terrorism. The first target of this war was Afghanistan, but this was only a sideshow. On January 29, 2002, the President announced his initial targets for regime change: the 'axis of evil' that included Iraq, Iran and North Korea.

The plan was to invade and consolidate control over Iraq as a base for operations against Iran, Syria and perhaps Saudi Arabia. This sequencing was based on two assumptions: that the invasion of Iraq would be a cake-walk and American troops would be greeted as liberators. The US invaded Iraq on March 20, 2003 and Baghdad fell on April 9, 2003. It was indeed a cake-walk, and it appeared to television audiences that American troops were also being greeted as liberators. Understandably, the mood in Washington and Tel Aviv was triumphant. The US is unstoppable: it was time for real men now to go to Tehran.

Nearly three years after the Iraqi invasion, the real men are still stuck in Baghdad. Yes, there has been a great deal of talk about attacking Iran: plans in place for air strikes on Iran's revolutionary guards, on its nuclear installations and other WMD sites, and even talk of a ground invasion. There have been reports of spy flights over Iran and operations by special forces inside Iran. Israel too has been goading the US to strike, and if the US shrinks from this duty, threatening to go solo.

---

1 Oded Yinon, "A strategy for Israel in the 1980s," *Kivunim, A Journal for Judaism and Zionism*; Issue No, 14--Winter, 5742, February 1982. <www.theunjustmedia.com/the%20zionist_plan_for_the_middle_east.htm>

What has been holding back the real men in Washington and Tel Aviv? One reason of course is that the 'cake walk' in Iraq very quickly turned into a quagmire. The apparent Iraqi welcome was replaced by a growing and hardy insurgency, which has exacted a high toll on US plans for Iraq even though it was led mostly by Sunni Arabs. As a result, close to 150,000 US troops remain tied down in Iraq, with little prospect that they can be freed soon for action against Iran. Most Shi'ites aren't resisting the American occupation, but they are ready to take power in Iraq, and want the Americans to leave.

While the US cannot mount a full-scale invasion of Iran without a draft, it does possess the capability – despite the Iraqi quagmire – to launch air and missile strikes at Iranian targets, using nuclear weapons to destroy underground weapon sites. On the other hand, despite its saber rattling, most analysts agree that Israel does not possess this capability on its own. Unlike Iraq, Iran has dispersed its nuclear assets to dozens of sites, some unknown. Then, why hasn't the US mounted air attacks against Iran yet? Or will it any time soon?

More and more, as the Americans have taken a more sober reckoning of Iran's political and military capabilities, they realize that Iran is not Iraq. When Osirak was attacked by Israel in June 1981, Iraq did nothing: it could not do anything. One thing is nearly certain: Iran will respond to any attack on its nuclear sites. Iran's nuclear program has the broadest public support: as a result, the Iranian Revolution would suffer a serious loss of prestige if it did nothing to punish the attacks. The question is: what can Iran do in retaliation?

Both the CIA and DIA have conducted war games to determine the consequences of an American air attack on Iran's nuclear facilities. According to Newsweek (September 27, 2004), "No one liked the outcome." According to an Air Force source, "The war games were unsuccessful at preventing the conflict from escalating." In December 2004, The Atlantic Monthly reported similar results for its own war game on this question. The architect of these games, Sam Gardner, concluded, "You have no military solution for the issues of Iran."

What is the damage Iran can inflict? Since preparations for any US strike could not be kept secret, Iran may choose to preempt such a strike.

According to the participants in the *Atlantic Monthly* war game, Iran could attack American troops across the border in Iraq. In responding to these attacks, the US troops would become even more vulnerable to the Iraqi insurgency. One participant expressed the view that Iran "may decide that a bloody defeat for the United States, even if it means chaos in Iraq, is something they actually prefer." Iran could also join hands with al-Qaida to mount attacks on civilian targets within the US. If Iranian losses mount, Iran may launch missiles against Israel or decide to block the flow of oil from the Gulf, options not considered in the *Atlantic Monthly* war game.

What are the realistic options available to the US? It could drag Iran to the UN Security Council and, if Russia and China climb on board, pass a motion for limited economic sanctions. Most likely, the US will not be asking for an Iraq-style oil embargo. Not only would this roil the markets for oil, Iran will respond by ending inspections, and accelerate its uranium enrichment. If Iran is indeed pursuing a nuclear program, then it will, per-haps sooner rather than later, have its bomb. Once that happens, one Israeli official in the *Newsweek* report said, "Look at ways to make sure it's not the mullahs who have their finger on the trigger." But the US and Israel have been looking for ways to remove the Mullahs since 1979.

It would appear that US-Israeli power over the Middle East, which had been growing since World War II, may have finally run into an obstacle. And that obstacle is Iran, a country the CIA had returned to a despotic monarch in 1953. Paradoxically, this has happened when American dominance over the region appears to be at its peak; when its troops occupy a key Arab country; when it has Iran sandwiched between US troops in Iraq and Afghanistan; and when it has trapped Iran inside a ring of US military bases running from Qatar, through Turkey and Tajikistan, to Pakistan.

Could it be that al-Qaida's gambit is beginning to pay off? It had hoped that the attacks of September 11 would provoke the US into invading the Islamicate heartland. That the US did, but the mass upheaval al-Qaida had expected in the Arab streets did not materialize. Instead, it is Iran that has been the chief beneficiary of the US invasion. As a result, it is Iran that now possesses the leverage to oppose US-Israeli aims in the region. Al-Qaida had not planned on a Shi'ite country leading the Islamic world.

It is possible that the US, choosing to ignore the colossal risks, may yet launch air attacks against Iran. President Bush could be pushed into this by pressure from Zionist Christians, by Neoconservatives, by Israelis, or by the illusion that he needs to do something bold and desperate to save his presidency. By refusing to wilt under US-Israeli threats, it appears that the Iranians too may be following al-Qaida's logic. We cannot tell if this is what motivates Iran. But that is where matters will go if the US decides to attack or invade Iran.

No one has yet remarked on some eerie parallels between the US determination to deepen its intervention in the Islamic world and Napoleons' relentless pursuit of the Russian forces, retreating, drawing them into the trap of the Russian winter. It would appear that the United States too is irretrievably committed to pursuing its Islamicate foe to the finish, to keep moving forward even if this risks getting caught in a harsh Islamicate winter. On the other hand, the Neoconservatives, the messianic Christians, and the Israelis are convinced that with their searing firepower, the US and Israel will succeed and plant a hundred pliant democracies in the Middle East. We will have to wait and see if these real men ever get to add Tehran to their next travel itinerary – or they have to give up the comforts of the Green Zone in Baghdad.

CHAPTER TWENTY-SEVEN

The Muslims America Loves

"The most potent weapon in the hands of the oppressor is the mind of the oppressed."
Steve Biko (1946-1977), Statement as witness [May 3, 1976]

May 2006

Being a Muslim today – in the middle of America's 'war against global terrorism' – carries some new hazards. But it is not without its bright side for a few Muslims who are eager to profit from this war.

Muslims need little tutoring in the hazards they now face. Many tens of thousands are already dead in wars imposed by the United States – on Iraq and Afghanistan. The death toll is expected to climb, perhaps steeply, as these wars are carried to Iran, Syria or Pakistan. Iranians also face the prospect – perhaps, imminent – of incineration in nuclear strikes.

Death or dislocation in wars are not the only hazards that confront Muslims. In principle, any Muslim can also become the object of 'extraordinary renditions.' No matter where they happen to be, they could be kidnapped by the CIA, hooded, and transported to secret off-shore US prisons, or delivered into the hands of US-friendly regimes with expertise in the fine arts of interrogation. No one knows how many Muslims have suffered this cruel fate – or how many of them are still alive.

By comparison, Muslims who are captured or bought, and imprisoned in Guantanamo as 'enemy combatants,' are lucky. After facing down several legal challenges to these detentions, the US now brings these prisoners before military review boards. Although many of them have been cleared of any terrorist connections, it is quite touching that the US is now refusing to release them – it says – because they could be tortured by their own governments. The prisoners can now thank the US for converting Gitmo into a sanctuary.

In fairness, America's 'war against global terrorism' has also created a few hard-to-resist opportunities. The chief beneficiaries of the new US posture are the Muslim rulers eager to get the US more firmly behind the wars they have been waging against their own people. They are happy to torture Muslims 'rendered' to them by the CIA, and, periodically, they capture their own 'terrorists' and put them on flights to Guantanamo.

The 'war against global terrorism' is also a war of ideas. In order to defeat the 'terrorists' the US must win the hearts and minds of Muslims. This is where Muslims can help. The US needs a few 'good' Muslims to persuade the 'bad' ones to reform their religion, to learn to appreciate the inestimable benefits of Pax America and Pax Israelica.

In the heyday of the old colonialism, the white man did not need any help from the natives in putting down their religion and culture. Indeed, he preferred to do it himself. In colonial times, the opinion of the natives carried little weight with the whites anyway. So why bother to recruit them to denounce their own people. As a result, Orientalists wrote countless tomes denigrating the cultures of the lesser breeds.

Today the West needs help in putting down the uppity natives – especially the Muslims. One reason for this is that with the death of the old colonialism, some natives have begun to talk *for* themselves. A few are even talking back at the Orientalists raising all sorts of uncomfortable questions. This hasn't been good: and something had to be done about it. In the 1970s the West began to patronize 'natives' who were deft at putting down their own people. Was the West losing its confidence?

The demand for 'native' Orientalists was strong. The pay for such turncoats was good too. Soon a whole crop of native Orientalists arrived on the scene. Perhaps, the most distinguished members of this coterie include Nirad Chaudhuri, V. S. Naipaul, Fouad Ajami and Salman Rushdi. They are some of the best loved natives in the West.

Then there came the 'war against global terrorism' creating an instant boom in the market for Orientalists of Muslim vintage. The West now demanded Muslims who would diagnose their own problems as the West wanted to see them – as the unavoidable failings of their religion and culture. The West now demanded Muslims who would take positions against their own people – who would denounce the just struggles of their own people as moral aberrations, as symptoms of a sick society.

So far these boom conditions have not evoked too copious a supply of Muslim Orientalists. Irshad Manji has made herself the most visible native Orientalist by cravenly playing to Western and Zionist demands for demonizing Muslims and Palestinians. I can think of a few others, but they like Irshad Manji have little to recommend themselves other than their mendacity. This must be a bit disappointing for those who had pinned their hopes on using Muslim defectors to win the battle for Muslim hearts and minds.

There are some indications that this disappointment is turning to desperation. On March 11 the New York Times published a front page story on Dr. Wafa Sultan, "a largely unknown Syrian-American psychiatrist, nursing a deep anger and despair about her fellow Muslims." Is self-hatred the only qualification that Muslims can offer to seize the attention of America's most prestigious newspaper?

If the only Muslims that the United States can recruit in its battle for ideas are at best mediocrities or worse – nobodies – what chance is there that it can win the battle for Muslim hearts and minds? The short answer is: very little. Muslims are not helpless children. You cannot molest them and then expect to mollify them with trifles and protestations of pure intentions. That may have worked for a while. It will not work for ever.

Muslims are too large and too dense a mass to be moved by wars. Military might could not break the spirit of Palestinians, Afghans, Bosnians, Chechens, Lebanese, Moros and Iraqis. What chance is there that West's military might will be more effective when applied against larger masses of Muslims?

The United States cannot expect to change Muslims unless it first thinks seriously about changing its policies towards Muslims. Americans must stop deluding themselves. Muslims do not hate their freedom: indeed, they want some of it for themselves. The United States and Israel seek to build their power over a mass of prostrate Muslim bodies. Stop doing that and then you will have a chance to win Muslim hearts and minds.

INDEX

mizan press publications
available from
Islamic Publications International

On the Sociology of Islam Lectures by Ali Shari'ati tr. by Hamid Algar
Paperback ISBN 0-933782-00-4 $9.95

Marxism and Other Western Fallacies: An Islamic Critique by Ali Shari'ati
tr. Robert Campbell
Paperback ISBN 0-933782-06-3 $14.95 Hardback ISBN 0-933782-05-5 $24.95

Constitution of the Islamic Republic of Iran tr. Hamid Algar
Paperback ISBN 0-933782-07-1 $7.95 Hardback ISBN 0-933782-02-0 $14.95

Islam and Revolution: Writings and Declaration of Imam Khomeini
by Ruhollah Khomeini tr. by Hamid Algar
Paperback ISBN 0-933782-03-9 $ 24.95 Hardback ISBN 093378-24-7 $ 34.95

Occidentosis: A Plague from the West by Jalal Al-i Ahmad tr. Robert Campbell
Paperback ISBN 0-933782-13-6 $14.95 Hardback ISBN 0-933782-12-8 $29.95

The Contemporary Muslim Movement in the Philippines by Cesar Adib Majul
Paperback ISBN 0-933782-17-9 $9.95 Hardback ISBN 0-933782-16-9 $19.95

Fundamentals of Islamic Thought: God, Man and the Universe
by Ayatullah Murtaza Mutahhari; tr. Robert Campbell
Paperback ISBN 0-933782-15-2 $9.95 Hardback ISBN 0-933782-14-4 $19.95

Social and Historical Change: An Islamic Perspective
by Ayatullah Murtaza Mutahhari; tr. by Robert Campbell
Paperback ISBN 0-933782-19-5 $9.95 Hardback ISBN 0-933782-18-7 $19.95

Principles of Sufism by Al-Qushayri tr. B. R. Von Schlegell
Paperback ISBN 0-933782-21-7 $19.95 Hardback ISBN 0-933782-20-9 $29.95

Sales Tax: Please add 6% for books shipped to New Jersey address.
Shipping: $4.00 for the first book and $1.00 for additional publication

Also published by
Islamic Publications International

Surat Al-Fatiha: Foundation of the Qur'an by Hamid Algar
Paperback ISBN 1-889999-00-8 $7.95

Sufism: Principles and Practice by Hamid Algar
Paperback ISBN 1-889999-02-4 $7.95

Jesus In The Qur'an: His Reality Expounded in the Qur'an by Hamid Algar
Paperback ISBN 1-889999-09-1 $7.95

Understanding The Four Madhhabs: The Facts about Ijtihad and Taqlid
by Abdal Hakim Murad (T.J. Winters)
Paperback ISBN 1-889999-07-5 $3.00

The Sunnah: Its Obligatory and Exemplary Aspects by Hamid Algar
Paperback ISBN 1-889999-01-6 $7.95

Imam Abu Hamid Ghazali: An Exponent of Islam in Its Totality by Hamid Algar
Paperback # 1-889999-15-6 $7.95

Wahhabism: A Critical Essay by Hamid Algar
Paperback ISBN 1-889999-13-X $12.95 Hardback ISBN 1-889999-31-8 $22.95

Path of God's Bondsmen From Origin to Return
by Najm A. Razi Tr. by Hamid Algar Paperback ISBN 1-889999-33-4 $39.95

Social Justice in Islam by Sayyid Qutb; tr. Revised & Introduction by Hamid Algar
Paperback ISBN 1-889999-11-3 $19.95 Hardback ISBN 1-889999-12-1 $29.95

Roots of the Islamic Revolution in Iran/Four Lectures by Hamid Algar
Paperback ISBN 1-889999-26-1 $14.95 Hardback ISBN 1-889999-27-X $24.95

Principles of Islamic Jurisprudence: According to Shi'i Law by Muhammad
Baqir al-Sadr; Tr. by Arif Abdul Hussain. Translation Revised by Hamid Algar
Paperback ISBN 1-889999-36-9 $19.95 Hardback ISBN 1-889999-37-7 $29.95

**Jihad & Shahadat (Struggle and Martyrdom in Islam) Essays and Addresses by
Ayatullah Mahmud Taleqani, Ayatullah Murtada Mutahhari & Dr. Ali Shariati**
Edited by Mehdi Abedi & Gary Legenhausen.
Paperback ISBN 1-889999-43-1 $24.95 Hardback ISBN 1-889999-44-X $34.95

What Is To Be Done (The Enlightened Thinkers and an Islamic Renaissance)
by Dr. Ali Shariati Edited & Annotated by Farhang Rajaee
Paperback ISBN 1-889999-41-5 $19.95 Hardback ISBN 1-889999-42-3 $29.95

Theoretical Studies in Islamic Banking and Finance Edited by Mohsin S. Khan
& Abbas Mirakhor Paperback ISBN 1-889999-40-7 $29.95

Man & Islam by Dr. Ali Shariati. Translated by Dr. Fatollah Marjani.
Paperback ISBN 1-889999-39-3 $14.95

Hajj by Dr. Ali Shariati. Translated by Ali A. Behzadnia & Najla Denny.
Paperback ISBN 1-889999-38-5 $14.95

Basic Principles of The Islamic Worldview by Sayyid Qutb.
Translated by Rami David. Preface by Hamid Algar
Paperback ISBN 1-889999-34-2 $24.95 Hardback ISBN 1-889999-35-0 $34.95

Sales Tax: Please add 6% for books shipped to New Jersey address.
Shipping: $4.00 for the first book and $1.00 for additional publication